PRIVATE PILOT BEGINNER'S MANUAL
(for Sport Pilots, Too)

by
Paul Berge, C

Ahquabi House Publishing, LLC
11872 G58 Hwy Indianola,
Iowa 50125 USA
Contact Us: paulberge.com

PRIVATE PILOT BEGINNER'S MANUAL
(for Sport Pilots, Too)
2nd Edition

by
Paul Berge, CFII

This is a work of non-fiction (mostly). The author relied upon FAA, US Navy, NWS and other government publications in public domain. All other passages and artwork are the property of the author and/or Ahquabi House Publishing, LLC and may not be copied without permission. That said, if you'd like to quote small portions of this book for instructional purposes, please follow FAIR USE guidelines and, please, credit the source. When in doubt, contact Ahquabi House Publishing, LLC, for reprint permission.

ISBN: 978-1-365-59977-4

Ahquabi House Publishing, LLC
11872 G58 Hwy
Indianola, Iowa 50125
paulberge.com

TABLE OF CONTENTS

INTRODUCTION

The *Private Pilot Beginner's Manual (for Sport Pilots, too)* is a flying primer. It can also serve as a refresher course book, because once you earn your pilot certificate the learning just begins.

The book's purpose is to introduce the student pilot to a new world full of unfamiliar terminology and strange regulations from even stranger regulators. You'll learn about aviation weather, cross-country flight planning, air traffic control, aerodynamics and more. Although the focus is on the airplane private pilot, sport pilots are expected to know much of what's included in this book. Sport pilot requirements are outlined in the appendix on page 281.

This book was not designed to teach you how to fly your airplane; flight instructors fill that vital role. You won't find everything you need to know to earn your pilot certificate from reading one book. This book is best used in a ground school course or in conjunction with self-study materials available from a number of suppliers such as King, ASA or Gleim. Additionally, your flight instructor will provide one-on-one ground instruction to fill in the gaps as you progress.

Speaking of gaps, this is a work in progress. The art and science of flight evolves and so will this manual with your help. If you have a comment or spot an error please send us a note, and we'll address the issue before you can say, "Wow, that was dumb!"

So, turn the page to begin your new life in the sky.

—Paul Berge, CFII
Ailerona, Iowa

Getting Your Private Pilot Certificate

Any journey begins with at least one known: The departure point; from there anything is reachable. For your Private Pilot journey, that point is right here. From this moment forward, you are no longer merely thinking about becoming a Private Pilot. Instead, you're on your way—cleared for takeoff to become a certificated Private Pilot. As with many adventures the destination may seem far off, shimmering in the mist with seemingly insurmountable obstacles between you and it.

Well, forget the obstacles. You now have wings to soar over them. The objective becomes learning how to use those new wings. This book is one tool in your quest and should be used in conjunction with one-on-one flight and ground instruction given by your flight instructor. Or as Benjamin Franklin once said: "Ya can't learn everything from a book, kid. Eventually, ya just gotta go fly a kite."

Let's begin with what a Private Pilot is and lightly address the Sport Pilot certificate.

The Private Pilot Certificate

The FAA-issued Private Pilot certificate allows you to fly as Pilot-In-Command (PIC) of almost any type aircraft you can imagine or afford. The FAA (Federal Aviation Administration) regulates flight in the United States, not the aerodynamic aspects (there's a higher authority controlling that), but the government rules—who gets to fly what, where and when. Once you earn your Private Pilot certificate you will be able to fly from Mooseguts, Maine to Rancho Suburbio, California and all points in between, day or night, at the controls of your own aircraft, whenever you want, free from airline schedules and TSA passenger screening.

For this course we'll focus on the Private Pilot rated to fly single-engine airplanes according to Visual Flight Rules (VFR). More on all of this in later chapters.

Day or night, the Private Pilot has access to thousands of public-use civil airports and countless private airstrips. The Private Pilot may carry passengers and cargo for business or pleasure. Granted, all flying should be pleasurable or what's an airplane for? But what about that "business" angle? Can a Private Pilot invite a few friends along for a trip to Orlando and charge each passenger a fee? Can you write off every flight as a business expense?

In a word—*No* to both. I'm no accountant or tax attorney, but I'll bet that mixing aviation with tax shelters puts a big bullseye on your IRS form 1040. Seek professional help before blending flight with business.

The Private Pilot may not, under most circumstances, "charge" a fee for pilot services. You can't fly for hire as a Private Pilot. To do so requires the pilot to hold a Commercial or Airline Transport Pilot (ATP) certificate. Even then, charging for flying services is a complicated affair. So for your Private Pilot ambitions, forget about making any money. You get to spend it—lots of it—and one day, perhaps, become a commercial pilot and make some of that back.

Not to be too discouraged, a Private Pilot may "share" some costs of flight with friends. We'll explore this "shared cost" notion later when we study the FARs (Federal Aviation Regulations). Also, a Private Pilot flying for business may accept certain compensation for flight costs associated with business travel. Again, more later.

If you're not yet a certificated Private Pilot, you'll fly using your Student Pilot certificate, which the FAA issues. You'll need the Student Pilot certificate before you can fly solo. To do so go online to the FAA's website (FAA.gov) and apply for your student pilot certificate through the IACRA (Integrated Airman Certification and Rating Application) link. Yeah, you're gonna encounter a boatload of acronyms while learning to fly. Don't be discouraged. The process is relatively easy, although the IACRA site doesn't work well with some computers, namely ones that most people use. Don't hesitate to call the help number; a human actually answers and will help. Good news: It's free, possibly the last free thing you'll find in aviation.

Complete the IACRA application for a student pilot certificate, hit submit and—hate to say it—wait up to three weeks for your plastic student pilot certificate to appear in the mail. In the old days, prior to June 15, 2016, all a student had to do was visit an Airman Medical Examiner (AME), submit to a simple physical exam and, on the spot, receive a Class 3 medical certificate, which doubled as the student pilot certificate. No more. The FAA "improved" the system by now requiring a plastic student pilot certificate in addition to the paper medical certificate, issued by an AME. You'll need both in your wallet before your instructor can authorize you to fly solo. The good news is you may begin receiving dual flight instruction with the instructor on board prior to receiving your student pilot certificate.

As of editing this second edition, the Class 3 medical certificate rules are undergoing a radical change—for the better—thanks (surprisingly) to the Congress and Senate, which ordered the FAA to reform the medical certification process. While we await the final wording, the big change is once you receive your Class 3 medical certificate it'll be good for life. Again, we're awaiting details, so check with an AME, whose name you'll receive from your flight instructor.

One more administrative hurdle: You must also show proof of US citizenship to your flight instructor prior to beginning any flight instruction. Plan to bring a valid US passport or birth certificate with you on your first lesson. Foreign students need to navigate past several more administrative dungeons and dragons before beginning flight instruction. Again, check faa.gov for more.

Other pilot certificates include: Recreational and Sport Pilot. Both have more limitations than the Private Pilot certificate. The Recreational certificate is fairly worthless, so stick with Private or Sport pilot.

Sport Pilot Certificate v. Private Pilot

If your goal is to fly small, single-engine, two-seat aircraft for fun on sunny days (not night), then the Sport Pilot certificate might be for you. To fly anything larger and to fly at night, you'll need a Private Pilot certificate. Here's a quick comparison of the two certificates.

Either certificate holds the potential to fly airplanes, gliders, hot air balloons and more. We'll stick with airplanes. The sport pilot (airplane) is limited to light sport aircraft (LSA) with a maximum of two seats, including the PIC (pilot in command) and a maximum gross weight of 1320 pounds, 1430 for seaplanes. The LSA choice is wide, including older two-seaters such as the 1940s Piper J-3 Cub, Aeronca 7AC Champ and several models of Taylorcraft. Good old airplanes all, but not exactly speed wagons or heavy haulers. Just fun. And that's the point of being a Sport Pilot—having fun in fun airplanes on nice days.

Sport pilots are not permitted to fly at night or in instrument meteorological conditions (IMC). You can't add an instrument rating to a Sport Pilot certificate. For that, you'll need the Private Pilot certificate. A Sport Pilot can fly just about anywhere in the USA, even into busier airspace (Class D, C and B) after receiving additional training.

Two big advantages to choosing the Sport versus Private Pilot path: A student pilot training for a Private Pilot certificate must pass a one-time class 3 flight physical. A sport pilot needs only a valid state-issued drivers license. Both Private and Sport Pilots must pass a written knowledge exam (70% is passing). The private pilot logs (records flight time in a logbook) at least 40 hours of flight time (dual instruction and solo) to be eligible to take the practical exam (check ride). The Sport Pilot needs only half that amount. In short, the Sport Pilot gets a pilot certificate in fewer hours—spending fewer dollars—but is restricted to smaller aircraft. You can always get a sport pilot certificate and then, later, train for the Private Pilot. It's a great way to begin flying on a budget.

Both Sport and Private Pilots need to understand the same basics of flight—aerodynamics, control input, airmanship, plus achieve a thorough command of aviation weather, airspace and Federal Aviation Regulations (FARs). Sport Pilots don't train at night or in simulated instrument conditions (hood work), plus cross-country requirements are less demanding than for Private Pilot applicants. But whatever the choice—Sport of Private—ya gotta know how to fly the airplane, and to master that you'll need a Certificated Flight Instructor (CFI).

What Is a CFI?

The Certificated Flight Instructor (CFI) is your shoulder-to-shoulder companion, teacher, mentor and guide for the next few months. The CFI provides the dual flight instruction required for solo as well as for taking your FAA written Knowledge Exam and Practical Test, or what's commonly referred to as the "check ride," during which a Designated Pilot Examiner (DPE) "rides" along with you to "check" your skills.

Above: Post-check ride relief. The Designated Pilot Examiner (DPE) and a newly minted Private Pilot.

During training, you may have one CFI from start to finish or, depending upon circumstances, several instructors along the way. Whatever the case, you choose who teaches you, and you must develop a good learning relationship with the instructor. Demand the best, it's your time and money.

What Does an Instructor Charge? Do They Take Checks?

Flight instructors aren't like plumbers, hired for a few hours and then sent packing. The CFI takes you above the two-dimensional planet, thousands of feet away from the place you've considered home for at least 16 years (minimum age to solo an airplane; 14 for glider) and introduces you to the stars and clouds. The CFI teaches you to read the sky and feel the wind while gazing down on bald eagles and mountain peaks you once only viewed from below. In short, the flight instructor expands your vision while elevating your mind, body and soul as you're guided through a maze of federal regulations and aeronautical lore. A plumber, by contrast, unclogs drains and usually charges considerably more than a CFI. Fees are negotiated between you and your instructor.

Your Private Pilot training is regulated under 14 CFR Part 61. CFR means Code of Federal Regulations; 14 is the Title number. CFRs are more commonly known as FARs or Federal Aviation Regulations. This book will help prepare you for the FAA written Knowledge Exam and introduce you to the basics needed to begin your flight training. Your personal flight instructor provides the rest, bridging bookwork with hands-on flight instruction.

According to FAR Part 61, Subpart E, you must *"log at least **40 hours** of flight time that includes at least **20 hours** of flight training from an authorized instructor and **10 hours of solo flight training"*[1] to become eligible to take the Private Pilot Practical Test (check ride). Most student pilots take longer, the good ones, anyhow. I was a slow learner and am chagrined to admit how many hours it took me to learn to fly.[2] Progress is based on individual ability, attitude, scheduling, weather, aircraft availability, funds, karma and a little luck. Don't be discouraged if it takes you 60 or even 80 hours to earn that Private Pilot certificate. It's worth the effort.

So, What Is a Student Pilot?

That's you. Temporarily. Armed with your Student Pilot certificate (and the medical certificate), you're ready to learn. Always carry your Student Pilot and medical certificates with you when you fly. Once you earn the Private Pilot certificate (passed the written and the check ride) you'll receive a new certificate. All pilots must carry their certificates (including medical, if required[3]) when acting as PIC. Students should also carry their

---

[1] Yeah, 10 + 20 =30, so figure a little more dual and a little more solo to get to 40 hours total time.
[2] OK, 80 hours…maybe 84.
[3] Sport pilots do not need a medical certificate.

logbooks in flight, although certificated pilots should not. It's too easy to lose a logbook, so lock it in a safe place, maybe a safe deposit box along with your passport and those embarrassing prom photos.

The student pilot is tethered to the instructor and learns by listening, asking questions and performing. Once the CFI judges the student ready to solo (fly alone), the instructor steps from the airplane (it's hoped while on the ground) and endorses the student's logbook for solo flight in the local area. Solo privileges are limited. The student may only fly where and when the CFI deems appropriate. Initial solo flights are referred to as "supervised solos," meaning the instructor stands on the ground nervously watching the fledgling navigate the airport traffic pattern alone. It's an instructor's loneliest moment.

Students also fly solo cross-country trips (over 50 nautical miles) as part of the training, but each flight must be approved and endorsed by the CFI. Of course, the student may not carry passengers or accept any compensation for any flight. That doesn't mean, though, that your rich Aunt Ophelia can't pay for your lessons; you just can't charge her for a ride once she buys you your first airplane.

Solo flight is limited to a particular make and model of airplane. If, for instance, you're learning in a Cessna 172, then the instructor will endorse your logbook for solo flight in the Cessna 172 only. The student pilot cannot then fly solo in, say, a Piper Cherokee or a Cessna 152, even though the airplanes have similarities.

A student pilot (we'll call, Dave) keeps his poker face after achieving solo flight

Once you pass the Private Pilot check ride your new pilot certificate will allow you to fly most single-engine airplanes that weigh 12,500 pounds or less, have fixed landing gear and pack no more than 200 horsepower. It's relatively easy to step-up, or transition, to higher performance or complex airplanes.

If, for example, you learned in a Cessna 172 (145-180-hp, fixed, tricycle gear) and want to fly a Beechcraft Bonanza with retractable landing gear and a 300-hp engine, you'd need further instruction and a one-time logbook endorsement from a CFI for "complex" and "high performance" privileges. Likewise if you want to fly a tailwheel airplane such as a Piper Cub, Aeronca Champ or Stearman biplane. Tailwheel airplanes require additional training (perhaps 5 hours) and a one-time sign-off from an authorized instructor. To fly multi-engine airplanes you'll need a multi-engine rating added to your pilot certificate. We'll assume you're learning in a single-engine airplane.

What Does VFR Mean?

You'll encounter a whole new language while becoming a pilot, including aviation weather terms. A sky may be "partly cloudy" to ground-bound earthlings, but to pilots it's referred to as "Few," "Scattered" or "Broken." An aviation airport weather observation is called a METAR, and a forecast for your airport is a TAF.

VFR means "Visual Flight Rules." Flying regulations are divided into two categories: VFR and IFR. In VFR you fly by visually looking out the window. In IFR, which means Instrument Flight Rules, you fly by reference to the flight instruments or what's often called, "flying on the gauges."

After achieving your VFR Private Pilot certificate, you may add an instrument rating to that certificate. This extra rating (after extra training) allows you to fly properly equipped IFR aircraft into thoroughly skuzzy weather. IFR flight, unlike VFR, relies upon the panel instruments to keep the pilot oriented. As a VFR student pilot you will receive three hours of basic instrument training, but this is given as an introduction only to IFR operations. Your basic instrument training is designed to aid you should you ever, inadvertently, stumble into Instrument Meteorological Conditions (IMC).

SAFETY TIP: Only a properly trained, rated and *proficient* instrument pilot should attempt flight into less than Visual Meteorological Conditions (VMC).

The VFR and IFR rules are many and varied but, broadly speaking, VFR weather usually means an environment in which the lowest cloud ceiling (broken or overcast) is at least 1000 feet AGL (Above Ground Level), and the visibility is at least three statute miles (SM). Lower weather conditions are permissible for VFR flight in what's called "uncontrolled airspace." Lots more on these rules later.

Although it's not weather related, you will need to know the acronym TFR. It means Temporary Flight Restriction and is usually not a weather restriction at all. TFRs are chunks of airspace temporarily closed or restricted to flight in order to protect the President, Vice-President, other toffee-nosed dignitaries or some unusual event such as the World Series or a disaster area where rescue operations are in progress..

Before beginning any flight every pilot needs to brief on all weather forecasts and reports as well as any navigational facility limitations or service outages plus airspace restrictions, such as TFRs.

But enough about rules for a while. You came here to learn to fly, so let's find an aircraft and decide if it's what we need in order to learn to fly. For that, we have to ask, "What is an airplane?"

Airplanes and Other Things That Fly

If you opened a hangar door and saw a machine with a cabin, wings, landing gear, tail at one end and propeller at the other, you'd state with some confidence, "That's an airplane." And the FAA might agree. Those passing your hangar might wonder why you're talking to your airplane. Ignore them. All good pilots talk to their airplanes.

We know it's an airplane because, well, it resembles an airplane. But the FAA regulates more than airplanes. It oversees helicopters, gliders, hot air balloons, powered parachutes, blimps and drones (to some extent), each of which has its own unique characteristics. Rather than simply lumping them all together as "flying machines," romantic though it may sound, the FAA composed a certification labeling system of **Class** and **Category**. These two groups are used to categorize both aircraft and the pilots who fly them, but the terms have different meanings depending on where they're applied. The FAA doesn't make this easy.

Category, as applied to aircraft, relates to the aircraft's intended use. There are nine broad aircraft certification categories: *Normal, Utility, Acrobatic, Commuter, Transport, Restricted, Limited, Provisional, and Experimental.*

Wow! That's confusing. As a student pilot you'll most likely be flying **Normal** and **Utility** category aircraft. Later, when you feel the urge to go inverted, you'll need to learn about the **Acrobatic** certification category. Should you heed the EAA's[4] siren call and build your own airplane, you'll become intimately familiar with the **Experimental** certification category. A student pilot may train in an Experimental aircraft; you just won't find many for rent (legally).

Staying with the aircraft certification theme for a moment, the **Category** is subdivided into four, more familiar **Classes**: Airplane, Rotorcraft, Glider, Lighter-Than-Air.

We'll ignore drones or UAS (Unmanned Aircraft Systems) in our studies here, although we'll watch for the pesky varmints in the air. FAR Part 107 regulates small UAS.

We're concerned with the **Airplane** Class.

---

[4] EAA: Experimental Aircraft Association

Still there? Good. Now that you have a Normal or Utility certified Airplane, we need to tell the FAA what **Type** of airplane that is. That's simple. Types (for aircraft certification purposes) are labeled by make and model, such as a Chevy Impala. Oh, wait, that's a car. Forget that. For airplanes Make and Model types would include, for example, these popular types: Cessna 180 (C180), Cessna 172 (C172), Piper Archer (P28A), Piper Warrior (P28A), Cirrus (SR22), Diamond Star (DA40).

Once we've identified the aircraft by its Category and Class certification status, let's label the pilot's certification using the same terms. (Confusing, ain't it? But hang in there.)

For pilot certification (not aircraft certification), the broadest group is **Category**. For pilot certification purposes (what appears on the pilot's certificate) Category includes: *Airplane, Rotorcraft, Glider and Lighter-Than-Air.* So, if you learn in a Cessna 172 (a Type of Airplane in the Normal and Utility Category of aircraft certification), the pilot will have the pilot certification Category "Airplane" on the pilot certificate. But what kind of airplane is this Airplane pilot certified to fly?

Airplanes, for pilot certification purposes, are further subdivided into **Classes**: *Single-Engine Land (SEL), Multi-Engine Land (MEL), Single-Engine Sea (SES),* and *Multi-Engine Sea (MES).*

Land means the aircraft lands on land, and Sea means it splashes upon water, although, not necessarily the sea.

So, if you learn to fly in a Cessna 172—with wheels, not floats—certified in the *Normal/Utility* Category and *Airplane* Class, then your pilot certificate will be for *Airplane* Category and in the *Single-Engine Land* Class. A Type will not be listed on your Private Pilot certificate, unless you learn in some behemoth with a gross weight over 12,500 pounds, but that's a whole other story. The smaller Cherokees and Cessnas top out around 2500 pounds, depending on models.

Got that? If not, don't worry, because you will if you reread the lesson and ask your instructor a lot of questions. By check ride time you'll be amazed what you know. Six weeks later, you'll be equally amazed how much you may have forgotten, which is why every two years pilots must complete a Flight Review to retain flying privileges. More on that rule (61.56) in the FAR Chapter.

For now, let's see how all these **Categories** and **Classes** bolt together to lift you into flight. But first, a few test questions you may encounter later.

Test Questions:

1. With respect to the certification of airmen, which is a category of aircraft?

a. Gyroplane, helicopter, airship, free balloon
b. Airplane, rotorcraft, glider, lighter-than-air
c. Single-engine land and sea, multi-engine land and sea

2. When referring to the certification of airmen, which is a class of aircraft?

a. Airplane, rotorcraft, glider, lighter-than-air
b. Single-engine land and sea, multi-engine land and sea
c. Lighter-than-air, airship, hot air balloon, gas balloon

3. With respect to the certification of aircraft, which is a category of aircraft?

a. Normal, utility, acrobatic
b. Airplane, rotorcraft, glider
c. Landplane, seaplane, rotorcraft

Answers:

1. **b.** Airplane, rotorcraft, glider, lighter-than-air.
2. **b.** Single-engine land and sea, multi-engine land and sea
3. **a.** Normal, utility, acrobatic

Principles of Flight

We've learned that an aircraft is something that flies; could be a copter, balloon or glider. Could even be an airplane. That's probably what you'll use, so let's define the word **Airplane,** and for that we read the FAA's FAR Part 1:

Airplane*: "An engine-driven, fixed-wing, aircraft heavier than air that is supported in flight by the dynamic reaction of air against its wings."*

Gliders don't (usually) have engines therefore aren't airplanes. Balloons, blimps and dirigibles don't lift with wings therefore aren't airplanes. Helicopters don't have anything that makes sense—especially a fixed wing—and as some wag once noted, "produce flight by beating the air into submission," so helicopters don't qualify as airplanes. Only the graceful, powered, winged machines you fly in this course meet all the criteria to proudly proclaim themselves "Airplanes."

> **_Note_**: Airplanes can, indeed, proclaim. In fact, they can think, speak and feel. Perhaps not the way the humans they support might, but an airplane—although it appears to be a collection of tubes, aluminum, fabric and steel—is really a conscious vehicle capable of the most amazing of conscious feats—Flight. So, get over any notion you might have of being superior to your airplane. Without a proper airplane/pilot relationship, the so-called inanimate flying machine will humble you in a flash. From the first lesson on, the pilot must respect the airplane's being. Then, as Humphrey Bogart noted, you'll have "the beginning of a beautiful friendship."

Airplane Parts

Airplanes come in many shapes and sizes. Some have one engine (**single-engine**), and others have two, three or more so qualify as **multi-engine**. Our focus is the single-engine airplane.

All airplanes have what appears to be at least one wing. Those airplanes we call **monoplanes**. The wings are usually two separate wing sections connected to fly as one.

Before we go any further, let's agree on terms. An **airplane** is not the same as a **plane**. A plane is a flat surface of some sort. An *air*plane is a vehicle utilizing planes to fly through air. "Plane," of course, is vernacular for airplane or in England, *aeroplane*. We'll stick with airplane.

> *Trivia*: While we're at it, the word "tarmac" is short for *tarmacadam*—named for John Loudon McAdam, who developed the macadam process in the early 19th Century. Someone then added tar and, *voila*—tarmac. Tarmac is used on some airport surfaces. Tarmac is not a US aviation term; using it makes you sound like a TV reporter who's watched too many British spy movies.

Wings are **airfoils** and are the primary lifting surface providing support in flight. On the ground they provide shade. Wings may be mounted below, above or in the middle of the fuselage, resulting in High-wing, Low-wing or (wait for it...) Mid-wing designs. Cessnas are generally high-wing and Piper Cherokees low-wing. It's a matter of pilot preference—you choose.

Chord Line

Leading Edge

Trailing Edge

Wing (Airfoil) Cross Section

The wing itself is usually a box-like construction. Curved ribs are attached to long spars running from wing tip to wing root. The ribs are webbed together with wires and struts into a semi-rigid form before the entire airfoil structure is covered in fabric or aluminum skin. Some airfoils use a thin wood veneer with a fabric overlay to produce a strong, smooth surface. Some airplanes, such as Cirrus or Diamond, are constructed with composite materials. We'll discuss airfoil shapes in more detail later.

All airplanes need fuel, and that's stored in fuel tanks, which ideally are located in the wings. Older airplanes store fuel inside the fuselage. High-wing airplanes generally use gravity to flow the fuel to the engine, while low-wing airplanes need one or more fuel pumps to pump the avgas uphill to the engine.

Attached to the wings' trailing edge are **Ailerons** and **Flaps** for controlling the airplane in flight. Attached to the wings' leading edge are smashed bugs.

Some airplanes have what appear to be two wings extending from either side of the main body. These are called **biplanes** and are really cool to fly. Biplanes are not limited to old flying movies or the air show circuit.

If you see an airplane with three wings, that's a **triplane**. If it's painted scarlet red and on your tail, it's the Red Baron in his Fokker DR1, and unless his guns jam, you'd better *jink* right or you'll be in deep *kimchi*. [5]

Chances are you're learning in a single-engine, monoplane, and even though the Red Baron died in 1918 and is commemorated, for some bizarre reason in a frozen pizza line, you shouldn't need to dodge machinegun bullets. But you will need to constantly scan the skies for other aircraft.

---

[5] *Jink* and *kimchi* are military slang. Go ask your mother.

Back to dissecting and labeling your airplane. Airplanes have **landing gear**. The gear may be comprised of wheels, skis or floats. Your airplane probably has wheels but even if you fly with skis for landing gear (a real giggle, by the way), you're still in a **Land Airplane.**

The landing gear usually has three legs—two beneath the wings or fuselage and one either under the nose (tricycle gear) or the tail (tailwheel or "conventional" gear). If you learn to fly in a tricycle-geared airplane and wish to transition to flying tailwheel airplanes you'll need additional training and a one-time endorsement as per FAR 61.31. To fly floats you'll need a Seaplane rating added to your Private Pilot certificate.

Left: This biplane has a tailwheel, so the confused, but snappily dressed, pilot must receive tailwheel training and a logbook endorsement from a qualified tailwheel CFI before acting as PIC (Pilot-in-Command).[6]

Let's concentrate on tricycle-geared airplanes. The two main gear legs are the actual landing gear upon which the airplane touches the earth in landing. The remaining nose wheel is there to keep the propeller from striking the runway.

> **SAFETYTIP:** *You don't land a tricycle-geared airplane on the nose wheel. It hurts. The airplane will "porpoise," and you'll soon learn that there's no fun with a porpoise in aviation.*

Some nose wheels are steerable with the nose wheel linked to the rudder pedals. Some tricycle-geared airplanes have castering nose wheels that swivel somewhat like shopping-cart wheels. Slightly different taxi techniques are required, and your CFI will explain.

Landing gear is classified as either **Fixed** or **Retractable**. As the terms imply, the fixed gear is bolted in the down position, while retractable gear is retracted in flight to reduce drag and

---

[6] The biplane is a 180-hp Marquart Charge

dramatically increase speed and maintenance costs. Your choice. As with tailwheel flying, if you learn in a fixed-gear airplane and switch to retractables, you probably will need additional training and a one-time logbook endorsement (FAR 61.31).

Wings, and sometimes landing gear, are attached to the **fuselage**. Fuselage is a French word. The French didn't invent flight; they merely acquired many of the naming rights.

The fuselage is the airplane's main body; beginning at the **firewall** and moving aft, it includes the cabin or cockpits plus the long hollow structure leading to and including the tail or the **empennage** (another French term).

The empennage comes in several shapes but most have vertical and horizontal fins in the tail. The vertical plane consists of an immovable vertical **stabilizer** with a hinged **rudder** attached. Perpendicular to this is the horizontal stabilizer, and hinged to that is the **elevator**. Attached to the elevator you may find a smaller hinged device called the **trim tab (or servo tab)**. Trim or servo tabs move opposite to the elevator to make the control input feel lighter and fine-tune or "trim" the elevator's input.

Some airplanes have a one-piece horizontal **stabilator** (Piper Cherokees for instance). It works like an elevator to control pitch but is a single piece, rather than two hinged planes, with an **anti-servo tab**, which decreases stabilator sensitivity, so the pilot doesn't over control pitch and acts, in part, like a trim tab. Pitch is the up and down movement of the nose.

Some airplanes have a V-tail. The Beechcraft Bonanza was the classic example of an airplane with two V-shaped **ruddervators** in lieu of the three-planed tail. Regardless of shape, pilot input is the same for any of the above tail arrangements. Rudder controls yaw and elevator or stabilator controls pitch. Ruddervators combine tasks.

The wings attach to the fuselage in several ways. Some are a single piece with the spars passing through the fuselage. Others are two sections (left and right wings) bolted to a carry-through center section in the fuselage. Some, like the Cessna 172, have struts that support the wings the way flying buttresses support the walls of Notre Dame cathedral. The Cessna 172, however, flies noticeably better than a medieval cathedral.

A fuselage can be constructed in a number of ways. Generally, the designs are divided into three groupings: *Truss, Monocoque* and *Semi-monocoque.*

Truss design (think bridge construction) is either metal tubing or wood connected in triangular shapes—trusses—that provide tremendous strength. A bit boxy, so the airframe is usually rounded out with stringers and formers to *form* a more pleasing shape before covered with either an aluminum or fabric skin. The goal is to achieve a strong, and yet light, airframe.

Many aircraft, particularly older ones, were covered in cotton or linen fabric (never canvas as non-pilots like to say) and glued or "doped" in place. The finish was light, strong and beautiful. Today, most fabric airplanes such as the Citabria, Pitts, Eagle, Husky and Maule, are covered in synthetic polyester fabrics with many brand names, but *Ceconite* ® is the brand name most often tossed about. Aluminum-covered airplanes are referred to as "Spamcans" by fabric-flying pilots. Spamcan drivers retort by calling fabric airplanes "Rag wings." It's all in good fun. Airplanes can also be made of plastic, but that's just silly. A Cessna 172 or any of the Cherokees are aluminum-skinned.

Monocoque (again with the French) is a round tube design wherein all the strength is in the stressed skin. Picture a beer can—light and strong but can't handle too many dents. So….

Enter **Semi-monocoque**, which combines stressed skin with a truss design. The best of both worlds and still very French.

Something has to motivate the airplane of whatever design to fly through the air, so every airplane has a **powerplant**. That sounds like a big coal-powered generator, but we're usually talking about a relatively small piston engine, spinning a propeller. Together with the engine's accessories (starter, alternator, vacuum pump) and propeller they form the powerplant.

Only FAA-certificated mechanics are permitted to work on your airplane (with some preventive maintenance exceptions outlined in FAR 43 Appendix A). Certified mechanics are dubbed "A&P" mechanics, not because they got their licenses from the *A&P* grocery store, but instead A&P here means "Airframe & Powerplant." (DistractingSideNote: *A&P,* the grocery store chain, means *The Great Atlantic & Pacific Tea Co* ™. You won't learn this stuff in any other aviation course.)

The powerplant (it's okay to call it the engine) is attached to the fuselage with an engine mount. The engine—hot from the constantly exploding gasses—is separated from the cabin or cockpit by a firewall. Common engines come in a range of sizes from the venerable 65-horsepower, four-cylinder engine produced by Continental and found on Champs, Cubs and Luscombes, to fire-breathing, 1500-hp Rolls-Royce Merlins on Spitfires and P-51 Mustangs. Most four-seat Cessnas and Pipers use the ubiquitous Lycoming 150 through 180-horsepower models. We'll skip all turbine (jet) engines in this course. Whatever engine your airplane sports, it most likely will be wrapped inside a **cowling**, which not only keeps off the rain but aids significantly in engine cooling and provides sparrows a place to nest.

An engine alone won't move the airplane, so a **propeller (air screw** to the Brits) is bolted to the engine's crankshaft. Through it, power is transferred from the engine to the propeller by turning the propeller at thousands of revolutions-per-minute (RPM). The propeller is an airfoil and, like the wings, produces a force when motivated. That force produced by the powerplant through the propeller is called **Thrust** and is one of four forces acting on the airplane in flight.

Let The Four Forces Be With You

The Four Forces acting on an airplane in flight are: **Thrust, Drag, Weight** and **Lift**.

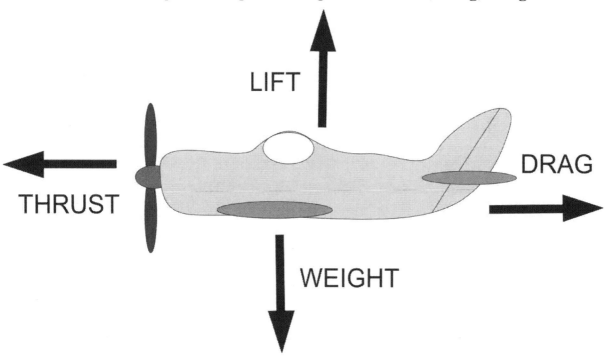

Thrust: It's the forward force produced by the powerplant and propeller. Thrust is opposed by its arch nemesis, Drag.

Drag: It's the rearward force that retards progress. Drag is caused by the disruptive flow of air over and around anything. Drag forms around wings, fuselage, struts, pilots' heads sticking above an open cockpit, flying wires, antennas, gear legs…anything that sticks into the relative wind.

Weight: This is the combined load of everything in and of the airplane. It includes, but is not limited to: The airplane itself, pilots, passengers, fuel, oil, baggage, charts, cheeseburgers or ice on the wings (**Safety Tip**: Never take off with *any* ice or frost on the airframe).

Lift: Ah, Lift, that sweet loosing from the surly bonds of gravity's (weight's) downward force that plagues the billions of planet crawlers who aren't pilots. Lift is created by the dynamic effect of air passing over a wing. No air movement, no lift. Lift acts perpendicular to the airplane's flight path.

It's The Law

Sir Isaac Newton, 17th Century Zen-master physicist and discoverer of many uses for the fig, wrote in his bestseller, *Newton's Third Law* ©, that there can be no unbalanced forces in steady straight flight. Or, when you're in cruise flight, holding altitude and airspeed, Newton's Third Law says you're balanced. This also applies if you're in a steady climb or descent. Everything must be balanced. The opposing forces (Lift v. Weight or that eternal grudge match Thrust v. Drag) must cancel each other out. Move one item out of balance and something else changes.

"In steady flight, the sum of all upward forces (not just lift) equals the sum of all downward forces (not just weight)." Plus, *"The sum of all forward forces (not just thrust) equals the sum of all backward forces (not just drag)."* [7]

Picture these forces as vectors or arrows of force. But these forces tend to wander about a bit, so in, say, a steady climb, since the nose is pointed up, a portion of thrust acts as lift. Meanwhile, with the nose up, a portion of the weight force acts as drag, pulling back or rearward not just downward.

In a glide, even with the engine off, a bit of the weight vector acts forward like thrust.

So, unless the airplane is flying perfectly horizontal to the flat plane of the Earth (no time to argue that Earth is allegedly round) you must subdivide these force vectors into two components as mentioned above. Don't sweat this too much, but keep it in the back of your mind for use when flying. This much detail won't appear on the written test. (*Phew!* The guy in the back row sighs….)

But you must understand the *Four Forces* acting on Flight: Thrust, Drag, Weight and Lift.

Add Three Axes

Balance is everything in flight, and all forces should balance together at the airplane's *Center of Gravity* (CG). Three lines (or axes) pass through this pinpoint of physical excellence and equilibrium. The airplane rotates around each of these axes to maneuver

---

[7] FAA-H-8083-25 3-1

about the sky. The three axes are: *Longitudinal, Lateral* and *Vertical.* You'll use them the rest of your flying life so embrace them.

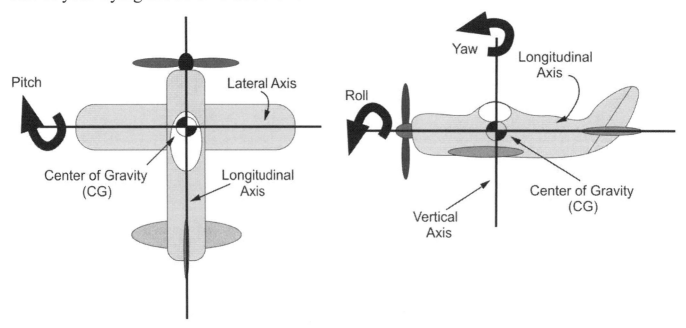

Longitudinal Axis: Picture a rod running from the airplane's tail to its nose. That represents the longitudinal axis. Now, imagine the airplane rotating, like a spitted hog, around that axis (for vegans picture a roasting zucchini). That rotation around the longitudinal axis is called **Roll** and is controlled by the ailerons. That rolling motion is also referred to as **Bank.**

Lateral Axis: Visualize a rod running through the wings from left wingtip to right. That represents the lateral axis, and rotation around that axis is called **Pitch**. Pitch is controlled by the elevator (or stabilator).

Vertical Axis: Imagine a rod poking vertically through the airplane's floorboards and out the top of the fuselage, running between the pilot and passenger seats like a pole dancer's workstation. That's the vertical axis and rotation around it, by activating the rudder, swings the nose left and right (picture it) in a yawing motion. So rotation around the vertical axis is called **Yaw**.

All three axes live in harmony, and all three come together at the airplane's center of gravity (CG). As you fly, you control all four forces to balance the airplane at its CG. Whenever you turn, climb or descend, you rotate the airplane around that CG and around one or more of the axes. Rarely do you use one axis alone; usually any maneuver—however slight—involves gentle application of all controls to balance these forces.

What Is Flight?

You buy a ticket, get in a line, remove your shoes and trudge onto an airliner that smells like a high school locker room where you sit between two guys the size of New Jersey for three hours only to arrive in Atlanta exhausted, sick and 18 hours late. That's not flight. That's airline travel.

Flight is you slicing through the atmosphere on gossamer wings, because you understand air the way no airline prisoner, *er*, passenger can. The atmosphere is made up of air. Air is composed of gases (78% nitrogen, 21% oxygen, 1% stray thoughts) that normally can't support anything bigger than dreams. But thanks to dreamers like Newton and Bernoulli[8]— guys who never flew—you can climb into your Cherokee, turn a key and, provided Homeland Security hasn't grounded everything, fly. All because of the magical and predictable fluid properties of air.

Air, while seemingly flimsy stuff, has **mass**, and anything with mass is attracted by **gravity**, which gives it **weight**. The higher you go in the atmosphere, however, the less weight the air has or think of it this way: Air density decreases with altitude. Breathing atop Denali,[9] Alaska is significantly more difficult than on Jones Beach, New York, although the parking is easier.

Since air has weight it exerts force. We call that force **pressure**, and since air is also a fluid it exerts that pressure equally around objects such as wings, propellers and struts. As altitude increases, **air density** decreases and affects aircraft performance. With increased altitude, the airplane engine produces less power, because, like the hiker atop the mountain, it takes in less air. Thrust decreases because the propeller has less air to bite and becomes less efficient. And lift decreases because the thinner air exerts less force on the airfoil. Air density is directly proportional to air pressure. Double the pressure and you double the density (assuming constant temperature).

Temperature affects air density. Increase air temperature and air density decreases. Air temperature usually decreases with an increase in altitude (that guy atop Denali is mighty cold, you bechya), but that decrease in temperature and expected corresponding increase in pressure is offset by the rapid decrease in air pressure resulting in air density decreasing despite decreasing temperature. In short, it's cold up high, but that doesn't increase the air density by much. It's dang cold in outer space, but not much air density there.

Humidity is a real stinker in the air density realm. All air has some moisture, although you'd never believe it standing on the ramp at the Blythe, California airport on a summer day. As humidity increases the air density decreases even though some might say it feels "heavier." It's not heavier.

---

[8] Daniel Bernoulli, 18th Century Swiss mathematician
[9] Mt. McKinley to those who like their mountains named for Midwestern politicians

Water vapor is lighter than air, so **humid (moist) air is lighter than dry air**. Warm air is less dense than cold air, so on a warm, humid day—typical midwestern summer day—the air is both hot and humid. *Oh, yah, Ingrid, and that there airplane of yours, you know, won't climb so good, you bechya.* But at least it's not Blythe. [10]

Knowing a little about air's properties helps the pilot understand how airplanes use air to fly.

Bernoulli's Airfoils

The physicist, Daniel Bernoulli, handed us what's probably the best overview of why airfoils lift. He noted that as a fluid changes its speed, pressure also changes. Increase speed of a fluid, and its pressure decreases; decrease the speed, and pressure likewise increases. I'm simplifying significantly but picture a wing's profile as viewed from the end.

Most small airplane wings have a curved surface on top of the airfoil and a relatively flat surface on the bottom. Here's why: Picture zillions of invisible air molecules racing into the airfoil's leading edge in flight. Each air molecule wants to stay buddied up with its neighbor. However, as the air molecules contact the wing in motion, being fluid they split apart and wrap around the wing as it passes through the air mass. Imagine a wave hitting a pier's piling. The wave breaks around the piling and then reforms again on the other side. The wind—air mass—also splits apart and tries to reform on the other side. Some of the air moves over the curved top of the wing and the rest along the flatter underside. They both try to reunite at the trailing edge as the wing passes. Due to the wing's curvature (called **camber**) the upper half of air speeds up while traveling the longer distance.

Bernoulli said that as a fluid speeds up its pressure decreases. The air rushing across the upper wing surface has a slightly longer distance to travel than the air along the bottom. The air along the upper wing surface speeds up. As it speeds up, its pressure drops, resulting in relatively low pressure on top of the wing and higher pressure below. The wing lifts into the low pressure.

Ever noticed a shower curtain pull toward the rushing water/air mixture from the showerhead? Of course not, you'd get shampoo in your eyes. Well, rinse and observe: The curtain acts like an airfoil at that moment. The rushing fluid (air and water) causes pressure to drop, while on the other side the air pressure remains unchanged so is higher than the side with the rushing water/air. The curtain, in a sense, lifts toward the rushing water. Similarly, a wing lifts toward the low or negative pressure created above the airfoil and in the process sucks the entire airplane up with it in **negative lift**.

---

[10] "At least it's not Blythe," town motto for Needles, California

The wing (airfoil) passing through the air creates LOW pressure on top of the wing....

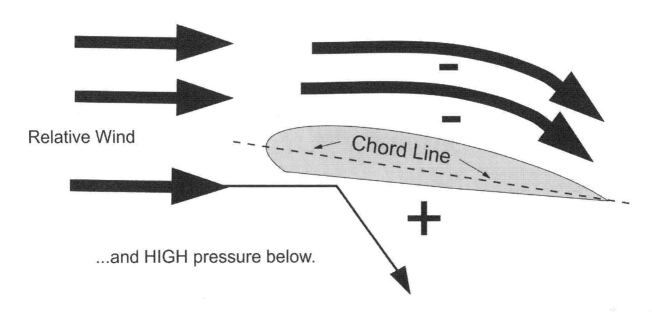

Relative Wind

...and HIGH pressure below.

The upper camber doesn't do all the work. The lower camber provides positive pressure, the way your hand does when you stick it out the window while driving 70 mph and trying to wave at a cop with a flat tire beside the road. (Safety Tip: Don't try this!) The hand, or the wing, is pushed upward by positive pressure from beneath. Applying Newton's law of **Action/Reaction** we see that as a force is applied to the lower side of the wing it deflects downward, and an equal and opposite reaction pushes upward in **positive lift**. The wing is pushed up into the low-pressure area. Studies have shown that the low-pressure force above the wing is larger than the high-pressure force below.

But, Wait, There's More...(music up)

As we increase the **angle of attack**, or the angle at which the airfoil (wing's chord line) attacks the air, the lift effect increases. Increase angle of attack (AOA) and you increase lift. Make a note of that and keep it throughout your flying life: *Increase angle of attack (AOA) and you increase lift. Plus, you increase Drag.*

So, a combination of high (positive) pressure below the wing plus low (negative) pressure above causes a lifting force that exceeds the airplane's weight and, *presto!* Flight. Almost. Read on, there may be some downside.

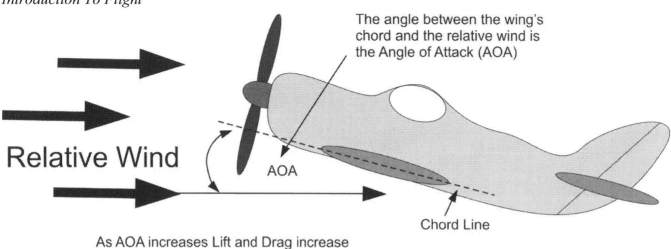

The angle between the wing's chord and the relative wind is the Angle of Attack (AOA)

Relative Wind

AOA

Chord Line

As AOA increases Lift and Drag increase

Wash This Summation Down

Bernoulli says, in part, that low pressure above, high pressure below causes our wings to lift. Newton reminds us in his Third Law that for every action there is an opposite and equal reaction (think of a shotgun being fired—pellets go one way, and your shoulder goes the other). In flight this means that as the low-pressure air flows across Bernoulli's upper wing camber when it reaches the wing's trailing edge it flows down. This downward, backward flow is called **downwash** and, invoking Newton here, that downward wash must have an opposite reaction that forces the wing upward. Imagine a wave of air flowing over the upper wing and washing down to push the wing up.

As air flows across the wing's upper camber it washes down, and...

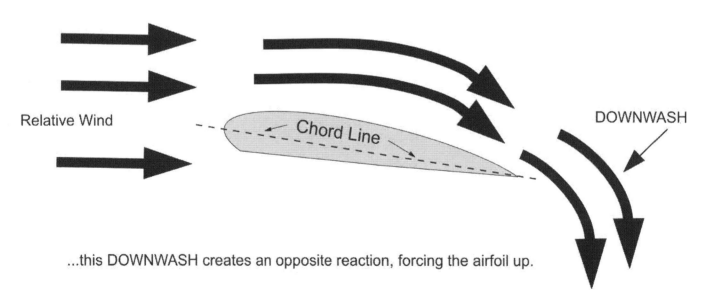

Relative Wind

Chord Line

DOWNWASH

...this DOWNWASH creates an opposite reaction, forcing the airfoil up.

So, Newton and Bernoulli can quit their longtime feud because, they're both right. Lift is caused (in part) by the Bernoulli pressure differential created by air flowing rapidly over an airfoil—low pressure on top and high pressure below. Plus, lift is produced using Newton's

Third Law, which says that for every action there is an opposite and equal reaction—if a downward force is created by an airfoil then an upward force must also be present.

I've greatly simplified what causes lift, mainly because I'm a deeply simple pilot. If you're more curious about aerodynamics—theory, physics, math, bigger words, Bernoulli's social life, and such—I recommend a thorough reading of the FAA's *Pilot's Handbook of Aeronautical Knowledge* (PHAH, FAA-H-8083-25, from which I glean much of my knowledge), and the US Navy's book on Aeronautics *Aerodynamics For Naval Aviators* (NAVWEPS 00-80T—80)

Coming Soon: In a future chapter we expand on chord line and AOA. Plus, we'll move these pressures about to maneuver the airplane—something Newton and Bernoulli never had the chance to do.

Test Questions:

4. How will frost on the wings of an airplane affect takeoff performance?

   a. Frost will disrupt the smooth flow of air over the wing, adversely affecting its lifting capability.
   b. Frost will change the camber of the wing, increasing lift during takeoff.
   c. Frost may cause the airplane to become airborne with a higher angle of attack, decreasing the stall speed.

5. The term "angle of attack" is the angle (complete the sentence)

   a. between the wing chord line and the relative wind.
   b. between the airplane's climb angle and the horizon.
   c. between the longitudinal axis of the airplane and the chord line of the wing.

Answers:

4. **a.** Frost will disrupt the smooth flow of air over the wing, adversely affecting its lifting capability.
5. **a.** between the wing chord line and the relative wind.

To Rent or To Buy?

It's hoped that at this stage in your studies you're either taking flight instruction or about to meet your instructor and apply book knowledge to your place in the sky. Either way, you'll need an airplane. Kind of a must. Sadly, not all airports have Fixed Base Operators (FBO) with flight schools and rental airplanes lined up and ready to serve. Many flight instructors operate freelance with one airplane or even with no aircraft available to rent. That's when you want to ask around at several airports about the availability of ***Flying Clubs.***

Flying clubs might comprise a few pilots who share the cost of buying and maintaining a single aircraft, or you might find a club with several airplanes and dozens of members, including a staff of mechanics and instructors. Visit nearby airports and ask, "Where can I learn to fly?" or contact AOPA at AOPA.org to search for flight schools and flying clubs in your area. We'll post suggestions on our website: paulberge.com

Consider the possibility of buying your own airplane in which to learn to fly. As with any plan there are plusses and not-so-plusses. On the plus side, if you own the airplane then it is only available to you, no waiting for another student to return it for you to fly. Likewise you don't have to sweat returning it to the flight school on time. It's yours. And that leads to the down side of airplane ownership while learning to fly.

If you own it you pay for everything: fuel, insurance, taxes, hangar rent, maintenance and more. When you rent or belong to a club, you indirectly pay for these things, but fixed costs are shared among all renters or club members. If something breaks on a rental airplane the owner fixes it. If it breaks on your airplane you pay the mechanic to fix it.

Owning an airplane is great. I've owned several. Paying for everything is not so great. The airplane in which you learn to fly might not be your ultimate love so get your pilot certificate in a rental and then begin the search for the airplane that will make you want to move into the hangar together for a lifetime. Relationships are tough so be picky selecting your aerial partners.

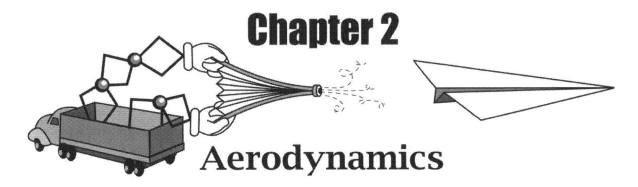

Chapter 2

Aerodynamics

Earlier we learned about pressures acting on a wing and, indeed, being created by the wing, or airfoil, moving through the fluid environment we call air. Now we'll move these pressures about to maneuver the airplane. Because without maneuverability, all airplanes would take off from Los Angeles, fly a straight line to Chicago and forever be stuck on the O'Hare ramp unable to move. That, once again, is airline travel and not flight. Never confuse the two.

We briefly discussed the **Center of Gravity** (CG), which is where all three axes (Lateral, Longitudinal and Vertical) around which the airplane maneuvers, come together. Think of it as the balancing point, the head of the pin upon which the angels of flight dance. The CG is a fixed point in the airplane based on how the airplane is built and loaded or where the total airplane weight is concentrated. Saying it's a fixed point is a little misleading since the CG will shift as fuel is burned or passengers bail out. More on determining the CG in the Weight & Balance chapter.

While it may sound like the site of headache, the **Center of Pressure** (CP) is, instead, a moveable point along the airfoil indicating where a force vector exists.

Center of Pressure
(or Center of Lift) vs...

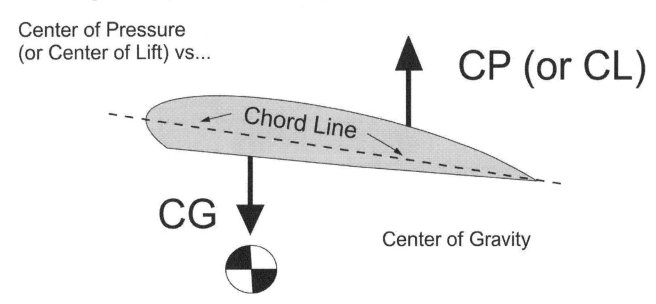

CP (or CL)

Chord Line

CG

Center of Gravity

It's not lift, per se, but CP exists as a part of the lift phenomenon. It's a combination of both the negative and positive pressure forces. It's a point where the resultant force vector of both positive and negative pressures applies. CP changes with Angle of Attack (AOA). Taking it one more step introduces the **Center of Lift** (CL), which is the location along the wing's chord line at which all the *lift* forces produced by the wing are concentrated. For simplicity, think of CP and CL as being the same thing. I know I will.

Terms: Angle of Attack (AOA) is the angle at which the wing's chord line (imaginary line from leading edge to trailing edge) *attacks* the relative wind. **Relative Wind** is the onrushing air created by the airplane moving through that air. Relative wind is not what blows through the trees and is not always parallel to the Earth's surface. In a loop, for instance, as the airplane's nose rises and descends, the relative wind is the airflow relative to the airplane's flight path, which in a loop is constantly changing.

Enough loops, back to the AOA and CP. From the FAA's own acronym-filled mouth: "For any given AOA, the CP is the point where the resultant force crosses the chord line."[11]

So?

So, normally, as AOA changes, the CP/CL changes. As AOA increases, the CP/CL moves forward, conversely, as AOA decreases CP/CL moves aft. Logic says that if the Center of Lift were placed directly over the Center of Gravity, the airplane would be balanced, like a model airplane hanging from the ceiling in the pilots lounge by a string. Right?

That's not completely true. Problem is, the wing is inherently unbalanced. The wings lift the airplane, and in stabilized, balanced, straight-and-level flight the CL remains aft of the CG. Picture it along the airfoil. If the Center of Lift, the upward force, is behind the downward, weighty CG, then the airplane will tend to be nose heavy. So, the airplane's tail is designed to exert a slight downward force—lifting the nose—to balance the longitudinal axis in level flight. The horizontal stabilizer is attached to the airframe with a negative AOA.

Huh? I thought we wanted to fly, you know, lift?

We do, and by balancing the nose-down force of the wing with a tail-down force that's trying to lift the nose, the airplane is balanced in straight-and-level flight...boring, straight-and-level-flight.

But we don't want to hang in space gathering dust. We want to maneuver, and in order to maneuver the balance must be disturbed, forces redirected and new balance achieved.

---

[11] FAA-H-8083-25 2-7

To maneuver the airfoil up and down the pilot moves the CL forward or aft. To do this, the pilot needs to decrease or increase the wing's AOA, by pitching the nose up or down to move the airplane's longitudinal axis up or down. Attached to the horizontal stabilizer is an elevator that's used to change the AOA and cause the CL to advance or recede along the wing. The pilot controls this by moving the yoke or stick fore or aft to move the elevator up or down.

The **elevator** (or stabilator in some airplanes such as Piper Cherokees) is a moveable control surface. It controls **pitch**, the up-and-down movement of the longitudinal axis around the lateral axis. Think about that: The longitudinal axis is that imaginary rod from tail to nose spinner. If we rotate around that axis, we call it roll. But if we force the longitudinal axis, instead, to tilt up and down, the airplane pivots or pitches around the lateral axis. The elevator deflects the relative wind to raise or lower the tail, which does the opposite to lower or raise the nose. That's pitch.

The ailerons, one located outward on each wing (usually) also deflect up and down, but they do so in opposite directions to control **roll** of the lateral axis around the longitudinal axis.

Each wing is an airfoil. An airfoil has certain lifting characteristics based in part upon its cross-section shape—flattish on the bottom, curved on top (camber). If we change the airfoil's camber, we modify its lift. Imagine the aileron at the end of the wing. As the aileron deflects downward, the chord line from leading edge to trailing edge changes its angle of attack to the relative wind. It increases as the aileron deflects down. In doing so, it changes the apparent shape, curve or camber of the wing creating more lift (and drag). If we deflect one aileron down while defecting the other aileron up or not at all, the increased lift on one wing will cause it to rise while the other wing does not or even descends. Result: The airplane rolls. As it rolls it turns. Or tries to.

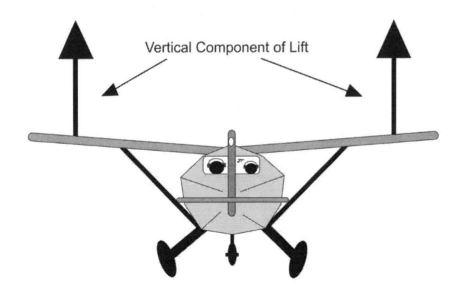

Vertical Component of Lift

In straight & level flight
the Vertical Component of Lift
prevails.

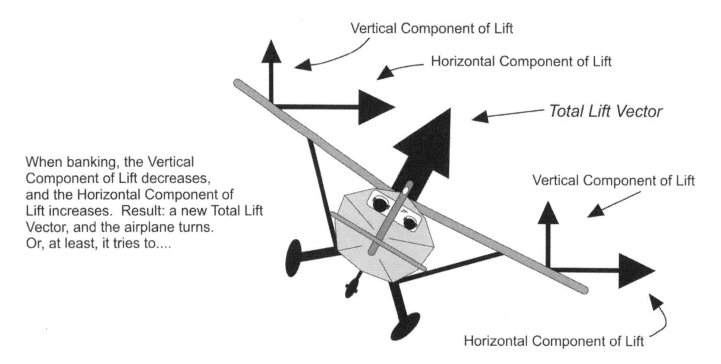

Vertical Component of Lift

Horizontal Component of Lift

Total Lift Vector

Vertical Component of Lift

When banking, the Vertical Component of Lift decreases, and the Horizontal Component of Lift increases. Result: a new Total Lift Vector, and the airplane turns. Or, at least, it tries to....

Horizontal Component of Lift

If life were simple, then aileron deflection would cause a smooth roll and a resulting turn. The reason the airplane turns is because the **Lift Vector** has changed from a **Vertical Component of Lift** to one with a horizontal component.

Huh?

Imagine an airplane in level flight. Both wings are lifting equally and the airplane cruises along. It stays aloft because the lift is being vectored (pointed) vertically up—we call that the vertical component of lift. As we bank the airplane we move the lift vector toward the horizon. In essence, we "lift" the airplane in a new direction other than perpendicular to the Earth's horizon. This increased **Horizontal Component of Lift** (a **Centripetal Force** that lifts inward) competes with the diminishing vertical component, and the airplane turns in the bank toward the new **Total Lift** component, which is a combination of the vertical and horizontal lifting forces.

So, a turn seems to be initiated by using ailerons. If so, why do we have a rudder? Boats turn with rudders, why not airplanes?

Boats generally operate on the horizontal surface of the water. The boat's rudder deflects forces to move the pointy end (You sailors know these terms. What is it, bow, stern, yardarm?). An airplane turns from the banking caused by deflecting the ailerons—one up, one down. But the same ailerons that seemed so eager to please us with a turn will also diminish the turn.

As one aileron goes up and the other down, the down aileron has a higher AOA and produces lift plus its annoying, tag-along cousin, drag. The down aileron, which is lifting the wing, produces more drag than the up aileron on the other wing. So, as the airplane tries to bank and turn, the lowered aileron encumbered by drag, pulls or **yaws** the airplane away from the intended turn. The result is an uncoordinated, slipping mess.

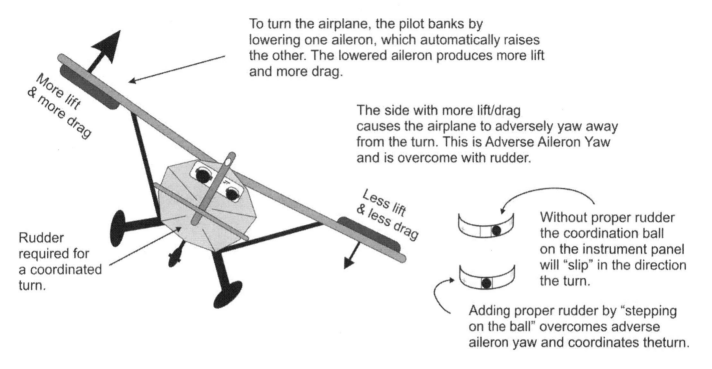

To turn the airplane, the pilot banks by lowering one aileron, which automatically raises the other. The lowered aileron produces more lift and more drag.

More lift & more drag

The side with more lift/drag causes the airplane to adversely yaw away from the turn. This is Adverse Aileron Yaw and is overcome with rudder.

Less lift & less drag

Rudder required for a coordinated turn.

Without proper rudder the coordination ball on the instrument panel will "slip" in the direction the turn.

Adding proper rudder by "stepping on the ball" overcomes adverse aileron yaw and coordinates the turn.

The down aileron's drag (by-product of its lift) adversely yaws the airplane's nose (around the vertical axis) away from the turn. This is called ***Adverse Aileron Yaw*** and must be understood in order to make a coordinated, smooth turn.

To overcome adverse aileron yaw, the pilot adds rudder to yaw the nose in the direction of the turn. How much? Enough to keep the **Coordination Ball** centered in the **Turn Coordinator** or **Turn-and-Slip Indicator**.

Something else happens when you bank an airplane—it wants to overbank. This **Overbanking Tendency** is caused by the additional lift on the raised wing (the one with the lowered aileron producing all that extra lift). In a normal turn, the pilot banks and adds a bit of rudder to overcome adverse yaw and keep the coordination ball centered. As desired bank angle is reached, the pilot rolls the yoke or joystick toward neutral in order to hold the bank. Especially at high bank angles (steep turns) the pilot needs to not only neutralize the ailerons but also perhaps add a little aileron input opposite to the turn. You can read about and intellectualize this all you want, but it won't make gut sense until you try it in flight, and, then, it'll seem easy.

For routine Private/Sport Pilot training banks won't exceed 60 degrees relative to the horizon. If you fly beyond 60 degrees of bank, FAR 91.307(c) says you might need to wear a parachute.

Load Factor or Ten Pounds of Flight In a Five-Pound Bag

What do you weigh? Think so? Let's take off, climb to 1500 feet above ground level (AGL) and roll the airplane into a 60-degree bank. Whatever you thought you weighed on earth, you now weigh double.

Hokey smokey, no more Twinkies and beer for breakfast!

Don't panic; simply roll back to level flight and your weight returns to normal. Magic? No, load factor. Although, you should really avoid the *Twinkie 'n Beer* breakfast diet craze.

Gs, Louise!

When an aircraft sits on the ramp, its weight exerts one force of gravity or **1G.** That's weight, or gravity pulling stuff down. We can simulate increased (and decreased) gravity or weight in flight. **Load Factor,** as it relates to flight, is the ratio of the load supported by the wings to the actual aircraft weight and everything in it or on it. In level flight the wings support all the weight (load) so the load factor is 1G. As you bank and change the vertical lift to horizontal lift, you know from several paragraphs back that Total Lift moves the airplane in the turn. Newton said that if we create a force in one direction (Total Lift) there must be an opposite force. In a banking turn centripetal force pulls the airplane inward into the turn. That's good. But an opposite centrifugal force acts outward of the turn from the center of rotation. That's not all bad provided the pilot balances these two forces to achieve a coordinated, constant rate of turn.

Pilot Lounge Bonus Points: Sideways force is called **Transverse G-force**.

Experiment 2.1: Find a bucket out by the airplane wash area. Half fill it with water (soap optional). Now, tip the bucket so water runs all over your shoes. No, don't get angry. Get Newton. Swing that bucket in a wide arc. Assuming you don't hit anything, the water won't spill. Why? Because centrifugal force sends the water toward the bottom of the bucket, trapping it. That water exerts more than 1G. Now, put the bucket down and go change your socks.

Imagine you're a bag of watery guts in the pilot's seat. As you bank the airplane, centripetal force pulls you into the turn, and the opposite centrifugal force yanks you outside the turn. Strapped into your seat, like the water in the bucket, you feel the **G-Force** or load factor increase, pressing you into the cushions. At 60 degrees of bank this force doubles the load factor, and everything in and including the airplane is now twice as "heavy." That's misleading because your actual weight has not changed, only the load factor seeming to magnify your weight. Your airplane, however, wonders if you're still on the Twinkie 'n beer routine.

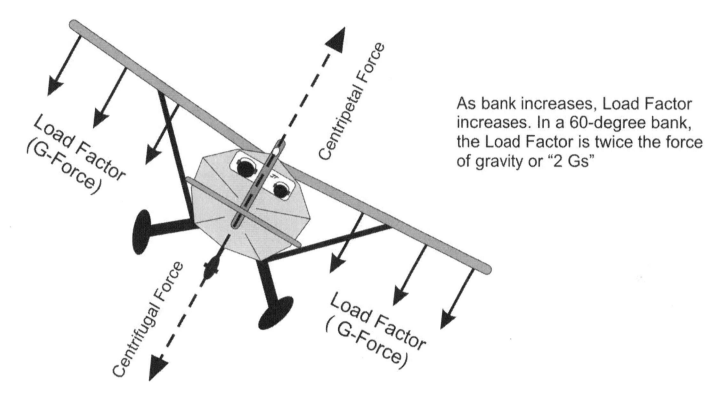

As bank increases, Load Factor increases. In a 60-degree bank, the Load Factor is twice the force of gravity or "2 Gs"

All type-certificated aircraft are designed, tested and certified to sustain certain load factors. In Chapter 1 we encountered the Normal, Utility and Acrobatic certification categories. Here's how they apply to your Private/Sport Pilot world.

Normal category airplanes are certified to withstand 3.8 positive Gs (3.8 times gravity) or 1.52 negative Gs. These are your basic family cruisers, designed to fly from Point A to Point B without a lot of commotion. Or they can be trainers used for non-acrobatic maneuvers not exceeding 60 degrees of bank. Yes, a 60-degree bank normally pulls only 2Gs, and Normal allows up to 3.8. That extra protection is a safety cushion.

Utility category airplanes are the pick-up trucks of the sky, the workers. They're certified to withstand +4.4 Gs or –1.76 Gs. Utility aircraft will handle the Normal category maneuvers plus extras, which usually includes spins.

Acrobatic category, as the name implies, are for loops, rolls, snaps, and whatever else stays within the higher load limits of +6Gs and –3Gs.

<u>*Note*</u>: Sloppy maneuvering can cause the airplane to exceed these limits. Built tough doesn't mean you fly 'em rough. For instance, a 60-degree turn in your Normal Category airplane pulls 2Gs—Fun. But add a mere 15 degrees more and at a 75-degree bank, you're pulling almost 4Gs. Normal is certified for, what? 3.8Gs? Hmmm.... Now add severe turbulence such as would be found when inadvertently penetrating a thunderstorm (no sane pilot intentionally punches into one), and a sloppy steep bank could pull the wings off. Ruins the entire flight.

Stalls

A wing moving through air lifts. A wing banks to produce a turn. And a wing without moving air can forget to be a wing and stall. Before we define a stall, it's *muy importante* to know what it is not. An aerodynamic stall is not caused by the airplane's engine quitting as non-pilots talking to TV news crews like to say, *"Why, I seen da airplane's motor stall, and then it smacked into da tavern; luckily, right after I walked out."*

A wing produces lift. When a wing quits lifting enough to overcome the airplane's load, it stalls. The engine could be running full power or at idle, doesn't matter. If the wing's angle of attack exceeds the **Critical Angle of Attack**, the wing stalls. An airplane can stall at any airspeed. Repeat: An airplane can stall at any airspeed, but will always stall when the wing's critical angle of attack is exceeded. (Memorize that.)

Increasing AOA does not cause a stall. It's when the AOA becomes excessive that the wing stalls. Each airplane has a certain—and almost invisible—angle of attack at which it will always stall. This AOA can be achieved at many different airspeeds and flight configurations, but there is always a certain AOA at which smooth airflow over the wing separates from the upper wing surface, and it stalls.

Picture three flight configurations: Low-speed flight, high-speed flight and turning flight.

In low-speed flight as airspeed is reduced, the airplane will descend unless pitch is increased to increase AOA. By increasing AOA, lift is increased. The slower you fly, the higher the AOA must be to maintain altitude. Unfortunately, this can't go on forever. Eventually, the AOA will become excessively high and smooth airflow over the wing burbles at the critical AOA. Result: Stall, wing quits lifting, passengers scream. So, it seems as though speed has something to do with stalls. It does, and it doesn't.

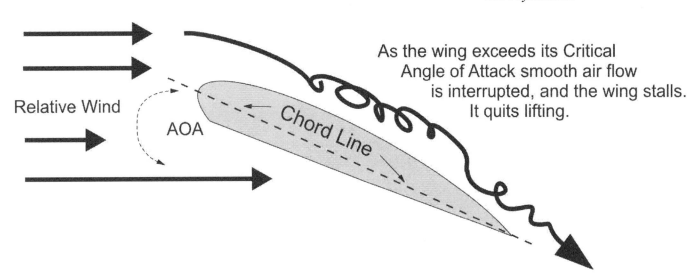

As the wing exceeds its Critical Angle of Attack smooth air flow is interrupted, and the wing stalls. It quits lifting.

Consider high-speed flight. When an airplane dives, it goes fast. With speed it won't stall, right? Don't believe that. If the pilot dives to gain speed and then abruptly pulls back on the control yoke or stick to increase pitch, a load is placed on the airplane. It's just like swinging that water bucket. The increased load factor puts more demand on the wing to lift. Gravity (in the dive) and sudden addition of centrifugal force inhibits the airplane from smoothly altering its flight path from nose-down to nose-up. The nose pitches up, the AOA increases rapidly. Load factor goes way up as the airplane momentarily continues along its diving flight path, and the smooth airflow over the wing is quickly interrupted even though the airplane is at a high airspeed: Stall.

Stick with load factors a bit longer and feel the increased load factor in a steep level turn. As load factor increases stall speed increases. Additionally, as the load factor increases while banking you need to increase the angle of attack to gain more lift to hold altitude that is lost to the excess load factor. This cycle repeats until with the excessive load, the wing reaches an excessively high angle of attack at a relatively high airspeed, and: Stall.

So, in a level turn, if the AOA becomes excessive—won't allow the smooth flow of air over the wing—the airplane stalls. Then what?

We know that the airplane's CL is usually located aft of the CG making most airplanes feel "nose heavy." We also know that the tail's downward force balances this in flight. As the wing stalls, these lift forces quit, and if the airplane is properly rigged and loaded, that nose-heavy condition will cause the nose to drop. That's a little disconcerting to the first-time flyer staring at the ground coming up. But it's actually good news, because if the nose goes down, pitch decreases, so the AOA decreases, allowing air to flow smoothly across the wing, and before you can say, "That's all there is?" (while relaxing elevator back pressure to prevent a second stall) the wing flies, the stall is defeated, and you breathe again while climbing to a safe altitude.

While you're catching your breath consider this aspect of stalling speeds: the higher the airspeed, the greater the load factor imposed before a stall occurs. The load factor squares as the stall speed doubles. Don't sweat the math, just realize that the faster you try to stall, the more load (stress) you exert on the airframe. Too much stress and it bends. Not good.

To avoid catastrophic failure, airplanes should not be stalled or flown in turbulence where an inadvertent stall might occur, when operating above the airplane's **Design Maneuvering Speed** (V$_A$). Design Maneuvering Speed is a function of stall speed, so it varies with the airplane's weight or load. However, in rough air, or when maneuvering, be certain to operate below the Design Maneuvering Speed found in the airplane's pilot operating handbook (POH). For older airplanes (Cubs, Champs and such) without an owner's manual, calculate V$_A$ as 1.7 times stall speed. If your Champ stalls at 43 knots, then V$_A$ would be ~73 knots. Bottom line: High-speed stalls exert tremendous loads. A normal stall entered from slow, straight-and-level flight exerts little excess load.

Spins Make The World Go 'Round

You learn about stalls not simply to pass the FAA written Knowledge Test or to impress the Designated Pilot Examiner (DPE) on the Private Pilot check ride. Every pilot must also understand stalls to avoid the consequence of unattended stalls—the spin.

The FAA defines a spin as "an aggravated stall, which results in autorotation."

To the first-time spinner, it looks more like *Earth-In-A-Blender* as everything outside the windshield twirls in a blur. Spin training is not required for a Private Pilot certificate. Perhaps it should be. I highly recommend spin training if only to see what spins look like, so you won't be so surprised should you stumble into one unassisted. They're actually kinda fun.

Spins are possible from any stall configuration. Unattended, they're deadly as the airplane rotates in a semi-stalled descent into the ground. Spins are also easy to recognize, avoid and recover from. Here's a simple power-off stall to an intentional spin entry and recovery. Consult your Pilot Operating Handbook (POH, aka the aircraft's owner's manual) for specifics and have your instructor demonstrate rather than experiment on your own.

From slow flight—with power off, airspeed low—the airplane's nose pitches up in a familiar stall entry. As the stall begins, the wings shudder, the ailerons get mushy, and the tail chatters from ragged downwash. In short, everything is ready to quit flying. With an overly high AOA, suddenly a wing stalls and the nose drops. To induce a spin, the pilot intentionally holds full aft yoke or stick to aggravate the stall.

As the nose drops it rotates (pivots), because one wing stalls before the other and remains more stalled. The less-stalled, outer wing produces more lift than the inner wing. So, around we go. And it's a fast around-we-go, too. You'll feel like you're pointed straight down. You're not. Surprisingly, although a spin seems violent the load factor is low because the airplane is stalled and airspeed is low.

Spin recovery is similar to stall recovery because you're recovering from (*what, class?*) an aggravated stall. Decreasing pitch stops the stall. Release backpressure on the stick or yoke. Air flows across the wings again, and the stall is over. Rotation (pivot) is corrected—*not with ailerons*—but with rudder. You're not done yet.

Recovery puts the airplane in a fairly steep nose-down attitude with airspeed screaming toward redline ("*Incredible ain't it?*"[12]), so the nose needs to pitch up smoothly after breaking the stall. Pull up too quickly and you'll overstress the airframe or induce a secondary—nastier—stall. As the nose raises through the horizon, and your instructor stops screaming, apply full power to climb back for another one. Repeat until your hat falls off.

Note: Not all airplanes are certified for spins and, except for flight instructor training, parachutes are normally required. Still, find a good CFI who likes spins and get at least one lesson.

Drag

With lift comes drag. Drag comes in two types: **Induced** and **Parasite.**

Induced drag results from flight. The wing develops lift and induces (causes to happen) drag.

Parasite drag is subdivided into three classes: form drag, skin friction and interference drag.

Form drag comes from anything that protrudes into the wind—gear legs, antennas, cowlings, cylinders, and struts. An airplane designer can limit form drag through streamlining.

Skin friction results from imperfect surfaces, such as the airplane's skin (fabric, wood, aluminum, composite). No surface is perfectly smooth, so all those microscopic imperfections plus rib stitching and rivet heads grate against the wind causing drag. A good wax job helps reduce the drag but won't eliminate it.

---

[12] Bugs Bunny, © 1943

When you place two objects in close proximity to each other, the elements of skin friction and form drag combine and magnify to create **Interference Drag**.

The pilot has no control over parasite drag in flight.

Induced Drag appears whenever an airfoil produces lift. Learn to live with it. We know that when the wing is in flight, there's a positive force on the bottom and a negative force on top. As the wing passes through the air that high pressure below tries to equalize with the low pressure above. The result is a lateral flow outward from beneath the wingtip. That flow rotates at the wingtips and trails behind—counterclockwise around the right wingtip and clockwise around the left. These vortices flow upward beyond the wingtip and in a downwash behind the wing. (This downwash is not the same downwash associated with downwash that produces lift.)

The induced downwash around the wingtips is induced drag. It actually bends the lift vector rearward at the wingtip.

As angle of attack (AOA) increases lift increases. As lift increases drag increases, so induced drag is greatest at slow speeds and high angles of attack. Induced drag varies inversely as the square of the airspeed. Or, skipping the math (so the author can understand it): Go faster and have less induced drag. Wingtip vortices intensity is directly proportional to the aircraft's weight. A heavy, slow airplane with a high AOA produces the worst (most violent) vortices and the most induced drag. This usually occurs in takeoff and landing phase. (See Chapter 5 for more on Wake Turbulence.)

Parasite drag, conversely, increases as the square of the airspeed. Or: Go faster get more parasite drag.

The pilot can't beat parasite drag in flight, but you can mute the effects of induced drag by utilizing the planet on which your airplane is based and taking advantage of what's called ground effect.

Ground Effect

Every flight begins and ends in the presence of the phenomenon called ground effect. Good students memorize the definition and pass tests. Good pilots use ground effect to their advantage.

Ground effect occurs close to the ground, within about a wingspan's height. The closer the wing is to the ground the greater the effect. That effect is the interference by the ground of the less desirable airflows around the wing. In ground effect the air flows unrestricted over the top of the wing, producing lift, but the ground mutes the downward forces (mainly wingtip vortices), so induced drag is reduced.

While operating in ground effect the wing will require a lower AOA than when out of ground effect. This means that close to the runway you'll experience lift at fairly slow airspeeds. Little in aviation is free, so as you leave the ground-effect region, induced drag returns with all its might, and that lower airspeed might not be enough to maintain flight. Ground effect is used to get the wheels, skis or floats off the surface allowing the airplane to skim along the surface for a short distance until proper climb speed (Vx—Best Angle of Climb or Vy—Best Rate of Climb) is achieved. Your instructor will teach this technique. Those of us who fly old, underpowered airplanes off grass or muddy runways know and appreciate ground effect. Those who try to land their airplanes too fast will not appreciate it.

A Few More Forces Acting On Flight

We've discussed the wing's ability to use invisible air to lift you, your airplane, three whining kids and a wet dog in the baggage compartment above the planet. We've utilized Bernoulli's principle about pressure differentials and nodded in unison agreeing with Newton's law of action/reaction, but we need to consider Newton's *First Law*, which he conceived as an undergraduate while he slept at his desk unable to move after studying all night for his alchemy midterms.

Newton figured out that "A body at rest tends to stay at rest unless acted upon by another force." Or: "Hey, Newton, wake up, Physics class is over, time to get to gym!" The other half of that law is that bodies in motion tend to stay in motion unless acted upon by another force.

Consider the first half. Your airplane sits on the ramp, wings intact, fuel tanks full, engine in fine shape, passengers loaded and flight plan filed. It looks like an airplane, but it isn't moving. So, what's it take to motivate this piston-engine flying machine?

A Propeller

Even the name is perfect. The **Propeller** *propels* the flying machine through the air. It's an airfoil, similar to the wing. It has a curved side and a relatively flat side. It attaches to a hub on the engine's crankshaft. The engine's crankshaft turns the hub, which turns the propeller blades. Looking at it from the back (pilot's view) one blade ascends while the other descends. Yes, propellers can have three, four or more blades, but we'll stick with the two-bladed types commonly found on trainers. Later, when you write your own best-selling Private Pilot manual you can buy a Hawker Sea Fury with a five-bladed prop.

The propeller blades act like airfoils if they're canted with a positive AOA. So, if you look down the tip of a propeller....

SAFETY TIP: Never consider a propeller to be safe. As with a gun, treat the propeller as though it will always bite you. It can lop off a hand before you can say, "Gee, the ignition switch said OFF!" The prop is always hot. Treat it with respect.

...without touching it, you'll notice that you're viewing an airfoil. As the propeller turns each blade attacks the relative wind (up and down), creating all the lift and drag forces found in a wing. Lift results, only it's called something else.

That force produced by the spinning propeller is called **Thrust**. Each side of the propeller produces thrust in two vectors (arrows) coming back from the prop blades and pushing along the fuselage. That thrust moves the entire airframe full of fuel, engine, passengers and bowling balls forward. Once the airplane reaches flying speed, it lifts. Amazing all the work that skinny prop has to do.

Propellers come in many styles and are made from several materials. Originally, props were wood, and many still are. Today, props are often made of high-tech carbon-fiber compounds—light and strong. Most propellers on trainers are aluminum.

For our purposes, propellers come in two flavors: **Fixed Pitch** and **Variable Pitch** (also called **Constant-Speed**). We'll concentrate on fixed pitch, but—quickly—a variable pitch prop has two or more independent blades attached to a hub, which has the ability to change the blade angles in flight the way a transmission allows a car driver to change gears. Variable-pitch props are more efficient than fixed-pitch props. To fly an airplane with a variable-pitch propeller, you'll need additional training, and a one-time logbook endorsement under FAR 61.31 if the airplane also has flaps and retractable landing gear. We'll stick with fixed-pitch prop here.

The fixed-pitch propeller is one solid piece of wood or metal. It's a thing of functional beauty with its cambered airfoil and a noticeable twist from hub to tip. The camber provides the pressure differentials that translate into thrust. The twist is there to balance the thrust along the spinning blades by varying the angles-of-incidence to maintain a relatively constant angle of attack along the blade's span.

Picture a spinning propeller's blurry disc. As the propeller rotates at, say, 2500 RPM, the tips turn as many revolutions per minute as the hub. The tips, however, are three or more feet away from the hub. Ever play crack-the-whip? Bunch of kids hold hands and spin in a circle. The little kid on the end has to travel faster than the anchor kid (the one usually picked last) in order to travel the same distance. Likewise the propeller tip. It has to travel faster than the hub in order to complete the same revolution in the same time. In order to equalize the angle of attack along the blade and provide relatively equal thrust, the blade is twisted. This changes the **Angle of Incidence**[13] of the propeller's airfoil. Angle of incidence (AOI) is the angle at which the airfoil (wing or prop blade) is attached to either the airframe (wing) or the propeller's hub. A changing angle of incidence allows for relatively constant angle of attack along the propeller. The hub should have a higher AOA (for slower speed) while the faster tip has a lower AOA.

Propellers, as we'll discuss further in chapter 3, are part of the airplane's powerplant, which consists of engine, accessories and propeller.

Left-Turning Tendencies

An Air Force F-16 pilot once told me that flying the single-engine jet fighter was easier than flying my Cessna 150. I didn't believe him, but why argue with someone who can drop a 500-pound bomb on your Volkswagen? His point, though, was that the jet engine produced a relatively straight line of thrust, "Like sitting atop a blowtorch," he said, and, again, I had to take his word for it, having never sat atop a blowtorch.

Propellers, by contrast, produce lines or vectors of thrust along the sides of the spinning arc. That thrust doesn't blow back in a straight force. The slipstream spirals, because a spinning blade produced it. This **Corkscrewing Effect** is compact when the airplane is at high power and low forward speeds, such as in a climb. Being compact, the corkscrewing slipstream strikes the airplane's vertical tail on the left side. This pushes the tail to the right and the airplane's nose to the left. The result: a left-turning tendency in climb.

The propeller imposes another left-turning tendency called **Asymmetric Loading (or P-factor)**. In climb, or other nose-high attitudes, the propeller "bites" the air unequally. From the pilot's seat picture the blade descending on your right and rising on the left. With nose high, the descending blade on your right gets more "bite" from the air than the opposite, rising blade on the left. The right side, then, produces more thrust than the left, so the airplane's nose yaws to the left.

The third cause of left-turning tendency is **Gyroscopic Action**. A spinning propeller is a mass of metal, wood or plastic in motion. It spins much like a gyroscope. Funny things about gyroscopes: **Rigidity in Space** and **Precession.** Okay, not funny—*Ha! Ha!*—but funny that something spinning will tend to remain rigid or funnier, still, that if disturbed this spinning gyro (the propeller) precesses or reacts 90 degrees ahead and in the direction of the rotation.

---

[13] Angle of Incidence AOI: For propellers it's the angle between the chord line and a reference plane on the hub. The wing's AOI is the angle between the wing's chord line and the airplane's longitudinal axis.

This means if we apply a force to one point along the spinning propeller arc, that gyroscopic reaction will appear 90 degrees (a quarter of the way around the arc) ahead of where the force was applied. So, as the pilot changes pitch (raises or lowers the airplane's nose) a force is applied to a point on the arc, and that force reacts 90 degrees ahead of where it was applied.

You really have to experience this to appreciate it. Tailwheel pilots encounter **Gyroscopic Action** or **Precession** on most takeoffs as they lift the tail, causing the propeller to shift its rotational plane. As the tail rises, the spinning propeller disc tilts forward at the top of the arc, and the reaction happens 90 degrees ahead of that on the right side of the prop. The right side suddenly has an extra boost. This causes the nose to pull left. The airplane yaws left around the vertical axis.

The engine itself produces a left-turning tendency. Back to Newton for help on this one. As the internal engine parts (and propeller, which acts like a flywheel) revolve in one direction (clockwise as seen from the pilot's seat), an opposite force **Torques** the airplane the other way. Manufacturers offset the engine mount slightly to compensate for this.

For all the left-turning tendencies, the pilot counters with right rudder. Some airplanes have rudder trim to assist the pilot's lazy feet. Mostly, though, there's just an instructor repeating, "Rudder! Right rudder!"

Experiment 2.2: Here's a way to feel gyroscopic effects without leaving home—assuming you live in a home with electricity. Plug in a small electric fan. Pick it up. While keeping your fingers and necktie away from the blades, turn it on. Walk across the room. (You may need an extension cord for this.)

Notice that the fan remains relatively stable as you walk. Now, tilt the fan as it spins. Move it as though it were an airplane's propeller—climb, descend, climbing turns….

Feel the way the spinning blades—the gyroscope—react to your input. Now, put the fan down, turn it off and never speak of this to anyone.

Repeat After Me:

The four Left-Turning tendencies are:

1. Corkscrewing Effect
2. Asymmetric Loading (or P-factor)
3. Gyroscopic Action (or Precession)
4. Torque

Review item: The four Beatles were:

1. John
2. Paul
3. George
4. Ringo (I will accept Pete Best)[14]

Fly The Turning Tendencies

Learning to fly means leaving the familiar two-dimensional world and maneuvering in a third dimension that expands the spirit in ways your flat earth friends might not grasp. On initial flights student pilots might feel overwhelmed by the academics of aerodynamic forces. The trick is to relax. Let your body slump into the seat with your hands and feet resting gently upon the controls. The more you relax, the better you'll feel the airplane. Don't fall asleep; this Zen approach to flying only goes so far.

As you relax, your vision expands. You see more than the blur of the instrument panel and will fully experience what the flying machine is trying to tell you. When tensed up your focus narrows when it should expand, your breathing tightens when you need oxygen flowing smoothly to that brain full of newly acquired aeronautical principles. On takeoff, for instance, as you add power, the single engine airplane will likely pull to the left. Solution: add right rudder. How much? Whatever it takes to keep the airplane's longitudinal axis pointed down the runway's centerline.

Pilots tend to lean forward in demanding situations, such as takeoff and landing. Don't. Be cool, lean back. From that posture you'll better sense the left-turning tendencies as you add power, and then, again, as you increase pitch. *Rudder, rudder, rudder*—almost all from right foot input.

On landing as you transition from nose-low glide, to nose-high touchdown attitude, you'll gently—but firmly—add right rudder. How much? Again, whatever it takes to keep the airplane's nose (not necessarily yours) pointed down the runway.

I tell my students, "The wind is our friend." They disagree at first, but that's because its tough transitioning to 3-D mind. Anticipating how wind affects your airplane is crucial to success. Here's a tip: If given the choice of a left or right crosswind on takeoff or landing, it's usually best to choose the right crosswind. A left crosswind will exacerbate the left-turning tendencies, while a right crosswind will act as right rudder input and help keep you pointed straight down the runway. Make friends with the wind early in your flying life.

---

[14] Ask your grandparents

Test Questions:

1. What are the four forces acting on an airplane in flight?

   a. lift, weight, thrust, and drag.
   b. lift, weight, gravity, and thrust.
   c. lift, gravity, power, and fiction.

2. Angle of attack is defined as the angle between the chord line of an airfoil and the

   a. direction of the relative wind.
   b. pitch angle of an airfoil.
   c. rotor plane of rotation.

3. During a spin to the right, which wing(s) is/are stalled?

   a. Both wings are stalled.
   b. Neither wing is stalled.
   c. Only the right wing is stalled.

Answers:

1. **a.** lift, weight, thrust, and drag.
2. **a.** direction of the relative wind.
3. **a.** Both wings are stalled. (Remember, in order to spin the airplane, both wings must stall. One wing, however, is more stalled than the other and causes the rotation.)

In the next chapter we learn to maneuver these forces about the sky while chewing gum.

Chapter 3

Controls

Or:
"Principles Are Fine, Mr. Bernoulli, But Will It Fly?"

As Pilot in Command (PIC) you must know what controls the airplane, or you're nothing more than a passenger warming the pilot's seat. Lift was understood well before the Wright Brothers tried to sue anyone for patent infringement. Making something leave the planet and return was not so difficult. Maneuvering the flying machine, however, took some genius, and the Wright Boys figured that out while everyone else was lobbying their governments for user fees.

To maneuver an airplane the pilot needs flight control systems. Those are divided into Primary and Secondary controls. **Primary controls** are those absolutely necessary for flight. Primary controls include rudder, ailerons and elevator (or stabilator). **Secondary controls** include flaps and trim systems designed to lessen the pilot's workload or enhance aircraft performance.

To review: The rudder controls yaw around the vertical axis, ailerons control roll around the longitudinal axis, and the elevator controls pitch around the lateral axis. All three should work in coordinated concert in flight. The goal is to maneuver the airplane in four fundamental ways. The four **Fundamentals of Flight** are:

1. Straight and Level
2. Turns
3. Climbs
4. Descents

We introduced flight controls in Chapter 1, so let's expand our knowledge.

Ailerons can be subdivided into three common types: Differential, Frise-Type and Coupled.

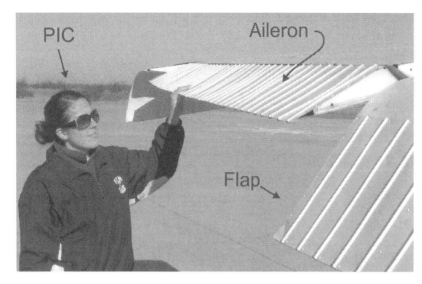

Left: *Ailerons control roll around the longitudinal axis.*

Generally, when ailerons are deflected one goes up and the other down. The lowered aileron produces more lift so that wing rises, causing the airplane to bank (roll) in a turn. But, that lowered aileron produces the byproduct drag that adversely yaws the nose away from the intended turn. Adverse aileron yaw is easily overcome with rudder.

Differential ailerons are designed so the up aileron rises further than the down aileron descends. This creates additional drag on the up aileron to offset the increased drag on the lowered aileron. It somewhat offsets adverse aileron yaw. Still need your feet on the rudder pedals.

Frise-Type (pronounced "Freeze") ailerons pivot on a hinge. So, as one aileron raises, its leading edge scoops below the wing and creates drag. It also flows air through a slot and over the top of the raised aileron making it more efficient at high angles of attack. Like differential ailerons the Frise-Type overcomes some adverse aileron yaw. The pilot still needs to apply rudder to offset this and fly coordinated.

When the ailerons are coupled to the rudder through interconnect springs, the **Coupled Ailerons** act in coordination with the rudder automatically overcoming adverse aileron yaw. Clever stuff for lazy pilots, and, as you'll learn, lazy isn't always bad. The Ercoupe has the ultimate in coupled ailerons with no rudder pedals at all (some Ercoupe models added rudder pedals to give the owners more input).

The **elevator** is linked to the control yoke or stick and controls pitch. Pull back, pitch up; push forward, pitch down.

Left: *The elevator controls pitch, and the rudder controls yaw.*

Rudder pedals control the rudder in the tail to yaw the airplane's nose left or right around the vertical axis. Rudder pedals also steer the airplane while on the ground. Brakes are usually attached to the rudder pedal toes with each wheel's brake operating independently to aid differential steering on the ground. In older airplanes the brake pedals (if they have brakes) might be heel-operated and are called heel brakes. Some older airplanes have a single brake handle and no brakes on the pedals. Many cockpits only include brake pedals on the pilot's side making for extremely nervous instructors: "Brakes, Mrs. Bernoulli. *BRAKES!*"

High Lift Devices

There are several ways to alter the airfoil shape in flight. In the early days the pilot actually warped the wing to alter the pressure differentials. Wing warping wasn't real practical, so ailerons were invented. Today, the pilot not only has ailerons to control bank but also has various lift devices to alter the airfoil's shape to improve slow-flight performance in takeoff and landing. Leading edge slats and spoilers are common devices on higher-performance jets, but the smaller Cessnas and Cherokees have flaps.

Flaps are high-lift devices commonly attached to the trailing edge of the wing. When deployed (lowered) the flap increases lift and drag allowing the pilot to fly at slower speeds (lower stall speeds, usually) than without flaps. Flaps allow for steeper approaches—ideal for landing over obstacles—and for slower touchdown speeds. This reduces rollout length and saves on tires and brakes as well as other wear and tear as the airplane touches the Earth more gently than without flaps. Partial flap deployment (maybe 10 or 25 degrees) is often used for soft or short-field takeoffs. The airplane's POH tells what to use.

Right: Flaps allow for steeper descents and slower approach speeds.

Flaps usually are controlled by either an electric motor or by a manual flap handle. Flaps are found on the wing's trailing edge inboard of the ailerons. Unlike ailerons, flaps should always operate in the same direction. There are four common flap types:

1. Plain
2. Split
3. Slotted
4. Fowler

All flaps change the wing's camber when extended. The **plain** flap, hinged behind the wing's trailing edge, is the simplest.

Split flaps extend from beneath the wing's underside. Both plain and split flaps produce lift and drag, but when fully extended they produce high drag without much added lift.

Slotted flaps are common on smaller airplanes. They're more efficient than the previous two and produce more lift when extended.

Fowler flaps are slotted flaps that change both the wing's camber and its area. To do this the Fowler flap not only extends downward but also rolls back on tracks.

Trim Some pilots simply work too hard. A good pilot needs to relax, be a little lazy and let the airplane fly.

Remember: "The airplane already knows how to fly, the pilot merely tells it where to go." – *Jake Hollow, barnstormer*

To lessen the pilot's workload, the primary controls have secondary trim devices. There are several trim types, but the most common in our single-engine piston world are trim tabs (servo tabs), antiservo tabs and adjustable tails or stabilizers. Some trim systems apply pressure directly on the elevator control cables.

The **Trim Tab (or Servo Tab)**—found on Cessnas, for example, or the Aeronca Champ—is an adjustable tab hinged to the elevator's trailing edge. It moves opposite to the elevator and *trims* away the excessive elevator pressures. Trim tabs are operated by a trim wheel, crank, lever or electric trim button on the control yoke.

Antiservo Tab—found on one-piece stabilators on some gliders and Piper Cherokees, for example. It moves with control input on the yoke and in the same direction as the stabilator's trailing edge to decrease stabilator sensitivity. The antiservo tab adds excess pressure to the control surface. This avoids unwanted pilot induced oscillations (PIO). An antiservo tab also acts and feels like a trim servo tab. From the pilot's operational perspective there is no difference. Set pitch with the yoke and then adjust trim.

Right: *The stabilator on a Piper Cherokee controls pitch. The antiservo tab is on the trailing edge.*

Some airplanes (Mooney, for instance) have an adjustable tail where the entire empennage rotates up and down as the pilot trims pitch. Some airplanes (older Pipers and Marquart Chargers) have an adjustable horizontal stabilizer, controlled by a jackscrew. The pilot rotates a trim wheel, crank or electric switch, and pitch is trimmed. In all cases, the pilot makes the same control trim input.

Learn to use the trim control in conjunction with all pitch changes. Make flight easy. Don't fight the airplane, because it already knows how to fly. You won't teach it a thing.

Tip: When adjusting trim, make your pitch adjustment first using the yoke or joystick and, then, adjust the trim. Don't chase pitch with trim.

Powerplants

The powerplant consists of the airplane's engine, accessories and propeller, everything that powers the machine. Chances are you're learning to fly in a single-engine, piston airplane. If you're learning in jets, you're in the wrong ground-school class. Have your Learjet instructor pick you up and good luck on your training.

The piston engine is a reciprocating engine. Its pistons pump back and forth in a reciprocating motion. This technology was pioneered well before the Wright Brothers flew and with a few improvements is still powering the GA (General Aviation) fleet. There are several types of piston engines, designated In-line, V-Type and Opposed.

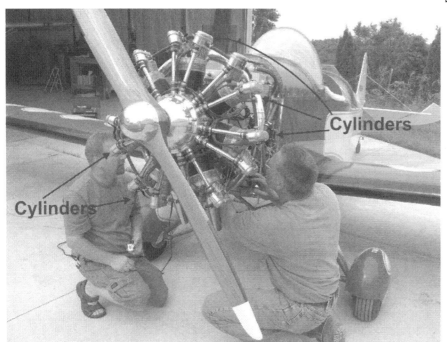

Left: Mechanics working on a radial engine. Cylinders are arranged in a circle.[15]

The **radial engine** is commonly found on older airplanes through W.W.II. It's easily identifiable with the cylinders arranged like daisy petals in a circle around the crankshaft. Radial engines have powered a wide variety of airplanes from two-seaters such as the Fleets, Rearwins and Ryans through the powerful P-47 fighters plus multi-engine bombers and transports. The sound of a radial engine at sunrise is the closest thing to audio perfection many pilots will hear this side of *Ailerona*.[16] Lindbergh crossed the Atlantic in 1927, alone, behind a Wright J-5 radial engine. Never missed a tick.

Radial engines are air-cooled and tend to be a bit draggy, what with all those cylinders poking out fanlike to catch the wind. **Inline engines**, such as the Ranger or Menasco, in which the cylinders are arranged in a line, provide a smaller frontal area against the wind—streamlined, less drag. Getting air to cool the rear cylinder is a problem therefore size is often limited.

---

[15] A Warner Sportster at Nash Field (IA66), Indianola, Iowa
[16] Ask your CFI about *Ailerona*

The **V-Type** engine squeezes in more cylinders in a V-shape along a single crankshaft. This allows for more horsepower and a streamlined nose. Usually V-engines are liquid cooled much like a car engine. This adds weight and the potential for over-heating if a coolant line or radiator leaks. P-51s and Spitfires had V-type engines. The sound of their Rolls-Royce engines at sunset is almost as stirring as the radials at dawn. Something to argue over in the *Ailerona* pilots lounge.

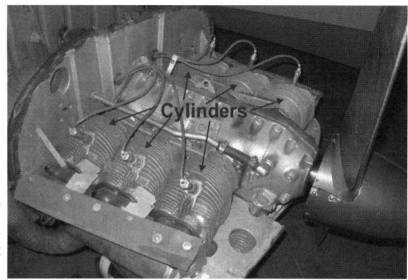

Right: *A six-cylinder, 145-hp, Continental O-300 engine. The cylinders oppose each other.*

Most GA airplanes are powered by **opposed-type** engines, which provide favorable power-to-weight ratios. The cylinders are arranged flat, in two banks opposing each other. The smaller GA airplanes will normally have four or six cylinders. Opposed arrangement allows for a fairly compact unit with semi-favorable streamlining. Opposed engines are normally air-cooled, meaning the onrushing air flows through baffling (duct work) and cooling fins to remove heat produced by combustion. It's important to inspect all cooling baffling in the engine compartment before flight.

Engines are commonly labeled not by horsepower but, instead, by size and configuration. For instance: A Lycoming O-360 engine was manufactured by Lycoming, has Opposed cylinders (O-) and displaces 360 cubic inches (O-360). A Lycoming IO-360 is the same as the O-360 except it has fuel injection instead of a carburetor, so the letter "I" is added to the designation. Adding a "T" designates Turbo. A Pratt & Whitney R-2800 is a radial engine (R) and displaces 2800 cubic inches. "F" stands for FADEC or Full Authority Digital Engine Control. So, a Continental FIO-240 has FADEC, is fuel Injected with Opposed cylinders and displaces 240 cubic inches. And so it goes….

Engine Parts

A pilot who's not an FAA-licensed mechanic might never see the inside of the airplane's engine. That's a shame, because the more you know about your airplane—the thing that carries you, your friends and family through the sky—the better you'll fly. Plus, knowledge is power against the rare unscrupulous or incompetent mechanic trying to butcher your airplane and wallet. The following overview is basic, and in no way pretends to be the ultimate in airplane engine knowledge.

The average airplane piston engine[17] consists of **cylinders** bolted to a **crankcase**, which has an **accessory housing** where accessories such as alternator/generators, vacuum pumps, tachometer cables and starter motors are connected. The **carburetor** mixes fuel and air before sending it to the cylinders through an intake manifold. It's commonly attached beneath the engine, so the air/fuel mixture is drawn up. This is called an updraft carburetor. **Fuel injection** delivers fuel from fuel pumps, through a fuel/air controller unit and into the fuel manifold valve and then in fine mist through the discharge nozzles and into the cylinders. Fuel injection is considered more efficient than carburetors, but can be a challenge to start on a hot day, particularly if you haven't read the POH hot-start procedures.

Carburetors are further divided into Pressure or Float-Type. Most likely you'll use a **Float-Type** carburetor, which as the name implies, operates using a float controlling a needle valve. Open a toilet tank and you'll notice that the flush mechanism is remarkably similar—crude but effective. It works like this: Air flows to the carburetor through a filter (which you inspect before flight). The air goes through the carburetor's **venturi.** That venturi uses Bernoulli's genius because it has a narrow throat, which constricts the airflow, causing pressure to drop. This sucks fuel through a jet and mixes it with the air and sends it into the intake manifold—a spider-like bit of plumbing where the air/mixture is sent to the appropriate cylinders on demand. Crude but it works.

Four-Stroke Engine

Cylinders are hollow tubes capped on top by a **cylinder head** and at the bottom by the constantly moving piston that compresses and exhausts the gases in four repetitive cycles or strokes.

Inside the cylinder head are intake and exhaust **valves** operated by cams, lifters and springs. **Spark plugs** (two per cylinder) provide the, well, the spark to ignite the compressed fuel/air mixture, giving this entire device the name "internal combustion engine."

Today's **Four-stroke** (or four-cycle), reciprocating engine operates on the same principle used for over 100 years:

1. As the piston travels down the cylinder, an intake valve opens to draw in the fuel/air mixture for the **Intake** stroke.
2. The valve closes as the piston reverses course at the end of the stroke and moves up the cylinder to compress the gases in the **Compression** stroke.

---

[17] This applies to avgas and mogas engines. Newer diesels offer new possibilities.

3. Once properly compressed, spark plugs ignite the mixture, which releases the energy and pushes the piston back down in the **Power** stroke. That power turns the crankshaft, which in turn cranks the propeller.
4. Finally, that same piston heads back up the cylinder to push out the spent gases through the opening exhaust valve in the **Exhaust** stroke. And the whole process is repeated hundreds of times per minute.

Engine RPM are recorded on the **Tachometer** located on the instrument panel. The pilot controls RPMs using the **throttle** located either on the instrument panel (usually in the lower center section) or on a side panel. (Powerplants with constant-speed propellers will also have a manifold pressure gauge. Most trainers will not since they normally have fixed-pitch props.) The throttle controls fuel/air flow to the engine.

A red **Mixture Control** knob or lever is usually located near the throttle. With it, the pilot manually adjusts fuel/air mixture. The ten-year-old car you drove to the airport has a far more sophisticated and efficient induction system than is found on most airplanes at many times the cost. Go figure.

Carb Ice

It's not a frozen dessert high in carbohydrates. Instead, Carb Ice (real name: **Carburetor Ice**) is to be avoided. Remember that Bernoulli-inspired venturi in the carburetor? It lowered air pressure allowing fuel and air to mix. Great device, but with greatness comes an evil side. As the air pressure drops so does temperature—dramatically. So, that fuel/air mixture gets freezing cold at times, and that air contains water vapor. Mix cold and water together you get ice. Ice clings to the venturi throat and cuts off the airflow. Result: Engine failure. Solution: Heat the air with **Carburetor Heat** (aka, Carb Heat).

Note: Carb Ice can happen when the Outside Air Temperature (OAT) is well above freezing. In fact, it's most likely to occur when the OAT is 70 degrees F (21 C), and the relative humidity tops 80%.

The first indication of carb ice in an engine with a fixed-pitch propeller is a decrease in RPMs, usually followed by engine roughness and, if left unattended, dumbfounding silence. "Hmmm.....Carb ice?"

Solution: Apply carb heat at the first hint of RPM loss on those cool to warm humid days. Carb heat takes warm air from the exhaust manifold and directs it into the carburetor. The ice melts—with some accompanying coughs as the water is ingested—and the engine runs smoothly. The POH details when to use carb heat.

Controls

Funny thing: The constant-speed propeller is designed to maintain a preset RPM. So, as carb ice develops the prop governor automatically adjusts prop pitch to control RPM even though power is being sapped by carb ice. The first indication of carb ice in an engine with a constant-speed propeller is a loss of manifold pressure.

Solution: Apply carb heat.

Alternate solution: Get fuel injection. Fuel injection is not subject to carburetor ice because (think about it…) it doesn't have a carburetor.

Engine Super Heroes

Most trainers have normally aspirated engines with float-type carburetors. Power, in part, is a function of outside air density. As the airplane climbs it breathes less dense air—molecules get further apart. On a hot day, the air becomes even thinner, and the airplane operates as though it were at even higher altitudes. This phenomenon is called **Density Altitude**[18]. At high density altitudes the wings produce less lift, the propeller less thrust, the pilot—a two-pack-a-day Marlboro guy—gasps for breath, and the engine puts out less horsepower.

To overcome this wheezy engine condition a **Turbocharger** is added to compress the less dense air into denser stuff before it's blown into the engine. For our purposes we'll think of turbochargers and superchargers as the same thing, even though, technically, they're not. The supercharger is engine-driven, while exhaust gases drive the turbocharger (or turbosupercharger[19]). If you go for your commercial pilot certificate or fly a turbo'd aircraft as a private pilot, you'll need to know more about these. As a Sport Pilot don't plan on any turbo flying.

Ignition

An internal combustion engine needs three things to operate: Air, fuel, and spark. Fuel and air we've already discussed. Spark, we know comes from the spark plugs, and those are powered by the 19th Century's finest technology—**Magnetos**.

Unlike a car, your average GA airplane engine does not need a battery to run. It does not need a battery to start. Many older airplanes have no batteries. To start a 1946 Aeronca Champ, Piper J-3 Cub or any number of older airplanes without electrical systems, the pilot "hand props"—or spins the propeller by hand—to start the engine. Perfectly legal and safe when performed correctly.

---

[18] Density Altitude: Pressure altitude adjusted for non-standard temperature.

[19] Turbosupercharger: Has a certain Mary Poppins ring to it, donchya think? Go ahead, say it fast: "Turbo-super-charger-expialodotious…"

> **SAFETY TIP:** Unless you want the nickname, *Stubby*, don't try hand propping without proper instruction from a qualified instructor. Not every CFI is qualified.

By turning the propeller by hand (hand-propping) the crankshaft turns, which rotates gears, cams and whatnot and eventually spins the magnetos that supply the spark to the spark plugs, and the engine starts. It's hoped.

By adding a battery, generator/alternator and starter motor to the engine accessory housing, the pilot now has an electrical means to spin the prop to start the airplane. The battery, et al, supplies electricity for lights, radios and other accessories. Magnetos still provide the ignition spark in most GA airplanes.

Usually an engine has two magnetos with two separate sets of ignition wires leading to the spark plugs (two per cylinder). Two of everything provides even combustion and the safety of redundancy should one set fail.

Bad Combustion

Avgas is finicky stuff. It must be blended in a perfect ratio of air and fuel to burn properly. It must be compressed and then ignited at exactly the correct moment to release the energy in a controlled burn that smoothly pushes the piston back down the cylinder so the energy can be transferred through the connecting rod to the crankshaft, which turns the propeller. And it must do this hundreds of time per minute for thousands of hours of operation. As with comedy, when it comes to perfection, timing is everything.

Almost everything. The magnetos must be timed to match the valves' openings and closings during intake, compression, ignition (power) and exhaust stokes. Any slippage in timing or sloppy mixture control and the engine can react adversely in two ways called Detonation and Preignition.

Detonation: "An uncontrolled, explosive ignition of the fuel/air mixture within the cylinder's combustion chamber. It causes excessive temperatures and pressures, which, if not corrected, can quickly lead to engine failure."[20] Less dramatically, detonation causes overheating, roughness and power loss. It's detectable by high cylinder head temperatures, particularly at high power settings.

Detonation can be caused by:

1) Lower than required fuel grade
2) Too high manifold pressure and too low RPM

---

[20] FAA-H-8083-25

3) Excessively lean mixture at high power settings (above 65% power)
4) Running the engine for too long on the ground (such as awaiting an ATC clearance) or in a steep climb when air doesn't cool the cylinders as well

Preignition: When the fuel/air mixture ignites too soon, guess what that's called? Yes, Preignition. A hot, glowing bit of carbon on a spark plug can theoretically cause preignition. Your expensive airplane engine suddenly runs like an old diesel. Proper fuel grade, sparkplug maintenance and good leaning technique helps mitigate these issues.

Fuel Systems

Most airplanes store fuel inside wing tanks, one or more per side. Older airplanes often had fuselage tanks, not the most ideal location in the event of a crash but motivation enough not to do so.

The fuel system usually has vents so air can displace fuel as it's burned. Vents may be located in the filler caps or in a standpipe somewhere above or below the wing. They may be hard to find but find them nonetheless. If the vents get plugged the fuel stops flowing with predictably depressing results. Vents must be inspected before each flight. Vents are ideal places to attract mud, ice and bugs—living or dead.

In a high wing monoplane with the fuel tanks in the wings high above the engine, gravity flows the fuel through a **fuel (tank) selector** valve and a **fuel strainer** and into the engine using a simple plumbing system designed in the late Stone Age. Low-wing monoplanes with the fuel tanks below engine level need a fuel pump (or two) to pump the avgas uphill. Your POH explains which system you have and when to use the auxiliary electric (or manual) fuel pumps.

There's usually a **fuel primer** somewhere in the cockpit. It's a hypodermic-like plunger that sucks avgas from the tank or fuel strainer and squirts it raw into the intake manifold to prime the engine prior to start. Make certain it's locked in place after engine start, because, unlocked, it can mess with your fuel air mixture, causing the engine to run rough. Fuel-injection systems usually have an electric boost pump to prime the engine. Again, check the POH.

Each tank is required by FARs to have a **fuel quantity gauge**. Modern airplane fuel gauges are notoriously crappy. Never trust them. Estimate your fuel quantities based on known fuel quantities and fuel burn rates. The best fuel gauges were made from a cork float with a wire poking through the gas cap: *See wire, got gas. See no wire, got no gas.*

Fuel is often stored in several fuel tanks or cells. **Fuel valves** allow the pilot to select individual tanks (*Left* or *Right, Main, Aux*) or *Both* tanks or *Off* for no tanks. Managing fuel between tanks can be challenging and if left unattended you may gasp at the sudden sound of silence when a tank runs dry while another tank is full of fuel. As always, consult the POH for proper fuel management.

Fuel theoretically comes in several grades, but in reality you'll most likely only find **100LL** avgas (100 is the octane and LL means Low Lead) or **auto gas** (or mogas) for your piston airplane. Auto fuel can be used provided your airplane has a **Supplemental Type Certificate** (STC) approving its use. That STC paperwork plus placards must be in the airplane and checked as a part of your preflight inspection. Leaded aviation fuel will eventually be outlawed so testing is underway for alternatives to 100LL. Jet fuel (Jet A) should never be used in a piston airplane. Jet fuel is kerosene. It's straw colored and stinks. By contrast, 100LL avgas is blue and smells of Alpine meadows on a dewy morning just as a Piper Cub lifts from the earth spitting billions of sparkling water droplets from its wheels….
Okay, so I like the smell of avgas.

Auto fuel can be any color and any quality. Stick with major brands and no ethanol (Sorry, Iowa ethanol lobbyists). Auto gas stinks but has one major advantage over 100LL: it costs way less.

During the preflight inspection the pilot should drain a fuel sample and inspect it for clarity, aroma, color (almost like wine tasting but don't drink it), plus dirt or water. There should be no dirt or water. Water is heavier than oil (or avgas) so will sink to the bottom of a sampler cup. If you find a few drops of water, simply take another sample or two, until the sample is clean. If you can't get a clean sample, it's time to call the mechanic and clean the fuel system.

The question begs: After taking a fuel sample what do you do with it? At many dollars per gallon it's tough to simply toss away. I can't recommend pouring it back into the fuel tanks. Yes, it's probably as clean as it was the day it left the rusty old fuel truck, but you may be introducing contaminants into the fuel system by dumping it back. Toss it on the ground? Not at that cost, I don't. Plus, that fuel kills the grass and eventually seeps into groundwater supplies. Airports need to be good neighbors to the thousands of subdivision homebuilders trying to strangle the airfield and close it down, so pour your samples into a waste gas fuel can. The FBO should have one or you should have one in your hangar. Then what? I use it in the lawn mower.

It's All About Oil

Sadly, aviation is heavily dependent upon oil and its derivatives. Oil itself is used for engine lubrication and cooling. Oil also removes contaminants—byproducts of combustion. Oil provides a seal between piston rings and cylinder walls. Each engine type has a unique oil system, and each requires a minimal oil level to operate. Your POH has this information. Don't skimp on oil—an engine overhaul is a lot more expensive than a quart of Phillips 20/50.

Unless your POH calls for it, never use car oil in an airplane engine. Most oil additives are not FAA-approved for use in an aircraft engine, either. Plus, some of that additive stuff is snake oil—useless.

Oil systems are monitored in flight by the oil temperature and oil pressure gauges. Normal operating ranges should be marked with green arcs. Operating outside the green arcs can cause engine damage.

Exhausting

Whatever burns inside the cylinders needs to be pumped overboard into the atmosphere to aid in global warming and sprinkle microscopic bits of vaporized lead onto flowerbeds below. One day, scientists may figure out how to make the internal combustion engine pollution-free but until then don't hold your breath.

Exhaust gases are expelled through the exhaust valves by the piston on its exhaust stoke. The exhaust gasses travel through the exhaust manifold and into one or more exhaust pipes or "stacks" and then into the cold night air. Not all airplanes have mufflers, so they can be quite noisy.

Exhaust gases are extremely hot and contain a witch's cologne of noxious vapors with the sneakiest of them being **carbon monoxide** (CO). This odorless, colorless—and generally useless—gas can seep into the airplane's cabin if the exhaust system is cracked or leaking in any way. A properly maintained and inspected exhaust system prevents CO poisoning. Those *stick 'em* CO detectors you see on some airplane panels seem about as effective at detecting CO as a pine-tree air freshener. Don't rely on them. Most are so out-of-date as to be considered antiques.

Instruments

Your Private Pilot Certificate alone won't allow you to fly solely on instruments or in Instrument Meteorological Conditions (IMC). You must have an instrument rating added to that certificate. Sport pilots cannot fly IFR at all. That caveat aside, all VFR pilots must have some instrument survival training. Plus, all pilots should have a working knowledge of the instruments in the airplane.

The airplane's three basic instrument groups are: Vacuum system, pitot-static and magnetic compass. Radios, VORs and GPS are all considered part of the avionics package. Our focus here is on the basic flight instruments used for maneuvering and navigating.

Pitot-Static

Pitot is pronounced "Pee-tow" and is named for the 18th Century French physicist Henri Pitot. It'd be easier if Henri's surname were Ram, because ram-static is a little more descriptive of how this system operates.

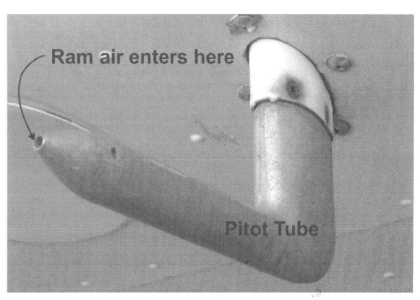

Common **pitot-static** instruments are: Airspeed indicator, altimeter and vertical speed indicator (often called the VSI). All three are on the **pitot-static** system but only one uses both ram and static air sources.

Ram air enters a **pitot tube** usually located in or below the wing's leading edge and pointing into the relative wind. The tube may stick quite a ways forward to get the best sample of undisturbed ram air. Ram air, as you've surmised, is air ramming into the airplane and into the pitot tube. That air pressure is measured against air from a static source to determine indicated airspeed (IAS).

Static air pressure is sampled through small holes located in some portion of the airframe protected from onrushing wind. These static ports can be located along one or both sides of the fuselage or on a back portion of the pitot tube itself. On many Pipers the static source is on the same blade that collects the ram air. Static ports allow the instruments to sample undisturbed atmospheric pressure. It's vitally important that both ram and static ports be inspected and open prior to flight. Either can become clogged in flight (rare), so the pilot needs to learn to recognize a malfunctioning pitot-static instrument and fly accordingly. For instrument flight, most instrument airplanes have an alternate static source inside the cabin. Ice can block a ram pitot tube so most are heated. Look for an electric switch labeled **Pitot Heat** on the instrument panel. Warning it gets really hot so don't put your tongue on it.

The **airspeed indicator** is a differential pressure instrument that measures the difference between ram and static air pressures. It then indicates that differential as the airplane's indicated airspeed. Or this is how fast the onrushing air molecules are moving when compared to static air molecules doing nothing.

There are four types of airspeed the Sport and Private Pilots should know: Indicated Airspeed (IAS), Calibrated Airspeed (CAS), True Airspeed (TAS) and Groundspeed (GS).

1.   **Indicated airspeed (IAS)** is what you see on the airspeed indicator—it's a direct reading in knots[21] or miles-per-hour (MPH). It's an uncorrected value. KIAS means Knots Indicated Airspeed. And don't get me started on Kilometers Per Hour.

2.   **Calibrated airspeed (CAS)** is the indicated airspeed corrected for installation and instrument error. Meaning: No instrument is perfect or perfectly installed, so a tiny correction factor is noted in the POH. One example is the error that shows up in some airplanes when the flaps are lowered. These errors are usually minor.

3.   **True airspeed (TAS)** is calibrated airspeed corrected for altitude and nonstandard temperature. Since the air gets thinner with increased altitude, the airplane must be flown faster in higher air in order to achieve the same pressure effects found at lower altitudes. This includes effects on the pitot-static system. You need to move the airplane faster in order to ram and compare enough thinner air molecules. So, for a given calibrated airspeed (CAS), true airspeed (TAS) increases as altitude increases. Or, for a given TAS the CAS decreases as altitude increases. In other words, at high altitudes your airspeed indicator may show a low speed, but your true airspeed will be much higher. A flight computer figures the difference. More on that in a later lesson. *RuleofThumb:* To get TAS add 2% to the CAS for each 1000 feet of altitude.

4.   **Groundspeed (GS)** is the actual speed of the airplane over the (*wait for it…*) ground. Or, "When do we get there?" speed. It's the true airspeed adjusted for wind. Groundspeed increases with a tailwind and decreases with a headwind. *Travel tip:* Groundspeed is inversely proportional to the amount of coffee you drank before takeoff.

The airspeed indicator uses both ram (from the pitot tube) and static air. The altimeter and VSI use static air only.

Airspeed Markings

Small airplanes (12,500 pounds or less maximum certificated takeoff weight) should have color-coded markings (markers or arcs) on the airspeed indicator. Speeds are labeled using a

---

[21] Knots are nautical miles-per-hour

V- (velocity) system, as in Vx for the *best angle of climb* speed. You'll understand these better after a few hours at the controls, but for academic (and testing) purposes, here they are:

White arc: Flap operating range. Most approaches are made within the white-arc speed.

Lower limit of the white arc (VSO): This is the power-off stall speed in landing configuration or the power-off stall speed in smaller airplanes at max landing weight. Add 30% to VSO (1.3 VSO) and you have a ballpark figure for final approach speed.

Upper limit of white arc (VFE): Maximum speed with flaps extended.

Green arc: Normal operating range.

Lower limit of the green arc: (VS1): Power off-stall speed in a "specified configuration," possibly in the so-called "clean configuration" (flaps and gear up).

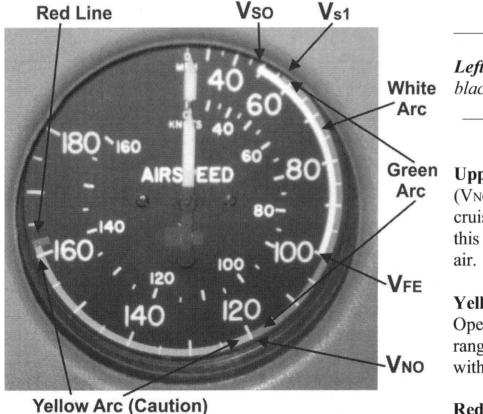

Left: *An airspeed indicator in black & white.*

Upper limit green arc: (VNO): Maximum structural cruising speed. Do not exceed this speed except in smooth air.

Yellow arc: Caution range. Operate within this speed range only in smooth air and with caution.

Red line (VNE): Never Exceed speed. You risk breaking the airplane when operating above this speed. The yellow arc ends at the red line.

Airspeed Limits That Don't Show on the Airspeed Indicator:

Design maneuvering speed (V$_A$): The so-called "rough air" speed or maximum speed for abrupt control input.

Landing gear operating speed (V$_{LO}$): Sport pilots don't worry about this, but Private pilots flying retracts need to know maximum speed for operating the landing gear—extending or retracting. It's not always the same value. See next....

Landing gear extended speed (V$_{LE}$): Maximum speed at which the airplane should be operated with gear extended (down).

Best angle-of-climb speed (V$_X$): The airspeed at which an airplane gains the greatest amount of altitude over a *given distance*. Used for short-field, obstacle-clearance departures.

Best rate-of-climb speed (V$_Y$): The airspeed, which provides the greatest altitude gain for a *given time* period.

Static-Only Instruments: Altimeter and VSI

The **altimeter** indicates the height of the airplane above—not the earth—but above a given pressure level. This pressure altimeter is a delicate gem of Jules Verne engineering. It's an **aneroid barometer** with several sealed aneroid wafers that expand or contract with changes in air pressure. These changes in the wafers push gears and needles to indicate altitude numbers on the instrument's face. Air at sea level is roughly twice as dense as air at 18,000 feet, so as an altimeter ascends (inside an airplane) from dense to thinner air the wafers—sealed from the outside atmosphere—expand. That motion transmits to the needle and shows the ascending altitude.

Kollsman Window

Turn knob to adjust altimeter setting in the Kollsman Window

The altimeter senses pressure change, and it's only accurate at standard sea level pressure of 29.92 inches of mercury and 59 degrees Fahrenheit (+15 Celsius). Most days aren't standard, so air traffic controllers, flight service or automated weather systems (AWOS, ASOS, ATIS) issue altimeter settings that correct for non-standard barometric pressure.

"Cessna Zero Eight Yankee," the controller will say, "Des Moines altimeter two niner niner eight." This means set the airplane's altimeter to the altimeter setting of 29.98 inches of mercury. How?

The pilot enters the **altimeter setting** into a small window (called a Kollsman Window) located in the instrument face by turning a knob. The altimeter setting is "station pressure reduced to sea level." If every aircraft flying in that area uses the same pressure reference level (altimeter setting) then all are referencing their altitudes to the same pressure value.

At airports where no altimeter setting is available, the pilot simply adjusts the altimeter to reflect the airport elevation. This, too, compensates for nonstandard barometric pressures. Your flight instructor will demonstrate this early in training. It's really easy and will make a lot more sense then. For now, remember that the altimeter measures the airplane's altitude above a pressure level or above Mean Sea Level (MSL). Above Ground Level (AGL) altitude is estimated by subtracting known ground elevation from your altimeter's indicated altitude reading. If you're indicating 5500 feet MSL and the charts say that central Iowa sits at 1000 feet above sea level, then you are 4500 feet AGL. Radar altimeters or GPS can measure how high above ground you are, too, although radar altimeters are rare in small airplanes.

Nonstandard Temperature and Pressure

Since altimeters rely upon static air pressure to indicate altitude, these instruments are subject to changes in barometric pressure. We know that as the airplane climbs or descends it moves through changing air pressure—the air gets less or more dense by going either up or down. Air pressure also changes over distance.

Look at any weather map on TV or the Internet (DUATS.com), and you'll see the letters L and H scattered about the country. L means Low Pressure and H means High Pressure. Barometric pressures and altimeter settings are lower in the Ls and higher in the Hs. If the pilot didn't make these adjustments to the Kollsman Window in the airplane's altimeter then as the airplane flew from one pressure area to another—without climbing or descending— the altimeter would show an altitude change nonetheless.

Huh? S'plain, Lucy...

Picture the altimeter sensing the outside air pressure and indicating an altitude, say 5000 feet MSL, on the instrument's face. Now move in level flight to lower pressure area (inside an L). The pilot wants to maintain 5000 feet. In order to keep the indicated altimeter reading 5000 feet, the airplane must gradually descend because as the altimeter moves into lower pressure it indicates a climb, a false climb indication, that is. The pilot would lower the nose to hold 5000 feet indicated altitude. In reality going from High pressure to Low pressure, the altimeter will indicate a higher altitude than the airplane really is, putting the airplane closer to the ground than the pilot might otherwise believe.

Remember: *"From High to Low, Look Out Below."*

Conversely, when flying from Low to High—without adjusting the altimeter setting, the altimeter will indicate an altitude *lower* than it really is.

Temperature has a similar effect on altimeters. Air expands at warm temperatures and contracts at colder ones. It takes more space to reach an indicated 5000 feet on a warm day than on a cold day when all the air molecules are taking up less volume. A colder than standard temperature puts the airplane lower than the altimeter indicates. **True altitudes** between the aircraft and sea level vary with temperature without changing the indicated altitude. The pilot sees only the indicated altitude on the altimeter. Temperature compensations are usually small and mostly affect extremely cold weather instrument operations. I'm looking at you, Canada....

Altimeters are good devices but subject to pressure vagaries in the atmosphere. The pilot must have an altimeter setting from a nearby station to get reasonably accurate altitude readouts. On a cross-country trip it's required to reset the altimeter every 100 miles.[22] ATC (air traffic control) issues a local altimeter setting on initial contact. Always use whatever altimeter setting ATC provides, because every other aircraft on that ATC frequency will be using that setting so the controller can provide accurate separation between aircraft. When flying over mountains, add another 1000 feet to your altitude if possible (with ATC's permission, if necessary) to compensate for weird mountain altimeter shifts. Above 18,000 feet (where Sport or VFR Private Pilots don't operate) all traffic is IFR and all altimeters are set to 29.92.

For The Test and Beyond....

There are five types of altitude commonly used by pilots: *Indicated Altitude, True Altitude, Absolute Altitude, Pressure Altitude and Density Altitude.*

1. **Indicated altitude** is what the pilot reads directly from the altimeter.
2. **True altitude** is the vertical distance between the aircraft and sea level, sometimes called the *actual altitude*. Given in feet MSL, charts depict obstacle heights, such as a mountain peak, in true altitude, because that's truly where it is.
3. **Absolute altitude** is not an altitude sponsored by a vodka distiller. Instead it is height (vertical distance) above an obstacle or terrain expressed in feet above ground level (AGL).
4. **Pressure altitude** is what is indicated on the altimeter when the Kollsman window is set to standard pressure 29.92 inches of mercury (Hg). This is an altitude above the

---

[22] FAR 91.121

standard datum plane. Theoretically this standard altitude plane is where air pressure, at standard temperature (59F, 15C) equals 29.92 inches Hg. Pilots use pressure altitude to compute true airspeed, true altitude and density altitude.

5. **Density altitude** is the aforementioned pressure altitude corrected for non-standard temperature. At sea level, 59F (15C) pressure altitude and density altitude should be the same. They rarely are. When temp rises, density altitude rises; when OAT lowers, density altitude goes down, too. Airplane performance is based upon density altitude. Your Cessna 150 won't perform at 5000-foot density altitude as well as it did at 2000-foot density altitude.

All altimeters need to be checked for accuracy. For VFR flight, while on the ground set the altimeter to the given altimeter setting (from AWOS, ASOS, ATIS). The altimeter should reflect airport field elevation, plus or minus 75 feet.

Vertical Speed Indicator (VSI)

The altimeter shows indicated altitude. The vertical speed indicator (VSI) displays altitude trends and rate. It instantly shows the beginning of a climb or descent and how quickly you're changing altitudes. Once level, the VSI should read 0. It should also read 0 when on the ground.

Like the altimeter, the VSI works off the static port. And like the altimeter it, too, has a diaphragm that expands or contracts with changes in outside air pressure. The big difference between an altimeter and VSI is the VSI's diaphragm has a calibrated leak allowing air to escape as pressure changes. This permits it to register change, rate and trend.

The VSI is under appreciated in VFR flight, especially when maneuvering. For instance, when the instructor or examiner asks for a steep turn (45-degree bank), you're expected to hold your assigned altitude throughout the maneuver. The altimeter will show if you're on or off the mark, but by the time it shows a change you might be heading even further off altitude so work the VSI into your altitude scan on almost all maneuvers. The VSI is the snitch: "Hey, Dave, you're starting to descend, add more back pressure before the examiner notices!"

Gyros (Not a Greek Pita)
We learned to control gyroscopic effects caused by the propeller. Now, we'll harness smaller gyroscopes to power some instruments, including the attitude indicator (aka, artificial horizon), the heading indicator (aka, directional gyro or DG) and the turn indicator.

The gyroscopic instruments are powered by a vacuum pump, electric motors or, in older airplanes, a venturi. Vacuum pump is the most common. A vacuum gauge on the instrument panel measures vacuum pressure.

Gyros are spinning things that exhibit two important properties: **rigidity in space** and **precession**. We saw how precession affects the left-turning tendencies on takeoff. Inside a gyro instrument, precession allows it to sense a rate of turn. Turn indicators come in two types: turn and slip indicator (aka needle-and-ball) and the turn coordinator.

The **turn and slip** is found on older airplanes and has a turn needle that indicates the direction (left or right) and rate of turn. By adding a curved smile-shaped tube with a metal ball rolling in fluid (**inclinometer**), the pilot can coordinate rudder and aileron in the turn. A centered ball indicates a coordinated maneuver.

The electric **turn coordinator** is commonly found in newer airplanes and displays the rate (not bank angle) at which an airplane turns and rolls. A standard rate turn is 3 degrees-per-second. At that rate it takes 2 minutes to complete a 360-degree turn (360/3 = 120 seconds or 2 minutes). It also has an inclinometer to reflect the quality of the turn.

Flying Tip: *Step on the ball.* In a turn, aileron and rudder are coordinated to balance the forces acting on the turn—gravity, centrifugal force and adverse aileron yaw. Once bank is established if the pilot doesn't hold enough rudder pressure the ball will **slip** into the turn. By adding rudder on the side with the ball (stepping on the ball) it returns to the center of the curved tube to indicate a coordinated turn. From lesson #1 the VFR student pilot learns to glance at the ball (not stare at it) in every maneuver. Coordination is an important skill to learn. With that said, slips are a safe way to lose altitude on final approach, especially in older airplanes without flaps.

If the pilot uses too much rudder or not enough aileron in an uncoordinated turn, the ball will **skid** to the outside of the turn. A slow skidding turn in the traffic pattern, particularly when turning from base leg to final, can spell disaster. Solution: Fly coordinated.

When it's spinning, a gyroscope tends to remain fixed—or rigid—in space. If everything else moves, then that fixed item can be used as a reference to simulate a horizon or a heading.

By adding a miniature airplane to the instrument the pilot can reference the miniature airplane to the artificial horizon bar to maintain proper flight attitude. This gyro instrument is the **attitude indicator** or as it's sometimes called, the **artificial horizon**.

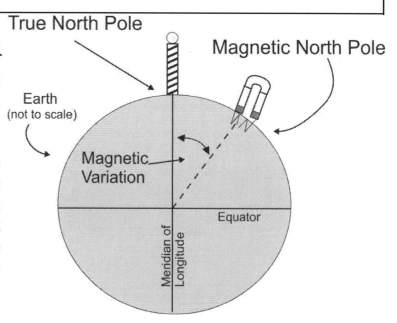

The Compass

Long before Bernoulli and Newton were born, sailors navigated around the world using magnetic compasses. Essentially this magnetic instrument points (roughly) at the **Magnetic North Pole**, which is located about 1100 miles from the **Geographic North Pole** that's depicted on maps. This is basically how a magnetic compass works: It's a direction-seeking instrument that aligns itself with the magnetic axis created by the Earth's north/south magnetic field. Two steel magnetized needles seek the earth's magnetic field. A compass card is attached to a float that rotates in a fluid. For that reason the airplane's magnetic compass is sometimes called a "wet compass." It's crude and suffers from errors, but it is required equipment in the airplane.[23] Since the compass is hard to read, the pilot, instead, uses the gyro **heading indicator** in flight. The pilot adjusts the heading indicator to the magnetic compass. The heading indicator gives a smoother depiction of heading and heading change.

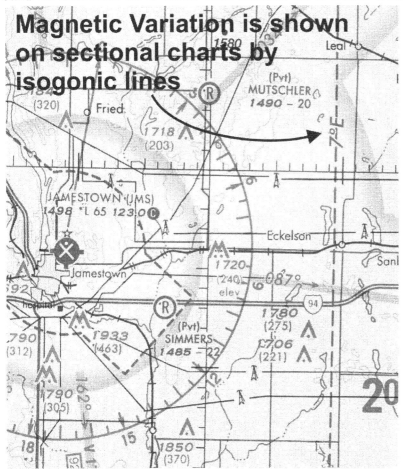

The angle difference between Magnetic North and Geographic (True) North is called **magnetic variation**. Lines connecting points of equal variation are called **isogonic lines**. The variation values are noted on aeronautical charts. The line of zero deviation is called the agonic line—where the compass points to both Magnetic and True North. In the USA that agonic line runs roughly from Duluth, Minnesota through Iowa and down the Mississippi. Everything east of that agonic line has a westerly variation and everything west of the agonic line has an easterly variation.

---

[23] 91.205 requires the aircraft to have a "magnetic direction indicator"

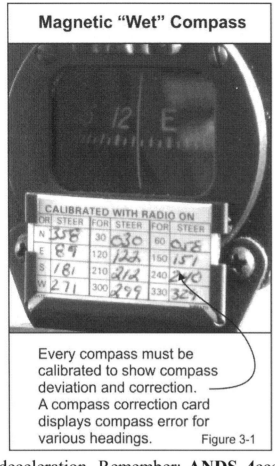

Magnetic "Wet" Compass

CALIBRATED WITH RADIO ON

FOR	STEER	FOR	STEER	FOR	STEER
N	358	30	030	60	075
E	89	120	122	150	151
S	181	210	212	240	240
W	271	300	299	330	321

Every compass must be calibrated to show compass deviation and correction. A compass correction card displays compass error for various headings. Figure 3-1

Compass Deviation is another error caused by interference inside the airplane itself. This deviation could be caused by airframe metal, avionics or wiring. A correction card showing the deviation for select compass points must be posted near the magnetic compass (Figure 3-1).[24]

Other annoying compass errors include: Acceleration/Deceleration Errors and Turning errors caused by Magnetic Dip.[25]

Magnetic Dip is caused by the earth's magnetic forces pulling the compass vertically. This force is negligible near the magnetic equator and strongest at the poles. *(Man, does that sound like a test question....)*

Magnetic dip causes fluctuations in compass readings as the airplane accelerates or decelerates. In the Northern Hemisphere (where Iowa is kept) the compass swings north when the airplane accelerates. It swings south in deceleration. Remember: **ANDS** *A*ccelerate *N*orth *D*ecelerate *S*outh. Flying down to Rio? South of the Equator reverses the phenomenon—**DNAS**.

When turning from a heading of north or south, the wet compass lags and leads. From a northerly heading the compass initially indicates away from the actual turn. Very disconcerting, but wait and it'll slowly indicate the correct direction although it will lag behind. This lag disappears as the airplane passes east or west.

When turning from south the compass leads and eventually catches up with itself around the easterly/westerly headings.

Remember: *Lag North, Lead South.*

In short, the magnetic "wet" compass is a thoroughly mediocre and frustrating—but required—piece of equipment. Be thankful for GPS (Global Positioning System).

That's the airplane; its flight controls systems and instruments. This has been a cursory introduction and by no means gives all the detail about the particular airplane you'll fly. For that refer to the POH and ask your instructor lots of questions. As you fly, all of these strange new items and forces will make sense as they burrow into your subconscious.

---

[24] FAR 23.1547

[25] Magnetic Dip is not something into which you dip a silicon chip at a computer party.

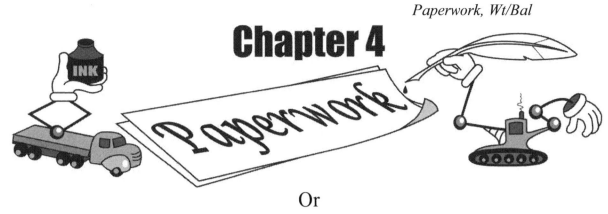

Chapter 4

Or

What Really Makes Things Fly

Barnstorming era pilot, Joe Pundzak, once said, "Kid, when the weight of the paperwork exceeds the airplane's gross weight, you're legal to fly." He then bit off the end his cigar, spit and waved his arm in a circle indicating to ground crew that he was cranking the DC-2's #1 engine before he disappeared in a swirling blue cloud of radial exhaust....

With only slight hyperbole, Captain Pundzak's statement is true. Paperwork makes the world fly 'round. You will never know enough to know everything. Despite this impossible concept, FAR 91.103 says, in part: "Each pilot in command shall, before beginning a flight, become familiar with **all available information** concerning that flight."

All available information? *All?* Everything that's ever been known about flight? How in heck is that possible?

It's not, so the FAA lists things that must be known and, frankly, should something go wrong because the pilot missed an unknown, well, the pilot may be to blame. Correction, the pilot is always to blame.

Here's the secret for handling paperwork stress: Don't sweat it. If you follow the rules and fly smart, you'll find that being legal flies in formation with being safe. You can never have too much of both to fly straight as an arrow.

ARROW

Aviation is built upon a mountain of acronyms and regulated through FARs by the mother of all acronymed government bodies—the FAA.[26]

As a private, sport or student pilot in solo flight, you are the Pilot In Command (PIC). As a student pilot on your check ride with the examiner, you are the PIC. As PIC you call the shots. You determine the airplane's airworthiness for that flight—not the mechanic, ramp

---

[26] Federal Aviation Administration or Funny Acronym Administration

rat or your instructor asleep on the pilots lounge couch. You, the PIC, have not only the right but also the responsibility to question and decline ATC instructions that may jeopardize the airplane's safety.

Each flight begins with a preflight inspection of the aircraft. Besides checking fuel, oil, aircraft condition and loading, the PIC examines the paperwork to make certain the proper documents are onboard.

To remember what documents should be carried onboard for all flights, use the acronym **ARROW:**

- **A**irworthiness Certificate
- **R**egistration
- **R**adio License (not required in the US)
- **O**perating Limitations
- **W**eight and Balance

The "A"

Airplane paperwork is not like car paperwork. When your airplane was manufactured, the builder (Cessna, Piper, Bellanca…) did years of research, engineering and testing to prove to the FAA, and prior to its existence, the CAA[27], that the design was airworthy. Once convinced, the FAA (or CAA) issued a Type Certificate (TC) to the designer/builder saying that the particular model airplane (say, a Cessna 172) was certified to be built with a specific list of parts and optional equipment—and nothing else. No aftermarket, Orange County pimping out your fly-ride at the pilot's or mechanic's whim allowed. Everything on that airplane must be FAA-approved. Each airplane built under that TC is delivered with an airworthiness certificate. That **Standard Airworthiness Certificate** must be displayed in the cabin so passengers can see it. (Not that they would know what it meant.)[28]

Homebuilt, or kit-built, aircraft receive a **Special Airworthiness Certificate** labeling them **Experimental.**

The First "R"

When a pilot buys an airplane, it must be registered with the FAA Civil Aviation Registry in Oklahoma City, which then issues a **Certificate of Aircraft Registration.** When the airplane is sold, the new owner must apply for a new registration. Most states require the owner to also register with the state DOT, so it can zing you for sales or use tax, plus more pointless registration fees.

---

[27] CAA: Civil Aeronautics Administration. Changed to FAA in 1958.

[28] FAR 91.203(b)

> ***Caveat Emptor:*** Let the buyer beware. Even though you register the airplane with the FAA, the FAA does not issue an ownership title as might be found with an automobile. Before you buy an aircraft have AOPA (an acronym that protects pilots—*Aircraft Owners and Pilots Association*[29]) perform a complete aircraft history (title) search. It's worth the money, because you might just be buying an airplane with a few liens attached or not even owned by the seller. Ask me how I know this….

The Other "R"

The second R in AR*R*OW means *R*adio and applies only to international operations. If you fly the airplane out of the country, you will need an FCC **Restricted Radiotelephone Permit** (plus federal Customs decals and such). More paperwork, more fees. *Ka-ching!$!*

"O" AFM, Where Art Thou?

Modern airplanes are certificated to include an **Airplane Flight Manual** (AFM). This is a detailed, FAA-approved book with many boring chapters. Buried in there are the important bits on **Operating Limitations** (the *O* of ARR**O**W) and procedures for that particular model (and serial number) aircraft. A Cirrus SR22 AFM, for instance, cannot be substituted for a Cirrus SR20 manual. The AFM may be included in the POH (**Pilot's Operating Handbook**). Older airplanes had generic owner's manuals that did not apply to a specific serial number aircraft. Many of these manuals were skimpy at best, more like sales brochures. If no manual is included with the aircraft, there should be sufficient **placards** and markings scattered about the cabin and on instruments to indicate appropriate operating limitations.

"W"

The airplane's *Dubya* (*W*): Every airplane has **Weight and Balance** paperwork. This may be included in the AFM/POH or might be some yellowed form jammed into an old folder. Either way, it must reflect the airplane's true weight and loading limits, include all equipment such as avionics, and it *must be current and should be carried* in the aircraft. It's also a good idea to know how to use the Wt/Bal data. More on that later.

That's *ARROW*.

Maintenance Paperwork and Responsibility

---

[29] AOPA, ask your instructor for a membership card application or go to aopa.org

This gets tricky. The FARs put the "primary responsibility on the (aircraft) owner or operator for maintaining an aircraft in an airworthy condition." [30]

Let's say that, you, a private pilot, rent an airplane from a seemingly respectable **FBO** (Fixed Base Operator). "Buddy," the aircraft owner, informs you. "It's a fine flyin' machine." And off you go, only to blow a tire on landing. No harm, no injuries but the runway is closed for 20 minutes while you call for a tow. And the control tower calls **FSDO** (Flight Standards District Office, aka: *The Feds*. Their motto: "We're here to help").

As we'll learn in the section on NTSB 830, a flat tire does not constitute an accident, but a pilot should be prepared at all times to present proper paperwork to authorized FAA representatives.

Each airplane is required to have a maintenance logbook for the airframe and one for each engine and propeller. The PIC is not required to carry the aircraft logbooks. In fact, it's a good idea to keep them safely locked in a fireproof cabinet. But the FAA can and will ask the PIC to present the logbooks at a later time as proof that the airplane was airworthy.

Hey, I thought the airworthiness certificate proved that!

You see, Timmy, an airworthiness certificate means the airplane is airworthy only if the required maintenance and logbook entries are up-to-date. So, if the FBO (airplane owner) swore that the airplane was airworthy but had not performed some required maintenance, perhaps the 100-hour inspection or hadn't complied with an **AD** (Airworthiness Directive), then the PIC is flying an un-airworthy airplane. The PIC is required to determine if the airplane is airworthy. The owner (FBO) might be responsible for *maintaining* the airplane in an airworthy condition, but it's the PIC's responsibility to ensure that the required maintenance was completed before flight. You can't say, "Gee, the mechanic said it was okay to fly." Well, you can say it, but the FSDO inspector will shrug as the violation paperwork is filed. (They're required to smile when they do that under an FAA enforcement program dubbed, *Smile 'n File*.[31])

Weight and Balance

Here is one of the most dangerous statements you'll ever hear on the ramp: "This thing'll fly with anything you can close the doors on."[32] Dangling preposition aside, too many pilots are impressed by what useful load the airplane can "carry" but not with how that weight affects flight characteristics when improperly balanced.

---

[30] FAA-H-8083-25 Ch. 7
[31] Unofficial program slogan: "We're not happy until you're not happy"
[32] #1 dangerous statement: "Watch this!"

Picture a teeter-totter ("seesaw" to those of us who grew up in New Jersey). It's a board balanced on a bar that acts as a pivot or fulcrum. Our seesaw—manufactured by the *Margery Daw See-Saw Company* of Sandusky, Ohio—is certified to hold up to 200 pounds gross weight. Put two 50-pound kids on either end, at equal distance from the fulcrum, and they sit there—balanced. Bored but balanced and under gross weight.

Now toss another 50-pound kid on one end and what happens? Yes, you get arrested for child endangerment, the school gets sued, and seesaws are removed from playgrounds everywhere as thousands of *Margery Daw Seesaw Company* employees (some close to retirement and with kids still in college) are laid off. Why?

Lawyers.

Be serious. Why really? Because the load, while below the max gross weight limit, was not balanced. Now picture the longitudinal axis through your airplane's fuselage. It's a seesaw with an engine at one end and tail at the other (assuming single-engine and no canard-types). The airframe itself counts in the weight-and-balance equation. Its weight is called the **empty weight**,[33] which includes: engine, avionics, seats, ashtrays... everything permanently attached to the airframe, including unusable (undrainable) fuel, hydraulic fluid and oil. The airplane must be balanced along its longitudinal axis (lateral, too, but we'll focus on longitudinal).

You can't hang a big engine on the airplane's nose and expect it to fly level unless the weight balances along the fuselage. Now add people, bags and fuel. The bags generally stay where they're loaded for the entire flight, so that weight doesn't shift. Passengers usually remain strapped in their seats, so their weight generally remains stationary, too. Skydiving airplanes routinely lose passengers in flight, but, normally, you should have the same number of passengers on landing as you did on takeoff. Fuel, however, disappears in flight.

Avgas weighs six pounds per gallon (6 lb./gal). Take off with 50 gallons, and that's 300 pounds of liquid power in the tanks. If the engine burns 10 gallons per hour in flight, then 60 pounds of blue 100LL escapes through the exhaust pipe as spent carbon and water vapor each hour, changing the weight-and-balance equation en route. The airplane weighs less on final approach than it did on climb-out. Is that good? Sometimes. Depends upon where that fuel was located along an arm referenced to the seesaw's fulcrum.

Weight

Consider the gravity: Every airplane is certified for a **Maximum Weight**, casually referred to as the **Maximum Gross Weight**[34]. In level flight, or parked on the ramp, everything in

---

[33] Three types of empty weights: Basic, licensed and standard. We'll often use the generic term empty weight.
[34] There are other types of gross weight: Max Landing, Max Takeoff, Max Zero Fuel. Don't sweat these.

the airplane, including the airplane itself, makes up the gross weight, and it's all pulled toward the Earth's core by gravity. Ignore load factor for a moment.

Lift overcomes weight. With an increase in weight it takes more energy, provided by fuel through the powerplant, to thrust the airfoil to lift the weight. More weight means higher stall speeds. More weight means longer takeoff and landing rolls. More weight means lower climb rates and lower maximum operating ceilings. Higher weight reduces maneuverability and lowers cruising speed. And excess weight adds stress to the airframe. An obese airplane is an unhealthy airplane. So, getting the weight off—and keeping it off—is vital…in flight.

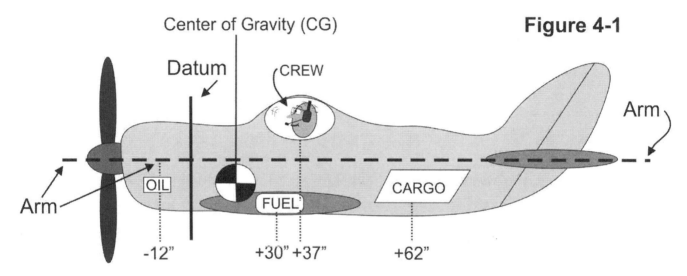

Figure 4-1

The datum is a reference line along the arm. Fuel, crew and cargo are added at various stations along that arm. Each item's weight is multiplied by its location on the arm to determine the item's moment. Add up all the weights and moments. Divide moment by weight to find the CG. Notice that some arms can be negative, such as the OIL at -12". The manufacturer determines the datum location. It could be anywhere.

Balance

The manufacturer handed you a relatively balanced airplane. Empty of fuel it sits proudly on the ramp, ready to receive avgas, people and bags. It's up to you to arrange these loads to keep the airplane balanced.

The place where the weight is located is called a **station,** or a specific place measured in inches from a defined reference point called the **datum line.** That's simply a line drawn perpendicular to the longitudinal axis on the side of the fuselage as a reference point. It's not the Center of Gravity (CG) location but is a place from which all distances are measured. The datum points are different on every airplane. Many are located at the firewall, some at the tip of the spinner and other datum points are located several inches ahead of the spinner untouched by the airplane. The datum line is an arbitrary line (defined by the aeronautical engineers) from which to measure distance along the longitudinal axis. Everything aft of the datum is considered plus (+) and everything forward of the datum line is minus (-). The distance from the datum point to an object is called the **arm** (or moment arm).

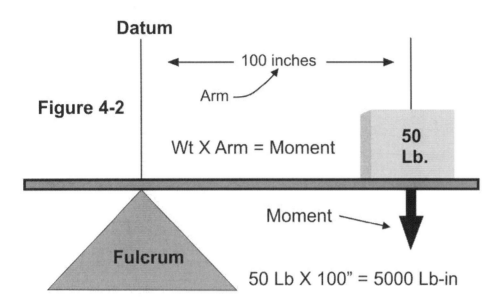

Datum

Figure 4-2

← 100 inches →

Arm

Wt X Arm = Moment

50 Lb.

Moment

Fulcrum

50 Lb X 100" = 5000 Lb-in

A weight suspended along an arm creates a **moment**. Think of it as a weight in motion, pivoting around a point or axis. It's an object exerting a force greater than its mere weight. Picture a five-pound weight held at your own arm's length. It sure feels heavier than five pounds. That's because its moment is 5 (Lb) x 36 inches (your arm's length) = 180 pound-inches (Lb-In). That five pounds exerts a greater force on your shoulder. Now apply that principle to airplane loading.

If we measure the arm where each item sits and multiply that arm times the item's weight we create a list of weights and their moments, or weights exerting forces on the airframe. The goal is to determine where all of those weights and moments come together in one Center of Gravity (CG).

Center of Gravity (CG) is the point about which an airplane would balance if it were possible to be suspended at that point. But if the CG is too far forward the airplane will be nose heavy. If it's too far aft, the airplane will be tail heavy. By adjusting the load we balance the airplane. We move the CG to a desirable location. Your airplane's POH has a loading diagram that shows the fore and aft CG limits or the range, called an **envelope,** within which the airplane should be loaded.

Lateral Pass

The airplane should be loaded properly along its lateral axis, too, but since fuel is usually the only adjustable weight in the wings (passengers object to wing seats—get bugs in their teeth), the only means the PIC has to balance the airplane laterally is by adjusting the amount of fuel in the tanks. If the pilot can select tanks in flight (Left or Right), fuel can be burned evenly from each to keep the airplane balanced. Our Wt/Bal calculations, however, will concentrate on balance along the longitudinal axis.

Why Balance?

Two big issues apply in balancing the airplane along its longitudinal axis: **stability** and **control**. A nose-heavy airplane would be hard to control on takeoff or landing when you need the nose held high. A tail-heavy airplane could become dangerously unstable, particularly in a stall. If the CG were too far aft, stall recovery would be difficult—or impossible—as it would be hard to lower the nose in order to reduce pitch and angle of attack to recover from the stall or a spin. That's bad. A tail-heavy airplane also has light control forces making it easy for the pilot to over-control and overstress the airplane. Again, not good.

The PIC must determine if the airplane is loaded safely before flight and forecast if it will still be safely loaded upon landing. Some airplanes, particularly high-performance models— can be loaded to Max Gross Weight and depart safely. But, during flight fuel burns off to lighten the load. This is good, except, in some aircraft if the fuel weight decreases the CG might shift aft, and the airplane will gradually become less stable even though it weighs less. Again, that's because it's not properly balanced.

The PIC can control balance by shifting cargo, including human cargo. Most fuel you can't move, although you can partially fill a tank, which may help with balance. Consult the airplane's POH.

If the airplane's CG is too far aft for takeoff, you may have to shift your…er, um…weightier passengers from rear seats to front. Remember to keep the pilot in the front regardless of weight[35]. Some baggage can be moved forward: "Here, hold this on your lap." Or simply leave the 40-pound fruitcake behind. You may have to depart with partial fuel and make an extra stop en route to accommodate excess passenger weight. It's usually safer to leave baggage behind rather than fuel.

W/B Terms

Here are terms every Sport or Private Pilot should know (from FAA-H-8083-25):

- **Arm** (arm moment): The horizontal distance in inches from the reference datum line to the CG of an item.

---

[35] Does not apply to some tandem-seat airplanes that require the PIC to fly from the rear seat

▪ **Basic Empty Weight**: The airplane's standard empty weight plus optional equipment installed.

▪ **Center of Gravity** (CG): Point about which the airplane would balance if it were possible to suspend it at that point. It's the mass center of the airplane, or the theoretical point at which the entire weight of the airplane is assumed to be concentrated. Expressed in inches from datum or percentage of mean aerodynamic chord (MAC). (We'll use inches from datum.)

▪ **Center of Gravity Range**: Distance between the forward and aft CG limits. Check the POH.

▪ **Datum** (reference datum): Imaginary vertical plane or line from which all measurements along an arm are taken.

▪ **Fuel Load**: The expendable part of the airplane's load. All usable fuel.

▪ **Licensed Empty Weight**: The airframe plus unusable fuel and undrainable oil, plus all installed equipment listed on the equipment list.

▪ **Moment**: Product of Weight times Arm ($M = W x A$), expressed in pound-inches.

▪ **Moment Index** (or index): This is a moment divided by a constant such as 100, 1000 or 10,000. The purpose of using a constant moment is to simplify weight and balance computations, where heavy items and long arms make for huge numbers.

▪ **Payload**: Weight of occupants, cargo and baggage. (In the airline business, this is the load that pays.)

▪ **Standard Empty Weight**: Airframe, engine(s), and all items of operating equipment that have fixed locations and are permanently installed in the airplane; including fixed ballast, hydraulic fluid, unusable fluid and full engine oil. (Slightly different than Licensed Empty Weight)

▪ **Standard Weights**: Let's agree that gasoline (avgas and mogas) weigh 6 pounds/US gal, Jet A—6.8 lbs/US gal, Oil—7.5 lbs/US gal and Water weights 8.35 lbs/US gal.

▪ **Station**: A location in the airplane that is identified by a number designating its distance in inches from the datum. The datum is *Station Zero* (which sounds like the title of a 1954 sci-fi movie starring Richard Carlson). An object placed 60 inches aft of the datum would be at Station +60.

▪ **Useful Load**: Weight of pilot, copilot, passengers, baggage, usable fuel and drainable oil. It's a GA term. It's Empty Weight subtracted from Max Allowable Gross Weight.

For The Test

The old FAA written exam would ask you to demonstrate your skill at balancing seesaws. The new Private and Sport pilot exams should have eliminated some of these questions, but they're still good ground school exercises. Here are two FAA-type questions:

1. Question (Refer to Figure 4-3): With 50 pounds of weight located at point X and 100 pounds at point Z, how much weight must be located at point Y to balance the plank?

a.   30 pounds
b.   500 pounds
c.   300 pounds

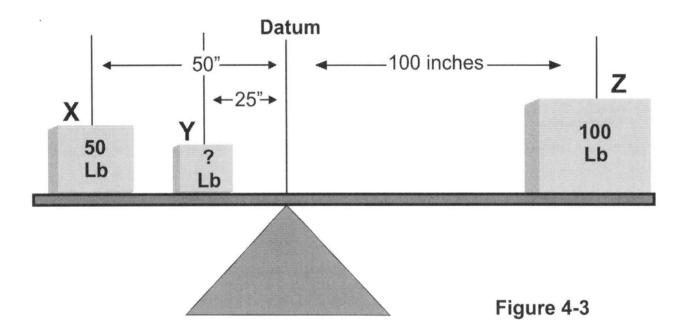

Figure 4-3

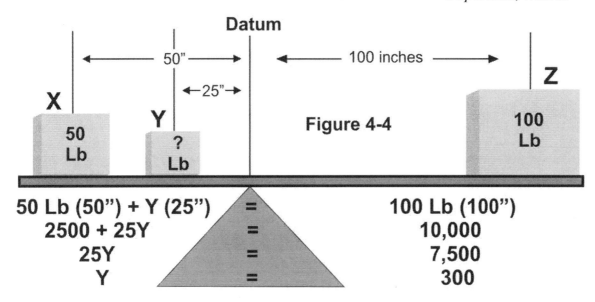

Figure 4-4

1. Answer (Figure 4-4):
Balance the left and right known values. Solve for the unknown Y:

$$\text{Left} = \text{Right}$$
$$50 \text{ lb. } (50 \text{ inches}) + Y (25 \text{ inches}) = 100 \text{ lb. } (100 \text{ inches})$$
This makes:
$$2500 + 25Y = 10{,}000$$
$$25Y = 7500$$
$$Y = 300 \text{ lb.}$$

Verbally the above process sounds like this:
On the Left side 50 pounds at X times 50 inches plus the unknown weight Y times 25 inches equals Right side 100 pounds at Z times 100 inches.

That computes to:
$$2500 \text{ plus } (25 \text{ times } Y) \text{ equals } 10{,}000$$
Eliminate 2500 from both sides gives us:
$$25Y \text{ equals } 7500$$
Divide both sides by 25 and:
$$Y \text{ equals } 300$$
Or

Question #1 answer is **c.** We need 300 pounds at Y to balance the 100 pounds hanging out there at Z.

Now, we'll add the weight of a plank itself to the weight and balance calculation. Here's an actual FAA question:

2. Question: (Refer to Figure 4-5) How far should the 500-pound weight be moved to balance the 200-Lb plank on the fulcrum?

a.   1 inch to the left
b.   1 inch to the right
c.   4.5 inches to the right

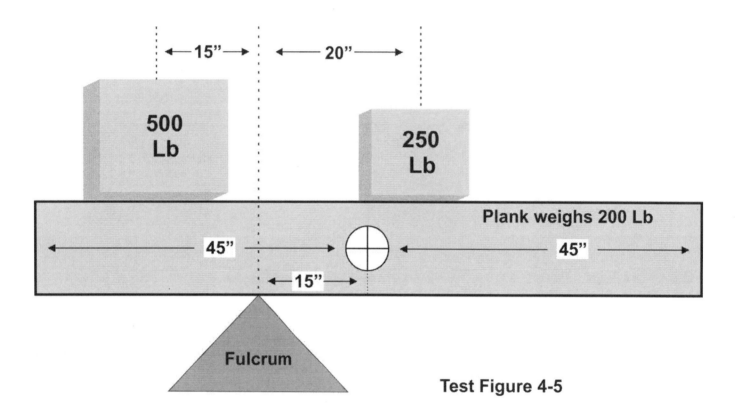

Test Figure 4-5

2. Answer:

$$\text{Left} = \text{Right}$$
$$500 \text{ lb } (X) = 250 \text{ lb. } (20 \text{ inches}) + 200 \text{ lb. } (15 \text{ inches})$$
$$500X = 8000$$

X = 16 inches or move the 500-lb block one inch left, answer **a.**

Just Compute It

Forget planks and teeter totters, we want to balance a real airplane. Finding total weight is easy. Add up all the weights of everything inside the airplane including the airplane. You'll find the empty weight in the AFM/POH. Now, the Zen of W&B: Let's see if all that weight is balanced. Here's a CG loading example from the FAA's *Pilot Handbook of Aeronautical Knowledge*:

✓   Max Gross Weight: 3400 lb
✓   CG Range: 78-86 inches

✓ Front seat occupants (pilot and instructor): 340 lb
✓ Rear seat occupants: 350 lb
✓ Fuel 75 lb
✓ Baggage Area 1: 80 lb

Here's the Step-by-Step **Computational Method**:

1. *List the airplane weight, occupants, fuel and baggage.*

2. *Enter the moment for each item listed (W x A = M)*

3. *Total the Weight and Moments (add 'em up in two columns)*

4. *Divide Total Moment by Total Weight to find the CG (M/W = CG)*

Item	Weight	x	Arm	=	Moment
Airplane Empty Weight	2100		78.3		164,430
Front Seat Pax	340		85.0		28,900
Rear Seat Pax	350		121.0		42,350
Fuel	450		75.0		33,750
Baggage Area #1	80		150.0		12,000
Totals	3320				281,430

281,430 divided by 3320 = 84.8

The airplane's Max Gross Weight is 3400 pounds, and our Total Weight for this flight is 3320 pounds, so we're under gross.

Is it balanced? Our CG (fully loaded) is 84.8 inches. The approved CG range is between 78 and 86 inches, so 84.8 is within range and we're good to go.

Graph Method

This is usually easier, not that the computation method was a brainteaser. The big advantage with graph method is that it presents an image of the CG. You can see how far over gross you are or if the CG is aft or forward and where it will travel as fuel burns.

Manufacturers may provide loading charts and graphs. You'll need to become familiar with your specific brand. They all share one common goal—find Total Weight, CG and determine if that CG is within load limits.

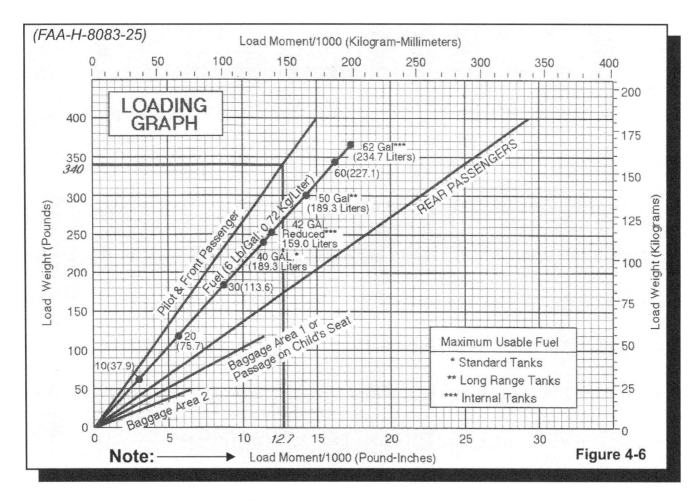

Figure 4-6

You begin with the **Loading Graph** (Figure 4-6, above) to find the moment for each weight.

> **Note**: The airplane's Empty Weight and Moment is always provided in the airplane's Wt/Bal paperwork or AFM/POH. For test purposes the FAA gives you these data.

Since you know the passenger and baggage weights you simply find the weight on the vertical axis of the graph and then trace across to the intersecting diagonal line that labels the item, such as *Pilot & Front Seat Passenger* or *Fuel* (remember fuel is ~6 lb/ US gal) or *Baggage*.

Where the weight line intercepts the item, trace vertically down again to find the Moment. Notice that it's usually listed as Load Moment/1000 (pound inches). Remember the Moment Index? That's a reduction factor to keep the numbers small, so in this case (/1000) three zeros are eliminated. For example, 11.5 would actually be 11500.0 (big number).

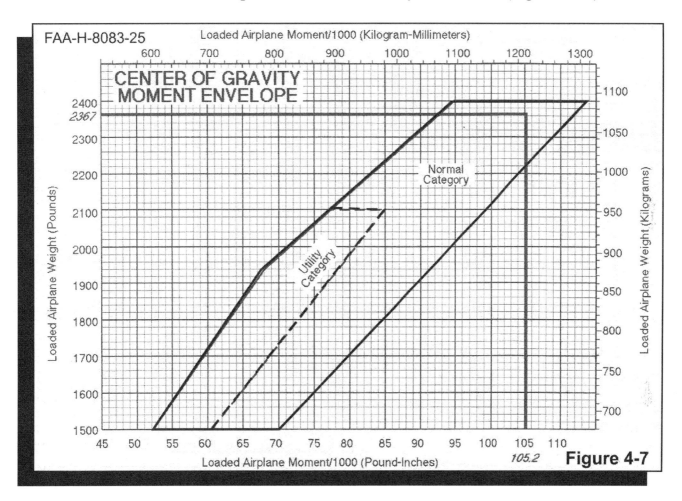

Figure 4-7

As before, add all the weights and all the moments but don't divide anything. Instead, refer to the **CG Moment Envelope (Figure 4-7)**. The vertical axis shows weights so find your total weight and draw a horizontal line to the right. The bottom horizontal axis depicts moments, so find your totaled moment and draw a vertical line up until it intersects the previous horizontal line. Where those two lines intersect is a graphic depiction of your weight and CG. If it's within the envelope, you're good to go. Remember to figure your landing weight and balance before you depart. Burning fuel might move you outside the envelope.

Wt/Bal Tables

Using the Table Method (Figure 4-8a), the manufacturer gives lists of various weights at each station, such as 170 pounds in the front seat and 190 pounds in the airplane's rear seat. The table multiplies the weight times the arm and gives the moment.

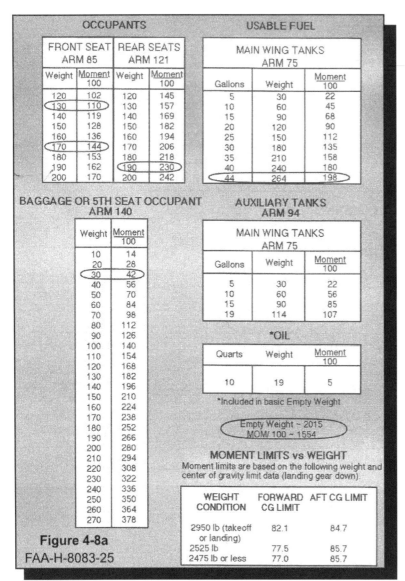

Figure 4-8a
FAA-H-8083-25

With total weight and moment figures, simply refer to the Limits Table (Figure 8b). For example, if the aircraft's gross weight is 2100 pounds, then the moment must fall between 1617/100 and 1800/100.

Old joke: How do you get to Carnegie Hall?

Answer: Practice.

Wt/Bal Computations: How do you get good at them?

Answer: Go to Carnegie Hall. Then, during intermission you can practice Wt/Bal computations. They're easy.

Moment Limits for Gross Weights

Weight	Minimum Moment 100	Maximum Moment 100
2100	1617	1800
2110	1625	1808
2120	1632	1817
2130	1640	1825
2140	1648	1834
2150	1656	1843
2160	1663	1851
2170	1671	1860
2180	1679	1868
2190	1686	1877

(From FAA-H-8083-25)   **Figure 4-8b**

Chapter 5

Airports

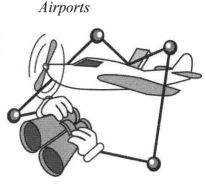

hy do pilots need to know so much about airports? The answer is obvious—to be self-righteous. Example: The next time you're in a crowded theater watching a thoroughly uninspiring action film with a climactic chase scene on an airport, when the air controller says, "Air Force One, cleared to land Runway 45..." You can stand up, thrust an accusing finger at the screen and shout: "*J'accuse!* There is no such thing as a Runway 45!"

After your date slinks beneath his seat, you'll then explain to the manager—as you're being ushered out—that runways are numbered from 1 through 36. There can never be a Runway 45, except in Hollywood. [36] And, the term "air controller" is strictly for non-flyers. The correct term is "air *traffic* controller." Air traffic controllers control air traffic. Air controllers maintain the heating/air conditioning systems in the air traffic control tower (ATCT).

Those are two of the things pilots know and the other 7 billion non-flyers shuffling about the planet's surface don't. Pity them.

Pilots need to know something—make that, *every*thing—about airports, because that's where flight begins and ends. It's where pilots hang around to drink bad coffee and swap flying stories. Airports are sacred places to be protected and understood. You can't know everything about airports, but that shouldn't stop you from learning everything you can. Let's begin the airport lesson by dividing airports into two broad groups: Controlled and Uncontrolled.

Controlled Airport

Broadly speaking, controlled airports are those with operating control towers. The same non-pilot moviegoers who believe that Bruce Willis can land a Boeing 747 (E-4) on Runway 45, think that all airports have control towers. That'd be like all road intersections having traffic cops. Luckily, only a small percentage of airports have control towers. Control towers exist at airports with complex or high volume traffic. The FAA's *Air Traffic*

---

[36] Note to Hollywood producers: If you offer me enough money to option this book, I'll turn my head and you can label runways whatever you want. Call my people. We'll do lunch. —*PB*

Airports

Organization (ATO) usually staffs air traffic control towers, but at slower airports these duties are often contracted out to private companies that provide the same ATC service, using the same air traffic control (ATC) handbook—the FAA-H-7110.65. Pilots may never know whether a controller is employed directly by the FAA or a contractor. It doesn't matter. "Cleared to land" has the same legal meaning regardless who's signing the paychecks.

Below: *Typical FAA ATCT Air Traffic Control Tower*

Tower Cab

Break Room

NATCA Office

ATC's job is to provide for the "safe, orderly and expeditious flow of air traffic." Pilots are required to communicate with ATC at controlled airports and to comply with ATC instructions. This doesn't mean controllers are all-powerful wizards in their dark towers with pilots as mere Hobbits groveling below. Hobbits...I mean, pilots have the right to refuse ATC instructions. If you decline an ATC instruction, though, be prepared to defend yourself in a Star Chamber Inquisition before a panel of black-hooded FAA attorneys and NTSB investigators. So, it's best to obey ΛTC instructions, keeping in mind that you do have the right and responsibility to decline an instruction if it endangers your flight.

Controlled airports exist inside Classes B, C or D airspace. More on that later.

Uncontrolled Airports (so called)

Just because an airport is so-called "uncontrolled" doesn't mean lawlessness reigns. Quite the contrary, regulations abound where ATC doesn't speak directly to pilots. Likewise on a freeway, simply because there's no state trooper in sight doesn't mean we drive any speed in any lane. At uncontrolled airports, pilots control themselves.

Uncontrolled airports are found in Classes G and E airspace. Uncontrolled airports can be large with several long paved runways or they can be small dirt or grass strips in the countryside. Uncontrolled airports might be publicly or privately owned. They might have runway lights or fade into darkness after sunset. An uncontrolled airport could have sophisticated instrument approaches or no published IFR procedures at all. Some uncontrolled airports even have airline service, while others have an old dog sleeping beside the gas pump.

Realty Reality Check: Normally, the FAA does not own or operate airports. Airlines, despite what they like the public to think, do not own or operate airports. Usually a municipal organization does that (while kowtowing to the airlines). Privately owned airports might be owned and operated by an individual or a corporation. Privately owned airports may have their own privately owned and operated control tower. Military airports are owned by the government and operated by folks with machine guns, so we'll avoid most of them in our routine operations.

Two-way radio communication is required at airports with control towers. It's not required when operating at uncontrolled airports. Radios are highly recommended at uncontrolled fields. Whether at a controlled or uncontrolled field, proper communication technique is a must. What's said to the tower controller or on the uncontrolled **Common Traffic Advisory Frequency** (CTAF) must be clear, concise and informative otherwise the frequency becomes a jumble of worthless noise.

Tip: The key to successful aviation communication begins with the ability to listen. Look, Listen, Think and, only then, Speak.

Some air traffic control towers provide radar service. We'll go into this in more detail later, but for now realize that not all control towers offer radar service. Many simply have radios and windows. The tower controller hears the pilot call, answers and looks out the window (perhaps with binoculars). By seeing the aircraft in and around the **traffic pattern** the controller applies visual separation between them. The controller assigns a runway and tells the pilot which aircraft to follow and how to enter the traffic pattern: "Make straight in runway 30, report two-mile final…" or: "Enter left base runway 12, report one mile out…" or, "Number two, follow a Cessna on base…" or, "Make right traffic runway 5, report crossing the river." The pilot responds to that last instruction with: "Make right traffic runway 5, report the river, Cessna Zero Eight Yankee,"[37] and complies. FAR 91.129 says, in part, that you can't operate on a runway or taxiway at a controlled airport without tower clearance.

Where a control tower has radar service the **approach controller** assigns a transponder code, called a **squawk**, and may issue **radar vectors** for a sequence with other traffic to a

---

[37] A readback is not required. Answering, "Wilco, Cessna Zero Eight Yankee," would suffice. Pilots shall read back all "hold short" instructions, though.

runway. Radar separation is not always provided between VFR aircraft even when receiving radar service.

In any case, when you're operating VFR, you are always responsible to **see and avoid** other traffic even if ATC has you in radar contact and on radar vectors.

Airport Markings

After World War I, when barnstormers like Jake Hollow flew around the Midwest in war surplus Jennies and Standards, airports were few and crude. (So were pilots, for that matter.[38]) Most airfields were just that—fields of grass and mud giving pilots access to the air.

As aircraft performance and sophistication improved, runways were paved with lights added for night flight, and navigational aids (navaids) installed for instrument approaches in poor weather. Today, the average municipal airport has one or two paved runways with connecting taxiways leading to an FBO's ramp and hangars.

The airport surface is divided into Movement and Non-Movement areas.[39] **Movement areas** include runways and taxiways, places where ground traffic, such as airplanes, trucks, and snowplows are subject to air traffic control. **Non-movement** areas are the parking ramps (aprons) around the hangars and FBOs. Aircraft and vehicles move freely about the non-movement areas without talking to the control tower. So, how does a pilot know if an area is movement or non-movement?

You can ask or look at the runway, ramp and taxiway markings. All airports should adhere to a standard set of airport markings. Private fields may not comply.

Runways

Runways are identified by thirty-six numbers—1 through 36—referenced to Magnetic North and rounded off to the nearest 10. So, a runway aligned to 334 degrees would be labeled Runway 33. A runway aligned to 006 degrees would be rounded up to 010 degrees and labeled Runway 1. A runway aligned to 060 degrees would be: (all together, class) "Runway Six" or Runway 6.

Runway Nomenclature: Runway 1 is called "Runway One" on the radio. It is not "Runway Zero One." So, Runways 1 through 9 are called: "Runway One," "Runway Two," and so forth through "Runway Niner." Runway 10 points roughly toward 100 degrees and is called "Runway One Zero," and not "Runway Ten."

---

[38] Want more? Read *Bootleg Skies*
[39] Won't appear on FAA written exam, but good to know

Decode the Runways:

Add one zero to a two-digit number painted on the runway to determine its approximate magnetic alignment (e.g.: Runway **10** + 0 = 100 degrees. Runway **23** + 0 = 230 degrees).

Add a zero in front and a zero behind a single digit painted on a runway to determine its approximate magnetic alignment. (e.g.: 0 + Runway **1** + 0 = 010 degrees. 0 + Runway **7** + 0 = 070 degrees).

Roman Numeral Runway **X** does not mean you're flying in ancient Italy. Instead it means that runway is closed—X'd off. Don't land (*non hic terrae*).

The runway's identifying number is painted in large numerals on the approach end of the runway. If you see a "2" on the runway, add a 0: 2 + 0 = 20, so the runway's magnetic alignment is toward 20 degrees (20 degrees is pronounced "zero two zero," but the runway is called "Runway Two").

Quiz: How do you say Runway 11? (See footnote for answer)[40]

(Red Background)

As you taxi and approach a runway you should see a red sign with the runway number in white. It may have two numbers separated by a dash, such as (see illustration at left):

This is a mandatory instruction sign—*ya gotta do somethin'*. Red means danger. *Danger, Will Robinson*, you're about to enter a runway where aircraft land and take off. The number 4 means Runway 4. Its reciprocal is 22. So, you're approaching one strip of pavement (or turf) that serves as two runways depending upon the direction. Runway 4 heads northeast and Runway 22 is opposite heading southwest.

Whatever sign you see, if it's red with white numbers it indicates a runway. At a controlled airport you must have a clearance to operate on or to cross that runway at any point. Without a clearance, hold short of the runway. If the tower controller tells you to "Hold short Runway Two Two…" You must (shall) comply and read back the hold short instructions: "Hold short Runway Two Two, Cessna Zero Eight Yankee." The FAA takes runway incursions real seriously and so should you.

---

[40] "Runway One One"

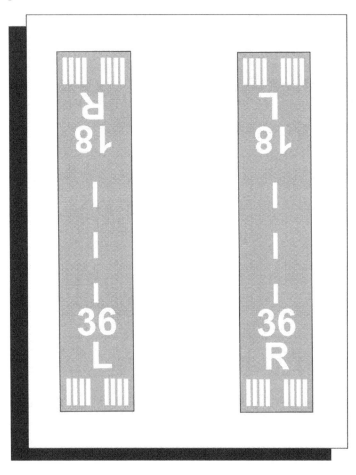

At an uncontrolled airport you're expected to look both ways and announce your intentions on CTAF (Common Traffic Advisory Frequency), if radio-equipped, before using the runway.

Runways Left, Right and Center

As a private pilot you'll be eligible to fly into the biggest airports in the nation, spending top dollar in landing fees and fuel prices there. Often bigger airports have parallel runways to squeeze in more traffic. If two runways are parallel and share the same magnetic heading, then one is the Left runway and the other the Right. So, two runways that point north would be 36L and 36R. That's pronounced: "Runway Three Six Left" and "Runway Three Six Right."

In the event of three parallel runways, the one in the middle is called "Center" as in "Runway 36 Center."

Displaced Ain't The Same As Lost

A runway is a rectangle, although on final it resembles a trapezoid. Its long sides are called the **runway edge**. The **threshold** is where the pavement stops and/or a large white line is painted across the runway. Beyond the threshold there might be an **overrun area**, used if pilots can't stop and need to overrun the threshold. Beyond that is usually a school, mall or housing subdivision built long after the airport was there, and its inhabitants are eager to close the airport.[41] As an aircraft lands it crosses a threshold. This is called the **approach end** of the runway. When departing, the last bit of runway the airborne aircraft crosses is the **departure end**.

Not all of a runway may be available for takeoff or landing. The runway could be, perhaps, 6000 feet long but because of obstacles, noise abatement issues (pesky neighbors) or poor pavement condition, a portion of that runway may be blocked off. The threshold is then moved down the runway. It's displaced. A **displaced threshold** may not be used for

---

[41] Sad political reality. Again, AOPA helps protect airports

landing; you can't touch down on it. In most cases it can be used for taxi, takeoff roll or as an overrun.

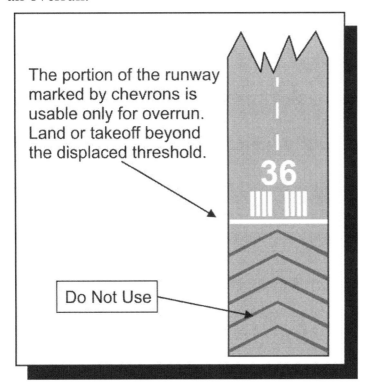

The portion of the runway marked by chevrons is usable only for overrun. Land or takeoff beyond the displaced threshold.

Do Not Use

could occur if brakes fail.

If the unusable portion of runway is marked with arrows pointing toward the displaced threshold, this tells the landing pilot to touch down beyond this segment. A painted fat line across the runway indicates the displaced threshold where the usable portion of the runway begins. The departing pilot, however, may use that section marked with white arrows for takeoff roll. If those arrows are yellow the pilot may only use the pavement to taxi to the displaced threshold (white line across the runway) and from there begin the takeoff roll. If the unusable portion is marked with chevrons, then it cannot be used for either takeoff or landing but will suffice for unexpected overruns such as

Each runway should have a dashed white stripe running down the middle. That line down the runway's center is called the (*wait for it…*) **runway centerline.** As you taxi onto the runway for takeoff you're expected to put your nose wheel or tailwheel on that centerline. Likewise on landing.

Call Me A Taxi [42]

To get to and from the runways on the ground, airplanes use **taxiways**. An airplane might also taxi on a runway when that movement is not associated with takeoff or landing. At a controlled airport you must have a clearance from the control tower in order to taxi on a taxiway or runway. We've already discussed runway markings for the VFR pilot, so let's look at taxiway markings.

Taxiways may run parallel to a runway. They may bend along the route. They often cross other taxiways, ramps (aprons) and runways. In short, taxiways can resemble a Parisian subway Metro map and like the *le' Metro*, you'll need to study the *Airport Layout* before operating at that airport. Layouts or **airport diagrams** are found in the **Airport/Facility Directory** (A/FD).

---

[42] Proper Groucho response: "Okay, you're a taxi."

Runways are numbered 1 through 36. Taxiways are lettered A through Z with some taxiway connectors labeled with a combination of letters and numbers, such as: T-1 or A-2, D-4. The ground controller will say, for example: "Cessna One Four Zero Eight Yankee, Runway Three One, taxi via Bravo, Delta, Delta Four."[43] The runway was easy enough to understand— "…Runway Three One (31)," but the taxi route in this clearance included two taxiways: Bravo and Delta, or taxiways B and D and a connector, Delta Four (D-4).

Before moving, you would consult your airport diagram and find where Taxiway B intercepts Taxiway D and how Delta leads to Runway 31 via D-4. If you are ever confused or lost, ask for "progressive" instructions along the route.

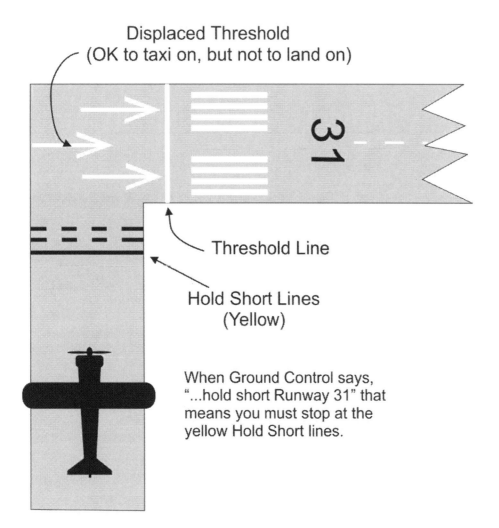

Displaced Threshold
(OK to taxi on, but not to land on)

Threshold Line

Hold Short Lines
(Yellow)

When Ground Control says, "…hold short Runway 31" that means you must stop at the yellow Hold Short lines.

Never fake it. Never hope that you understood the clearance. Always verify. Ask for "progressive taxi." Or if all else fails resort to using plain English: "Ground, I'm new here, how do I get to Runway Three One?"

Runways have a dashed white centerline stripe. Taxiways usually have a solid yellow stripe. Put your nose wheel on that stripe, and your wingtips should miss any known obstacles along the route. Tailwheel pilots may need to S-turn along that stripe in order to see past the nose. The yellow stripe leads onto the runway but ends where the white runway centerline takes up.

---

[43] Prior to June 30, 2010 ATC would've said , "Taxi to Runway…" That phrase "taxi to" is no longer used.

Some taxiways lead across open ramp (apron), making the taxiway edge indiscernible. In that case a taxiway edge line is painted. If the line is solid, it means do not cross. Possibly the shoulder is soft gravel. If it's dashed, you may use a portion of that pavement beyond the dashed line, perhaps, in order to give way to opposite direction traffic.

As you taxi toward your assigned runway ("…Runway Three One.") you'll see a set of yellow lines perpendicular across your taxiway: Two dashed lines and two solid. If the two dashed lines are on your side, you may cross. "If the lines are dashed, then dash across." If the two solid lines are on your side, hold short. These are the **hold short lines**. At tower-controlled airports there are usually two sets of alternately flashing yellow lights to mark the hold short position. Hold short means stop. Do not cross without a clearance from the control tower.

(Red Background)

At a tower-controlled airport (inside Class D, C or B airspace) a taxi clearance from ground control will sound like this: "Cessna Two Eight Eight One Lima, Runway Three One, taxi via Bravo." You are authorized, and expected, to taxi on taxiway B (Bravo) all the way to the approach end of runway 31 where you'll see the red sign with the runway's name in white letters. You are *not* cleared to taxi on any portion of the runway or any other runway en route.

You'll also see Hold Short lines. So—hold short, meaning STOP! You've reached your clearance limit, Runway 31. You then switch to tower frequency to get permission to use that runway.

You are authorized to cross any other taxiways en route, but you are not authorized to cross

(Red Background)

any intersecting runways. [44] ATC must clear you to cross each runway on the way to your assigned runway. You may hear something like this: "…Runway Three One, taxi via Bravo, hold short (of) Runway Two Three."

The controller says the name of the runway but only as a heads-up that eventually you'll get that runway. Meanwhile, ATC says, "hold short Runway Two Three." So, you know you should head toward Runway 31, but somewhere en route when you see a red sign for Runway 23…*(see figure above left)*…you shall (must) hold short of that runway. Perhaps tower has cleared another airplane to land on Runway 23, in which case, you need to stay clear.

---

[44] Prior to June 30, 2010, ATC would clear an aircraft to "taxi to" a runway. That clearance authorized crossing all other runways en route except the assigned runway. That rule has changed. "Taxi to" is no longer used.

Whatever the reason—and you might never know—you do not touch Runway 23 until cleared to "cross Runway 23," or, more correctly, the ground controller says: "Runway Three One, taxi via Bravo, cross Runway Two Three."

When in doubt…(*class?*) Verify. And always read back (repeat) hold short instructions.

Signs with yellow inscriptions on black backgrounds *(see figure at right)* with yellow borders are called **location signs.** They mean *You Are Here.*

(Yellow Letter) (Yellow Letter)

Imagine yellow letters or numbers on a black background. The left sign says that you're on Taxiway B. The right signs says that you're on Runway 4.

Other Signs:

▪ **Direction signs** have yellow backgrounds with black letters or numbers indicating runways, taxiways or ramps. An arrow is added to point toward that piece of pavement.

▪ **Destination signs** are black with yellow letters to indicate what a particular piece of airport real estate is. MIL indicates a *mil*itary ramp. CARGO is a cargo ramp. And so it goes….

▪ **Information signs** are also yellow with black inscriptions to pass along information about that segment of the airport, such as noise abatement departure procedures.

▪ **Runway distance remaining signs** are black with white numbers. Add three zeros to that number as you're whizzing past on landing, and you'll know approximately how many feet of runway remains before you have to either stop or call your insurance agent.

Wind Indicators

As much as possible, aircraft and birds land and take off into the wind. At an airport with an operating control tower the controller issues the wind direction (referenced to Magnetic North) and speed (in knots). The wind information is also broadcast on the Automatic Terminal Information System (**ATIS**), but that won't be the current wind. The ATIS is a recorded message updated every hour (more often in rapidly changing weather conditions). The ATIS gives wind direction and speed, sky cover, visibility, any precipitation or restrictions to visibility, altimeter setting plus the runway in use. Sadly, by the time you hear it, it's old news. To get a wind update the pilot simply states: "Wind check." The tower controller will answer (for example): "Wind one three zero at one five." That means the wind is coming *from* 130 degrees (magnetic) at 15 knots.

There are other means for judging wind direction and estimating its speed. Blowing smoke, dust from gravel roads, tall grass and fields of corn, sugar cane or mature soybeans—anything that reacts to the wind makes for a great wind indicator. Ponds and lakes show wind, too. Trucks blowing off the Interstate might be a good wind indicator.

Airport Lighting

Sport pilots are not authorized to fly at night.[45] Private pilots must receive at least three hours of night training prior to taking the practical exam (checkride)[46] and, once certificated, are authorized to fly at night. Night flight is often beautiful. The air is usually calm and traffic light. Plus, airports are easy to see because they have distinctive lighting.

The **airport (or aerodrome) beacon** is a rotating light with two or more beams marking the airport's location. Airport beacons are usually lit from sunset to sunrise (not always). In classes B, C, D or E surface area airspace, during daytime, the beacon should (not *shall*) be lit whenever the weather is less than what's needed for daytime VFR flight (1000-foot ceiling and 3 miles visibility). The beacon is not the definitive authority for indicating if an airfield's weather conditions are less than VFR. The pilot is responsible for determining that through official weather observations, such as AWOS/ASOS or ATIS.

The most common Airport Beacon flashes two beams: One green and the other white. This indicates a civilian land airport.

Other Airport Beacons:

- Flashing white and yellow indicates a water airport

- Flashing white, yellow and green is a heliport

- Two quick white flashes followed by a green indicates a military airport

Other Airport Lights of Note:

PAPI: Precision Approach Path Indicator and pronounced "Pappy" like some old west prospector. PAPIs usually appear in a single row, perpendicular and to the left of the approach end of the runway. Red or white lights indicate your position on the glide path. Ideally, you want to see two white lights beside two red lights, indicating on the glide path

---

[45]FAR 61.315

[46] In Alaska where the sun doesn't set for much of the summer, the night requirement is waived until winter (FAR 61.110)

(left to right or WWRR— *"Will Willie Reach Runway?"*). More red indicates getting lower. More white—getting higher. *Hint: All white—high as a kite. All red— you're dead.*

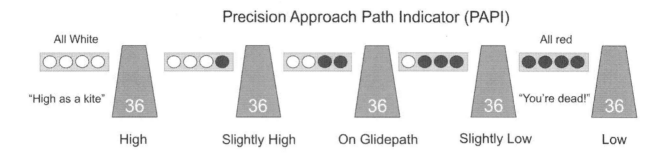

VASI: Visual Approach Slope Indicator. Like the PAPIs the VASI uses red and white lights to indicate height on the glide path. VASI lights are stacked in two or three bars. Each bar has two lights. Red on top and white on the bottom means on glide path. *Red over white is all right. White over white—high as a kite. Red over red—you're dead.* (Such grim mnemonic imagery) White over red doesn't exist. VASIs give a visual glide path. They do not align you (left/right) with the runway centerline. Some VASI units may have pulsating lights: **Pulsating** red means you're low. Steady white or alternating red and white means on glide path. Pulsing white—High as a kite.

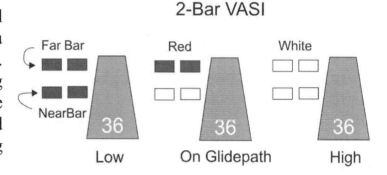

Other visual glide path indicators include a **tricolor** system. Below glide path—red. Above glide path—amber. On glide path—green.

VASI and PAPI are the most common visual glide path indicators.

FAR 91.129 (e)(3): "Each pilot operating an airplane approaching to land on a runway served by a visual approach slope indicator must maintain an altitude at or above the glide path until a lower altitude is necessary for a safe landing."

Taxiway lights are blue. Runway edges are marked with white and yellow lights. Yellow marks the last 2000 feet (caution) with red lights marking the runway's end. Runway lights are rated by intensity. High Intensity Runway Lighting (HIRL), Medium Intensity Runway Lighting (MIRL) or Low Intensity Runway Lighting (LIRL). Some runways have lights embedded into the surface. These look really cool at night, because you land on the lights. These include Touchdown Zone Lighting (TDZL) and Runway Centerline Light System (RCLS). Runway ends may have Runway End Identifier Lights (REIL) for quick and positive ID of the approach end of the pavement. These are synchronized flashing lights located on either side of the threshold.

Runways with Instrument Landing Systems (ILS) have **approach lights**. These come in several forms and point the arriving pilot toward the runway threshold. A moving and flashing light appears to "run" down the approach lights and resembles an electronic rabbit, so it's nicknamed the "rabbit." You'll hear instrument pilots occasionally ask tower to "Kill the rabbit." They're not being cruel. They just don't need the flashing bunny.[47]

At airports with an operating control tower, the tower controllers usually turn the runway, taxiway and approach lights on and off as necessary. When the tower is closed, or at uncontrolled airports there may be pilot controlled lighting (PCL). By keying (clicking) your microphone on a designated frequency (often CTAF) you can turn the lights on, off and change the intensity. Usually, to operate PCL the pilot keys the microphone seven times. That turns things on and at high intensity. For medium intensity key the mic five times. For Low Intensity, key three times. The A/FD tells if the airport has PCL.

Radio Controlled Runway Lights	
Key Mic	**FUNCTION**
7 times in 5 seconds	High Intensity
5 times in 5 seconds	Medium or lower Intensity
3 times in 5 seconds	Low Intensity

Airport Layout

Airports, as Richard Bach once noted, are "ports in the air."[48] Pilots roam the sky, returning to these ports to refuel, discharge passengers and be among fellow aviators. While airports vary in shape and size they share many characteristics.

Airport is defined in FAR Part 1 (Definitions and Abbreviations): "Airport means an area of land or water that is used or intended to be used for the landing and takeoff of aircraft, and includes its buildings and facilities, if any."

An airport can be Chicago's O'Hare or New York's LaGuardia with miles of pavement and thousands of distressed travelers slogging to make connections. Or an airport can be *Ailerona Muni*, a grass strip in the Midwest with a handful of hangars each with a small airplane owned by dreamers who believe in flight for flight's sake.

Usually there's at least one runway, the strip of land—paved or not—where aircraft take off and land. Taxiways, as we've seen, connect these runways to each other and to the parking ramps (aprons). Even at the quietest airport there must be a system defining how a runway

---

[47] Yes, tower controllers do sing the Elmer Fudd refrain: "*Kill da wabbit*" when hearing this request.
[48] "Gift of Wings" is mandatory reading.

is to be used. Airborne operations around an airport take place inside the **traffic pattern**. Pattern shape depends upon several variables. At non-towered airports traffic pattern shape is defined by FAR 91.126 (b):

Direction of turns. When approaching to land at an airport <u>without an operating control tower</u> in a Class G airspace area -
(1) Each pilot of an airplane must make all turns of that airplane to the left unless the airport displays approved light signals or visual markings indicating that turns should be made to the right, in which case the pilot must make all turns to the right; and
(2) Each pilot of a helicopter or a powered parachute must avoid the flow of fixed-wing aircraft.

The regulation says that, normally, aircraft make left-hand turns in the traffic pattern, and helicopters and powered parachutes stay clear of airplanes.

The traffic pattern is a rectangle above the airport and is aligned to a particular runway. Once inside the traffic pattern, all turns are made to the left unless a right-hand pattern is indicated. How would that be indicated? Several means:

The VFR navigational **sectional charts** contain a wealth of information on your destination airport, including runway alignment, shape, radio frequencies, airport elevation and, if non-standard right-hand traffic is required, a tiny note such as **RP 4, 36** appears in the airport data. RP means Right-hand Pattern. The number 4 means Runway 4, and 36 means Runway 36. So, at that airport, pilots are expected to make right-hand turns in the traffic pattern for Runways 4 or 36. If no RP appears, then the standard left-hand pattern applies.

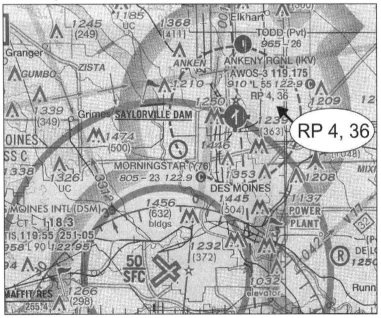

Some two-way, non-ATC radio communication is available at uncontrolled airports. The **UNICOM** operator (usually the FBO) on the CTAF might be available to tell a pilot whether left or right traffic is required. Note: UNICOM is not ATC. UNICOM is a nongovernmental, air-to-ground radio communication station. These **aeronautical advisory stations** are advisory only. The UNICOM operator should never say, "Cleared to land," "Cleared for takeoff" or sequence air traffic. UNICOM may be operated by the airport authority and therefore may have control of ground operations such as parking, curfews, noise abatement and law enforcement on the ground. MULTICOM is another CTAF used between pilots rather than between pilots and a ground base.

> **UNICOM** and **MULTICOM** frequencies include: 122.7, 122.72, 122.8, 122.97, 123.0, 123.05, 123.07, 122.9, 122.92, and 122.95.

"You don't need a weatherman to tell which way the wind blows."[49] **Wind direction indicators** are physical devices on the airfield that, as the name implies, indicate which way the wind is blowing. The **windsock** is the most common wind indicator. A cone-shaped rag tacked to a pole, it flaps in the breeze indicating wind direction and, to some extent, speed and gusts. The large end points into the wind. Some windsocks are illuminated at night. Windsocks may be located anywhere on the airfield including atop hangars.

A wind cone is another (rarely used) term for windsock.

Wind Tees and tetrahedrons are rigid wind indicators. The **Wind Tee** resembles a small airplane on a post. It usually has a fuselage and stubby wings (called a crossbar, it forms the T), plus a vertical tail. It pivots on the post so that the crossbar end points into the wind.

The **tetrahedron** is a four-sided pyramid on its side with the pointy end into the wind. It can either float on a pivot like a Wind Tee or be anchored in one position to indicate landing direction (pointy end into the wind). Both the Wind Tee and Tetrahedron are landing direction indicators used to indicate the suggested runway in use. Caution: Since Wind Tees and Tetrahedrons may be anchored or manually operated, check the windsock for the real wind direction. If a control tower is in operation, the ATC-assigned runway trumps any wind indicator. However, if ATC assigns a runway contrary to what you consider safe (too much crosswind or tailwind), request another runway.

A landing direction indicator may be located on the ground inside a large segmented circle, usually made with lengths of white pipe, logs or concrete, anything to form the circle. Viewed from overhead, if you see a segmented circle, it's a reminder that left-hand traffic applies. Likewise, the lack of a

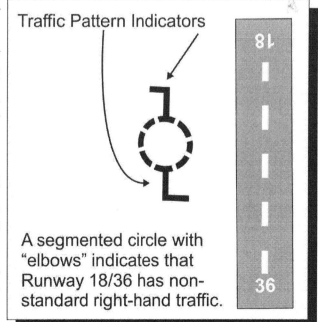

Traffic Pattern Indicators

A segmented circle with "elbows" indicates that Runway 18/36 has non-standard right-hand traffic.

---

[49] Dylan, and I don't mean Dylan Thomas.

segmented circle indicates left-hand traffic. If right-hand traffic applies to a runway, the segmented circle should have extensions or **traffic pattern indicators** that look like L-shaped arms. The L-shaped extensions indicate the base leg turn to final approach for that runway.

Traffic Pattern Segments

Upwind, crosswind, downwind, base, final and departure (or climb-out). Those are the legs of the traffic pattern. Picture the runway. Let's say it's Runway 36, pointing straight North. When flying parallel to the runway and opposite to the landing direction (tracking 180 degrees in this case) you're on the **downwind** leg. Turn 90 degrees (left or right) and fly perpendicular to the runway, while still approaching the runway, and you're now on the **base** leg. Turn 90 degrees until pointed directly at the approach end of the runway (heading 360 degrees in our case without any wind) and you're now on **final**.

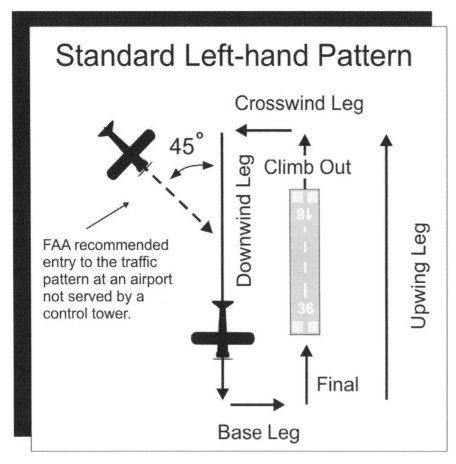

Standard Left-hand Pattern

When the airplane departs, the initial climb out is called the **departure** leg, sometimes called the **climb-out**. Turn 90 degrees, left or right, and the airplane is now on the **crosswind leg**. From crosswind, turn 90 degrees and you're back on the downwind leg. The downwind leg is so called because the aircraft flies with the wind or down wind. The opposite is the **upwind** leg, which is not found directly over the airport but, instead, on the opposite side of the runway (above the ground) from the downwind leg.

How To Enter The Pattern

There is no regulation way to enter or exit a traffic pattern. FAR 91.126 simply says to make left traffic unless otherwise advised. The *Aeronautical Information Manual (AIM)*, Chapter 4, however, suggests proper ways to operate in the pattern. If the *AIM* suggests, you can bet the FAA really, really wants you to take its suggestions to heart. So, based on that, it is recommended that pilots enter the traffic pattern on a 45-degree intercept angle to a midpoint on the downwind leg. That's sometimes unofficially dubbed **The Forty-Five**[50]. From that entry the pilot adjusts speed to follow other aircraft in the pattern as necessary. Don't be surprised to see other traffic entering the pattern on the crosswind, base leg or from just about any angle. Not everyone has read this book…yet.

> **Note**: "When two or more aircraft are approaching an airport for the purpose of landing, the pilot of the aircraft at the lower altitude has the right-of-way over the pilot of the aircraft at the higher altitude. However, the pilot operating at the lower altitude should not take advantage of another aircraft, which is on final approach to land, by cutting in front of, or overtaking that aircraft."[51]

Traffic pattern altitude is usually determined by the airport authority (airport management) and may be adjusted to appease neighbors. Most traffic pattern altitudes are between 600 and 1500 feet AGL. Military often run their heavy and faster aircraft at 2500 feet. Pattern altitude is usually maintained on downwind and upwind legs with descents made on base leg and on final. Aircraft are often climbing on the crosswind leg.[52]

Unusual Maneuvers In the Pattern

When a control tower is in operation, the tower air traffic controller establishes the traffic sequence and clears aircraft for takeoff and to land. The pilot's role is simple. Listen for your call sign and do what you're told. There's no need to enter the traffic pattern on a 45-degree angle to the downwind leg unless the controller assigns it by saying: "Make left/right traffic Runway 22." You may be told to "make straight in Runway 3," or "Enter right base Runway 17." If you can't do it, advise, and ATC will adjust the flow accordingly. What controllers absolutely hate are surprises. If after being assigned to "Enter right base Runway 5," you, instead, decide to enter on the downwind leg, you might upset the controller's plan. Sequence and separation (the tower's duty) of air traffic relies on pilots complying with ATC instructions.

Occasionally, a faster airplane overtakes a slower one and a sequence goes to pot. The tower controller may then tell the faster airplane to "make a right three-sixty," meaning turn right 360 degrees and roll out again on final (or wherever) to ensure proper spacing. This is the tower's call. The pilot should never (except in an emergency) make a 360-degree turn in the traffic pattern without first getting ATC approval: "Tower, Citation Zero Golf Charlie, request left three-sixty for spacing." Tower: "…approved." Keep surprises to a minimum. Controllers get gray hair soon enough from FAA management and don't need pilot help.

At an uncontrolled airport (Class G or E surface airspace) the pilot is the controller and, again, a "360" in the pattern is a thoroughly bad idea, because it means you'll be turning

---

[50] Not to be confused with the 1745 Jacobite Scottish rebellion against England, also called "The 45"
[51] AIM 4-3-4
[52] AIM 4-3-3

blindly into traffic behind you. If spacing doesn't work, if you overtake a slower aircraft, then make shallow, coordinated S-turns to maintain or widen the gap. If that doesn't work, and you're still overtaking the J-3 Cub on final, add power, pass the slowpoke and then fly the traffic pattern again. Don't get angry, don't make snide comments on the radio and don't collect $200. Simply go around and try again. If workload permits announce your go-around on the CTAF: "Cessna Eight One Lima going around, will pass the Cub on the right." If the pattern is so clogged with traffic to make this unsafe, exit the pattern and re-enter when it's safer.

Here are the *AIM*'s recommended steps for entering and exiting a traffic pattern when no control tower is operating:

Key to traffic pattern operations
1. Enter pattern in level flight, abeam the midpoint of the runway, at pattern altitude. (1000 feet AGL is recommended pattern altitude unless established otherwise. . .)
2. Maintain pattern altitude until abeam approach end of the landing runway on downwind leg.
3. Complete turn to final at least ¼-mile from the runway.
4. On departure, continue straight ahead until beyond departure end of runway.
5. If remaining in the traffic pattern, commence turn to crosswind leg beyond the departure end of the runway within 300 feet of pattern altitude.
6. If departing the traffic pattern, continue straight out, or exit with a 45-degree turn (to the left when in a left-hand traffic pattern; to the right when in a right-hand traffic pattern) beyond the departure end of the runway, after reaching pattern altitude.

Even though the above procedures are in the *AIM*, the pilot is in command, and if any procedure doesn't look safe, the pilot retains the right and responsibility to fly accordingly. Perhaps, as you enter an uncontrolled airport a standard 45-degree entry to the downwind would put you over alligator-infested bayou and you'd feel more comfortable remaining over dry land. Or, as happens along the Pacific Coast, a fog bank might block a portion of the pattern forcing pilots to enter on base leg. No problem, enter on the base leg. Or go somewhere else.

Maybe, you're in a position to make a straight-in approach to a runway, and rather than fly an extra five minutes with an already airsick passenger on board begging you to land, you elect to skip the downwind entry. Again, it's okay. Instrument approaches regularly make straight-in approaches to uncontrolled airports rather than circle-to-land. This is a good time to mention that IFR traffic DOES NOT have right-of-way over VFR traffic in the pattern.

A crosswind entry to the pattern often makes more sense than flying extra miles to the downwind leg, likewise with making an upwind leg entry. Whatever the case, if you fly a non-standard pattern entry realize that those making standard entries may not see you. So, as always, the pilot must see and avoid other traffic—IFR or VFR.

Flight involves risk. Pilots analyze and manage risk. The *AIM* cannot give a one-procedure-fits-all-situations ruling. It's a guide (a strong guide), and I suggest pilots follow the *AIM*, but remember that it can be modified for local conditions.

Pattern Hazard: Wake Turbulence

Some hazards the FAA can't regulate away. From the Aerodynamics chapter (Ch. 2) we learned that as a wing produces lift it also produces **wingtip vortices**. Every wing from an Ercoupe to a Boeing 787 produces wingtip vortices. These vortices are normally benign when trailing smaller aircraft. You'll feel an occasional bump following a Cessna or Bonanza on final. But if you tuck in behind a large airplane, these vortices in the airplane's wake become violent. This is wake turbulence.

The strongest vortex occurs when the airplane generating them is (remember this) **Heavy, Clean and Slow**. When is a Boeing 787 heaviest, clean (gear and flaps up) and slow? Usually after takeoff after the gear and flaps are retracted.

The vortex circulation around the wingtip is **Outward** and **Upward**.

The vortex sinks behind the generating airplane, so if you're trailing and below—watch out! These vortices are tiny tornadoes. They drift with the wind and can linger in your path for several minutes. Don't expect to see them unless they kick up a little dust.

So, when following a large aircraft, **operate above and upwind of its wake** to avoid its wake turbulence.

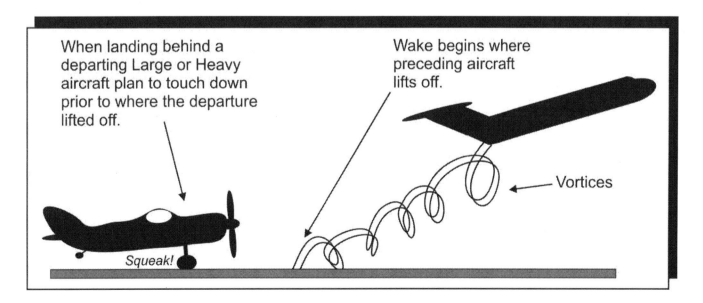

When landing behind a departing Large or Heavy aircraft plan to touch down prior to where the departure lifted off.

Wake begins where preceding aircraft lifts off.

Vortices

Squeak!

Here's a real stinker. When landing or taking off behind a large airplane, if the prevailing wind is a light, quartering tailwind, it will push the tornadoes (vortices) down the runway where you intend to land or rotate. Best solution: Go around and come back in a few minutes. If departing, hold short and wait.

ATC is required to provide minimal radar and runway separation between small aircraft following **Large** or **Heavy** aircraft. Large (for wake turbulence separation purposes) is anything more than 41,000 pounds maximum certificated takeoff weight, and Heavy is anything capable of a max takeoff weight over 255,000 pounds. [53] Although Boeing 757s are less than 255,000 pounds max gross, ATC treats them as Heavies. You will hear ATC use the word "Heavy" when talking to a Heavy: "United Twelve Fifty-Two Heavy, fly heading…."

When landing behind a Large or Heavy aircraft, plan your touchdown so as to touch beyond where the big beast touched, because once on the ground its wings stop producing lift and vortices. Caution: even on the ground a jet's massive power can toss your little Cherokee like an empty beer can in the wind, so don't taxi in a jet's wake.

Pattern Hazard: Collision Avoidance

"One midair collision can ruin your whole day."[54] Midairs are nasty. They're also incredibly rare and mostly occur—logically—in or near the traffic pattern in good VFR weather. Why? Because that's where the most aircraft are concentrated. Most happen on clear days, because—you guessed it—everyone's flying.

How do we avoid the ultimate traffic pattern hazard? *See and Avoid* is the running philosophy to which we add **See and Be Seen.**

Airplanes certified for night flight must have: Navigation lights and a red anti-collision beacon (rotating beacon or strobe). A landing light is required when operating for hire and is wise to have when not for hire.

Navigation lights consist of a Red light on the left wingtip, Green on the right and a White bulb in the tail. At night these three lights help the pilot tell which way another airplane is headed:

➢ If an airplane crosses in front of you from Left to Right, you'll see its Green right wingtip light.

---

[53] ATC manual, 7110.65 P/C Glossary
[54] Old ATC saying

➢ When an airplane crosses in front of you Right to Left, you'll see its Red left wingtip light.
➢ If it flies away from you, you should see its white taillight. You won't see its wingtip lights.
➢ Coming at you head-on (not good) you'll see, if only briefly, the Red and Green lights but no white light. Turn right—immediately!

Operation Lights On encourages pilots to turn lights on in the traffic pattern. Strobes and a landing light are the best in bright daylight. Always turn on your rotating beacon (ant-collision beacon) whenever the engine is running or about to run. Someone walking across a noisy ramp might not hear you call, "Clear prop!" but could notice the flashing red before seeing the propeller and should know to stay clear.

Scan, Baby, Scan

Stare at this dot: .
Keep staring…and staring…you're getting sleepy….(You're also cheating because you can't read this line if you're staring at the dot.)

Point is—if you stare in one place your brain goes numb. I know mine did in high school Algebra Class when I stared at the equations on the board. *Zzzzzzzzz*….

In flight, if you stare in one place, you won't see much of anything, including threats from other traffic. Two aircraft converging at 240 knots (your 120 knots plus its 120 knots) cover four miles per minute. That dot in the sky four miles away sixty seconds ago suddenly becomes a full-sized Cessna 182 in your windshield. *Yikes!*

Rule-of Thumb: If an object maintains no relative motion (stays in the same place in your windshield), you're converging. If it grows bigger, you're in imminent danger. Take evasive action.

Only a small center portion of the eye has the ability to process clear, sharply focused images to the brain—a brain that's preoccupied with interpreting charts, weather, deciphering ATC chatter, figuring fuel burns, remembering the lyrics to *Inagad Da Vida*….

At night your scan needs to utilize the off-center portion of your vision. Use your peripheral vision more at night. There are two types of light-sensitive cells in your eyes—rods and cones. **Cones** detect detail, while rods are better at detecting movement, particularly in dim light. The **rods** are located more to the side of the eyeball, so your peripheral vision—from rods—works best in low light.

The best way to spot traffic in daytime is to scan the sky "with a **series of short, regularly spaced eye movements** that bring successive areas of the sky into the central visual field. Each movement should not exceed 10 degrees, and each should be observed for at least 1 second to enable detection."[55] That sounds a bit mechanical, so develop your own scan that meets the intent.

Much of flight occurs en route between two points—straight and level with gentle climbs and descents at either end. The pilot can be lulled into thinking there's no other traffic, and, frankly, in the big sky you may never see another aircraft. When climbing or descending en route—particularly along an airway—make shallow banks to look for traffic.

Much of flight training, however, involves maneuvering—climbs, descents, slow flight, stalls. It's easy to become involved in the maneuver and forget to scan for traffic (that goes for us instructors, too). So, before beginning any maneuver, lift or lower a wing to scan for traffic. Watch for shadows on the ground, too. When performing ground reference maneuvers on a sunny day, find your shadow. If a second shadow appears you either have airborne company or you've suddenly developed weird vision problems.

Test Questions:

Question 1. Which is the correct traffic pattern departure procedure to use at a non-controlled airport?

a.   Depart in any direction consistent with safety, after crossing the airport boundary
b.   Make all turns to the left
c.   Comply with any FAA traffic pattern established for the airport

Question 2. The recommended entry position to an airport traffic pattern is

a.   45 degrees to the base leg just below pattern altitude
b.   to enter 45 degrees at the midpoint of the downwind leg at traffic pattern altitude
c.   to cross directly over the airport at traffic pattern altitude and join the downwind leg

Answers:

1. **c.** Comply with any FAA traffic pattern established for the airport
2. **b.** to enter 45 degrees at the midpoint of the downwind leg at traffic pattern altitude

---

[55] *Airplane Flying Handbook*, FAA-H-8083-25 ch 12

Chapter 6

Airspace & ATC
or
Who Controls the Air We Breathe?

In Kindergarten you learned your alphabet. Now, you'll see why it's so important. The air through which pilots fly is loosely classified as controlled or uncontrolled. More narrowly, all airspace is catalogued by the letters: A, B, C, D, E, (skip F in the USA) and G.

A Brief History of Air:
- ✓ 9 Billion Years Ago, 5:32 AM CDT—Rather large bang in Immense Void creates building blocks of aviation.
- ✓ December 17, 1903—Dawn of Human Flight. The Wright Brothers fly the first controllable powered airplane.
- ✓ December 18, 1903—Governments panic at the thought of free-thinking citizens leaving the planet without permission so announce that only bureaucrats can control the air through which all aeroships may one day sail.
- ✓ Today's date—We pilots still defy gravity, if not bureaucrats, and fly. To fly legally and safely we must understand what rules control our airspace. And, yes, it's *our* airspace. The FAA simply regulates it, much like the IRS regulates *our* money.

The terms **Controlled** and **Uncontrolled Airspace** are misleading, so we'll briefly mention their meaning and then abandon them to the pilots lounge trash bin. All air is controlled. If you lift off the Earth's surface, some government regulation will touch your wings. However, for air space purposes, "controlled," means airspace in which ATC has some level of interest, authority or control. Uncontrolled means that air traffic controllers don't have much interest in dealing with air traffic inside uncontrolled airspace. Now, let's dissect the airspace particulars as they apply in the United States.

Class A Airspace

This is (generally) all airspace from 18,000 feet MSL (FL180) up to and including 60,000 feet (FL600). Altitudes are called Flight Levels (FL180 through FL600) inside Class A airspace. All flights must operate IFR in Class A. Class A does not apply over Hawaii. Chances are you won't be operating inside Class A in your Cessna 150 while earning your Private license.

Class B Airspace

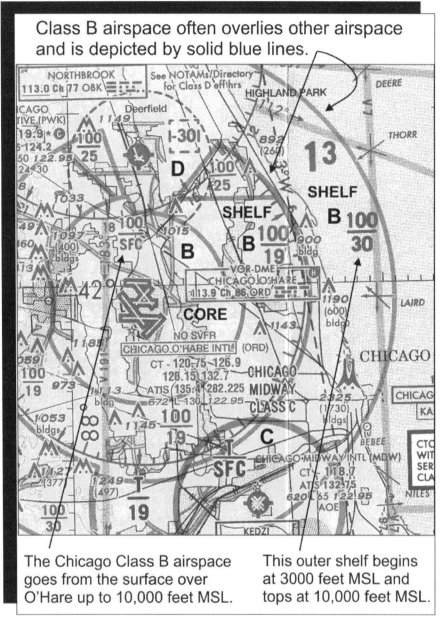

Class B airspace often overlies other airspace and is depicted by solid blue lines.

The Chicago Class B airspace goes from the surface over O'Hare up to 10,000 feet MSL.

This outer shelf begins at 3000 feet MSL and tops at 10,000 feet MSL.

Think *B Busy*. Or *B* for *Big City* airports. Generally, this airspace reaches from the surface to between 7000 to 12,000 feet MSL around busy US terminals such as New York City, Chicago, Dallas, Los Angeles and more. Toronto's Class B airspace reaches to 12,500 feet MSL. Class B airspace is configured to match local traffic needs. Often the airspace, when viewed from the side, is said to resemble an "upside-down wedding cake." The wide top might touch 10,000 feet, as it does over Chicago, but lower "layers" have bases at various altitudes. A private pilot certificate is needed to operate inside Class B airspace; students aren't permitted inside without special training and logbook endorsements; likewise for Sport pilots.[56] Both IFR and VFR traffic operate inside Class B (Bravo) Airspace. A clearance is required to operate inside Class B Airspace. ATC must say: "Cleared to enter Bravo Airspace." A transponder with altitude encoding is also required.

---

[56] FARs 61.95 and 61.325 also apply to class C and D airspace

Class C Airspace

Usually Class C extends from the surface to 4000 feet AGL around select moderately busy airports with control towers and radar service. Class C usually is depicted on sectional charts by two concentric magenta rings. The first ring, called the **Surface Area (or Core)**, has a five-mile radius. The Class C airspace inside that ring reaches from the surface to 4000 feet above the airport. The second ring is the **Outer Circle**, informally called the **Shelf**, and stretches to 10 miles from the core airport. It usually begins at 1200 feet AGL and reaches to 4000 feet above the primary airport's elevation. An **Outer Area**, which is not depicted on navigational charts, stretches from 10 miles to 20 miles and from the surface to roughly 4000 feet above the core airport's elevation. ATC provides radar service inside this Outer Area, but pilots are not required to participate here.

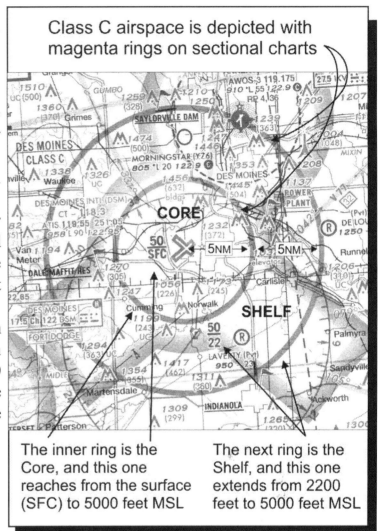

Class C airspace is depicted with magenta rings on sectional charts

The inner ring is the Core, and this one reaches from the surface (SFC) to 5000 feet MSL

The next ring is the Shelf, and this one extends from 2200 feet to 5000 feet MSL

Pilots must establish two-way communication with ATC prior to operating inside Class C Airspace (excludes Outer Area). When departing a satellite airport (non-towered) within the Class C airspace, you must contact ATC as "soon as practicable"[57] after takeoff. A clearance, however, is not required to operate inside Class C. You should not hear: "Cleared to enter Charlie airspace."

Class C airspace is smaller than Class B. Student and sport pilots may operate inside Class C airspace with proper training and logbook endorsements. The aircraft must be equipped with a transponder with altitude reporting capabilities. Two-way radio communication is also required.

---

[57] Practicable is one of those unpronounceable words the FAA likes. Think *practical* instead.

Class D Airspace

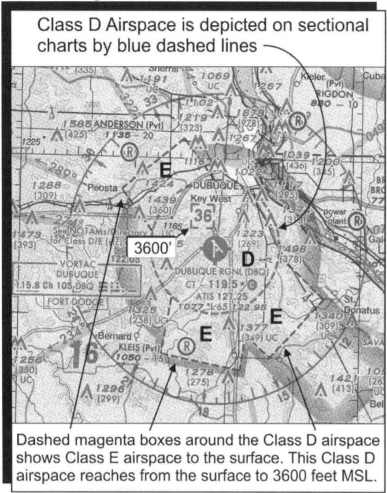

Class D Airspace is depicted on sectional charts by blue dashed lines

3600'

Dashed magenta boxes around the Class D airspace shows Class E airspace to the surface. This Class D airspace reaches from the surface to 3600 feet MSL.

Airports with operating control towers, but not busy enough to qualify for Class C airspace, are designated as Class D. Generally, Class D airspace extends from the surface to 2500 feet above the airport elevation and usually covers a 4 NM radius. Dimensions can vary. Class D is depicted on sectional charts with a dashed blue circle.

Some Class D control towers have radar service, but pilots may decline the service by saying, "Negative radar service." Student pilots and sport pilots may operate inside Class D with proper training and instructor endorsements. Transponders are not required. As with B and C airspace, two-way radio communication is required inside Class D.

When the control tower is closed, the Class D airspace becomes Class E or G (check A/FD) to the surface. Tower frequency usually then becomes the CTAF.

Class G and E Airspace

Most VFR flight occurs inside Class G or E Airspace. Class E is considered controlled and G uncontrolled. That's confusing, since ATC generally isn't involved with VFR operations in G or E. The big difference between G and E airspace is the weather requirements. It takes better weather to operate inside Class E than it does inside Class G. On sunny clear days, essentially, there is no difference. Let's define them beginning from the ground up.

Class G airspace begins at the earth's surface, or the ground. It's easy to operate inside G airspace; that's good. So, class *G* is *G*ood *G*round-loving airspace. Most of the country is covered in Good G Airspace. All other airspace is built atop G or carves out chunks from the G. Class G is the foundation.

Generally, Class G extends from the surface to **1200 feet AGL**, except over some (many) non-towered (meaning no operating control tower) airports where instrument approaches exist. There, the uncontrolled Class G reaches from the surface to **700 feet AGL**. On a VFR sectional chart, airports with Class G reaching only to 700 feet AGL are encircled in shaded magenta. These are also known as *transition areas* where IFR traffic transitions from the instrument approach environment to the VFR traffic pattern environment around the airport. IFR traffic does not have the right of way over VFR traffic here.

All pilots may operate in Class G airspace. No radio or transponder is required to operate inside Class G airspace.[58] Private Pilots may operate VFR (daytime) inside Class G with as little as 1-mile visibility provided they remain clear of clouds. Sport pilots need 3 miles visibility.

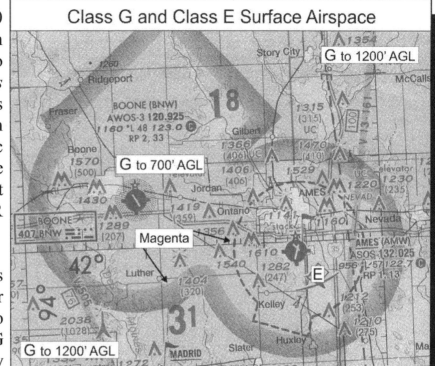

Class G and Class E Surface Airspace

Within the magenta shading Class G extends from the surface to 700' AGL. Outside the shading G reaches to 1200 feet AGL. Within the dashed magenta lines around Newton airport the Class E airspace goes to the surface.

At night the visibility requirement is 3 miles, plus the flight must remain at least 500 feet below or 1000 feet above or 2000 feet horizontally from the clouds.[59] Should you encounter Class G airspace above 10,000 feet the flight visibility minimum is 5 miles and cloud clearance minima increase to 1000 feet above or below or 1-mile clearance horizontally.

Caution: IFR approaches and departures do penetrate Class G airspace. The IFR pilots may be speaking to ATC, and the controller will have no idea who else is operating VFR inside that Class G airspace. What's the survival rule? Answer: *See and Avoid.*

*E*verything above Class G is **Class E.** Well, almost everything. C or B could overlie G but, generally, you'll find E above G. So, that means that Class E (generally) begins at either

---

[58] Exception: Transponders are required within the 30-NM Mode-C rings around Class B airspace, even inside Class G
[59] Night VFR exception: You may operate VFR if the visibility is less than 3 statute miles but not less than 1 statute mile during night hours and you are operating in an airport traffic pattern within 1/2 mile of the runway. (FAR 91.155)

700 or 1200 feet AGL and extends upward to the overlying airspace, which could be C, B or A. Class E is considered controlled airspace because ATC controls IFR traffic inside that airspace. That does not mean that VFR traffic can't operate in Class E without speaking to ATC. It means that the weather requirements are stricter. The VFR pilot needs at least 3 miles visibility inside Class E airspace and a wide clearance from clouds is required. Above 10,000 feet MSL 5 miles visibility is required.[60] More on that later. No radio is required in Class E airspace. Transponders with altitude encoding are required in class E when operating at or above 10,000 feet MSL. Let's linger on

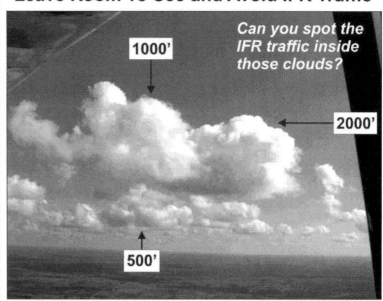

Leave Room To See and Avoid IFR Traffic

Can you spot the IFR traffic inside those clouds?

1000'

2000'

500'

When flying VFR inside Class C, D or E airspace below 10,000' MSL, remain at least 1000' above clouds, 500' below or 2000' to the side. At or above 10,000' increase that to 1000' above and below or 1 mile horizontally, plus increase flight visibility from 3 to 5 miles. (FAR 91.155)

the transponder requirements a bit. Any aircraft that has an operable (and properly certified) transponder must use that transponder (have it ON) inside any controlled airspace. If your hot air balloon, glider or 1946 Piper J-3 Cub doesn't have an electrical system and never had a transponder, you're largely exempt from this rule. You can make yourself crazy trying to fathom transponder rules, so if you have one, keep it certified (inspected every 24 months) and turn it on in flight.

Class E reaches to the surface over some airports where instrument traffic is complex enough to warrant a little more restriction than a Class G airport but not enough to spend the immense cost to build and staff a control tower. **Class E Surface Airspace** is defined on a sectional chart by a dashed magenta circle, possibly with extensions. VFR flight is not permitted beneath a ceiling inside Class E Surface Airspace when the reported ceiling (broken or overcast cloud layers) is less than 1000 feet AGL. Likewise, VFR flight is not permitted in controlled airspace if the visibility is less than 3 statute miles (SM)[61]. An IFR clearance or a **Special VFR (SVFR)** is required from ATC when weather is below VFR minima (1000-foot ceiling or 3 miles visibility). SVFR allows VFR traffic to operate inside Class C, D or E Surface Areas with ceiling or visibility less than minimum VFR, provided the pilot can operate clear of clouds and with 1 mile flight visibility. SVFR is not permitted for students or Sport Pilots. A SVFR clearance sounds like this: "Cessna One Four Zero

---

[60] Sport pilots are not permitted to act as PIC above 10,000 feet MSL
[61] FAR 91.155 and 91.157

Eight Yankee, cleared to enter the Echo Surface Area, maintain Special V-F-R conditions…" SVFR is not permitted at night unless the pilot is instrument rated and the aircraft is instrument equipped. The pilot must request SVFR; ATC will not initiate it. SVFR is usually prohibited inside Class B airspace with the notation, NO SVFR, on charts to indicate that.

Special Use Airspace

Some airspace is so special pilots aren't welcome. Special Use Airspace (SUA) includes:

- Prohibited Areas
- Restricted Areas
- Military Operations Areas
- Warning Areas
- Alert Areas
- Controlled Firing Areas

Prohibited Areas

You ain't getting in unless folks inside the DC Beltway regularly address you as "Mr./Madam President." Prohibited Areas exist mostly for security reasons, although some nature preserves are included. The White House and Camp David are inside Prohibited Areas.

Restricted Areas

All sorts of hazards, such as machine-gun and artillery ranges exist inside Restricted Areas. Stay out. The hours of operation as well as the dimensions are listed on aeronautical charts.

Military Operations Area

When you have a ramp full of F-16s you send your pilots to Military Operations Areas (MOAs) to practice dog fighting, refueling and various other airborne military exercises that take up large chunks of sky. IFR pilots may not fly through an active MOA, but VFR flights are not so restricted.

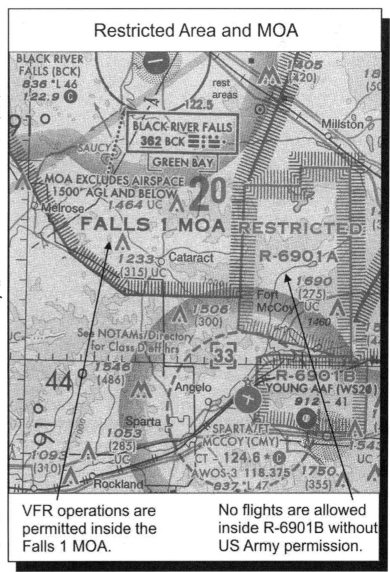

Restricted Area and MOA

VFR operations are permitted inside the Falls 1 MOA.

No flights are allowed inside R-6901B without US Army permission.

You may fly VFR through an MOA but keep your head on a swivel, because those F-16s might go whizzing past at speeds you can't begin to match even in your Cirrus SR-22. Dimensions and hours of operation are posted on sectional charts.

Warning Areas

These are similar to Restricted Areas—bombs, guns and such—but are located in international waters (beyond 3-mile limit), so the government has no authority and little responsibility beyond warning pilots away.

Alert Areas

These are areas where unusually high levels of training traffic (usually military) exist. You may go through an Alert Area but be (go ahead and say it aloud) *alert* for traffic. Scan, scan, scan….

Controlled Firing Areas (CFA)

Inside these areas someone wants to shoot something— perhaps, a rocket—into your sky. The shooters are required to have a spotter on duty to call off the firing should an aircraft penetrate. Feel free to fly through a controlled firing area. Feel free to say, "Ooo, look at the rockets' red glare!" should the spotter not spot you. CFAs are not charted.

Here are some other airspace areas that counsel extra vigilance:

Airport Advisory Area: These are rare and getting rarer. If you can find an airport with a Flight Service Station on the field (Alaska perhaps), then a 10-mile radius Airport Advisory Area will surround that airport. FSS (or AFSS— Automated Flight Service Station) is *not* ATC. FSS provides airport advisories (wind, altimeter and such) inside these rare Airport Advisory Areas.

Parachute and Glider Operations

The parachute symbol indicates that, yes, folks may be falling through your traffic pattern. Monitor CTAF for updates.

The glider symbol means that silent wings routinely operate in the area. Watch for gliders as well as their tow-planes.

Military Training Routes: One of the great things about being a military pilot is the chance to fly fast. Real fast. And sometimes, real low. Military Training Routes (MTR) allow pilots to practice this. These routes are depicted on aeronautical charts. IFR MTRs are called IRs. VFR MTRs are VRs.

Temporary Flight Restrictions

These are tricky devils. TFRs exist wherever the government deems them necessary. TFRs block some or all traffic from a small or large area. Whenever the President of the United States (POTUS) flies to some natural or political disaster, a huge TFR (30-mile radius) surrounds him/her. You are never welcome, and fighter jets and helicopters enforce the presidential TFRs.

Other TFRs exist around relief efforts, fire fighting and space launches. Check NOTAMs (Notice To Airmen) before every flight to find out if any TFR exists en route.

Parachute Jump Areas

Some people are nuts and jump out of airplanes, usually while wearing a parachute. When they do, they must notify the FAA first, post a NOTAM and announce the jumps on CTAF. You may operate inside a Parachute Jump Area, just watch for falling nuts.

Published VFR Routes

To help VFR pilots navigate through Class B airspace without interfering with congested instrument traffic routes, the FAA publishes VFR Routes—flyways or corridors. Your GPS may have these routes inside its database, if so, it's easy to follow one through the airspace. *VFR Terminal Area Planning Charts* display these routes.

National Security Areas

Rare. These are areas where something sensitive exists and yet, not so sensitive to command a Prohibited Area. They're marked on sectional charts with a thick magenta dashed circle or square. Avoidance is voluntary.

Terminal Radar Service Area

Shortly after the last dinosaur died, **TRSA**s were born. These are large radar service areas around semi-busy Class D airports. Black encircling lines on a sectional chart mark them. Pilots are encouraged to receive radar service, but it is not required. On a workload-permitting basis, radar approach controllers provide safety alerts, traffic advisories and some vectoring. TRSA controllers provide some sequencing to participating VFR arrivals. Pilots on the ground should contact ground control to "request radar traffic information" prior to taxi.

Transponder Codes and Terms

A transponder enhances your primary radar return on the air traffic controller's radar display. The transponder produces a secondary target plus a data tag capable of displaying the aircraft's call sign, groundspeed and altitude. In the radar identification process, the controller may ask the pilot to "Ident." Like this: "Cessna Zero Eight Yankee, Ident." The pilot should push and release the Ident button on the transponder. Do not push it unless asked.

Important Transponder Codes (memorize):

1200—VFR
7500—Hijack
7600—Lost Communication (Lost Comm)
7700—Emergency
7777—Military Intercept

Class D Airspace with TRSA

Muskegon's Class D airspace is shown encircle in blue dashed lines

Radar service is available within the TRSA's solid black rings.

Note: "When making routine transponder code changes, avoid inadvertent selection of: 7500, 7600 and 7700."[62] If you squawk 7500, ATC will ask you: "Cessna Zero Eight Yankee, verify squawk." Meaning, confirm you're being hijacked. If it's a mistake, say, "Ooops! Sorry..." and change to 1200 or your assigned code. If you're really being hijacked, say nothing, and the controller will take your silence as a plea to have the police meet you upon arrival.

Radiospeak or Phraseology

How well you speak on the radio determines how good your relationship with ATC will be. Here are a few basics:

Flight Service is not ATC; they don't control air traffic. When calling FSS say, "(name of station) Radio." Example: "Princeton Radio." This harks back to the 1930s. FSS is now contracted out to Wal-Mart or some other non-FAA low-bidder.

Your airplane's registration probably begins with the letter N if it's US registered. Example: N85607. When calling FSS or ATC drop the "N" and add your make of aircraft. Example: "Cessna Eight Five Six Zero Seven." Do not say: "November Cessna Eight Five Six Zero Seven."

State call sign digits individually. Cessna N1122G is "Cessna One One Two Two Golf." It is not "...Eleven Twenty-Two Golf." Airlines call signs do group the numbers, e.g., "United Eleven Eighty-Four."

Homebuilts and Experimental aircraft add "Experimental" to the call sign.

Student pilots should add "student pilot" to the initial transmission to ATC: "Des Moines Approach, Cessna Eight Three One One Juliet, Student Pilot, five south, 3500...." This should elicit some sympathy from the controller.

ATC Calls Traffic

Air traffic controllers have many jobs, one of which is to inform pilots of threatening traffic. Note: It's not ATC's responsibility to guarantee that you won't hit other traffic. Since pilots are in a constantly moving, three-dimensional environment, a system was devised to describe where traffic is located. It's based on the old-fashioned round-faced clock, the kind your grandmother used to have in her airplane. In a digital world, this can be an issue.

---

[62] AIM 4-1-19

When an aircraft appears on the controller's radar display it creates a "blip" that's usually reinforced (digitized) with a "slash." These are called **Targets**. Radar's early use was in WWII helping the RAF find Luftwaffe targets. In more peaceful use the radar controller tells the pilot where the target is, based on the target's position from the pilot's aircraft. This is based upon your ground track and not your heading (corrected for wind). Calls are made from 12 o'clock clockwise through 11 o'clock: [63]

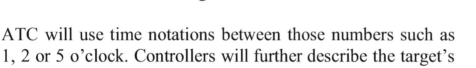

"Traffic 12 O'clock..."

12 o'clock is straight ahead—on your nose.
3 o'clock is off your right wing
6 o'clock is on your tail
9 o'clock is off the left wing.

ATC will use time notations between those numbers such as 1, 2 or 5 o'clock. Controllers will further describe the target's (traffic's) movement by giving its distance, direction of flight and altitude, if shown.[64] Example: "Cessna Eight One Lima, traffic, two o'clock, three miles southwest bound, converging, altitude indicates 3500."

When you hear your call sign, listen. When you hear it followed by "traffic," quit staring at ForeFlight and look outside, where you should be looking most of the time anyhow. When ATC gives the traffic's position ("two o'clock), look ahead and to the right and expand your scan from there. If the radar controller has verified the target's Mode C altitude, it will be given as "altitude 3500 (or whatever)." If the target is not talking to ATC, then the controller cannot verify the Mode C altitude encoding accuracy, so the controller will issue the altitude as "altitude indicates…."

ATC LIGHT GUN SIGNALS

COLOR AND SIGNAL TYPE	AIRCRAFT ON THE GROUND	AIRCRAFT IN FLIGHT
STEADY GREEN	Cleared for takeoff	Cleared to land
FLASHING GREEN	Cleared for taxi	Return for landing (to be followed by steady green at the proper time)
STEADY RED	STOP!	STOP!
FLASHING RED	Taxi clear of runway in use	Airport unsafe, do not land
FLASHING WHITE	Return to starting point on airport	N/A
ALTERNATING RED AND GREEN	Exercise Extreme Caution	Exercise Extreme Caution

Low Tech ATC Signals

Let's drift back to the 1930s when most airplanes didn't have radios. As a pilot approached a busy airport, he'd (rarely she'd [65]) enter the traffic pattern and look

---

[63] Does not change with Daylight Saving Time
[64] ATC can only derive altitude information from aircraft operating altitude-reporting transponders.
[65] See: *"Inside The Circle"* the story of Kate Strauss, for one notable exception.

at the control tower. The control tower operator would point a powerful light gun at the airplane and flash a color code. Some of this still exists today as a semi-emergency backup should a pilot (or controller) lose radios.

To acknowledge light gun signals rock your wings (daytime), if you're airborne. Or the move the ailerons up and down if taxiing. At night, blink your lights to acknowledge.

ELT

Emergency Locator Transmitters (ELTs) are required on most GA aircraft. In the unlikely event of an accident, the impact should trigger the device, which then broadcasts a *whoop-whoop* sound on the emergency frequency 121.5 (UHF 243.0). If bored in flight, monitor 121.5 (recommended for TFR notices). If an ELT sounds, you'll hear it on the frequency. Report it and your location to the nearest ATC facility or FSS. Newer style ELTs transmit signals that will also be acquired by satellite, and search and rescue operations will commence.

ELTs have a bad habit of triggering on hard landings or if bumped by pilots, mechanics, dogs, whatever. So, as you shut down after a flight, tune 121.5 to check your ELT. Ideally, the frequency will be silent.

ELTs must be tested annually. Batteries must be current usually with a sticker on the ELT of the panel-mounted ON/OFF switch, indicating battery expiration date. Testing may only be done during the first five minutes after the hour and never when airborne.

LAHSO

LAHSO sounds like a small dog breed, but it really means Land And Hold Short Operations. Or: How a busy tower squeezes more airplanes onto the same airport without building more runways. LAHSO allows the tower controller to clear an aircraft to land on a runway with a restriction to "Hold Short" of an intersecting runway where another aircraft lands or takes off.

A Few LAHSO Rules:

1. Student pilots are not permitted to participate in LAHSO.

2. Any pilot can decline LAHSO: "Unable hold short."

3. Runways must be dry or, if damp, no standing water or ice.

4. There can be no tailwind component for the restricted airplane.

5. Visibility must be at least 3 SM, ceiling no less than 1000 feet AGL.

6. Available Landing Distance (ALD) must be known (found in A/FD or ask tower). Tower will issue the ALD if you ask.

ATIS

Airports with operating control towers usually have an ATIS (Automatic Terminal Information Service[66]). Don't confuse ATIS with ASOS or AWOS. ATIS is a recording made by the tower controller. It's a continuous broadcast of non-control information such as weather, wind, altimeter, braking reports, taxiway closures and runway in use. While the information is important it is routine enough to be posted on a looping broadcast. This saves the controller from repeating the information to each pilot. It is important that you advise ATC (tower, ground, clearance delivery, approach control) that you have the current ATIS.

What's current?

The ATIS is updated hourly or whenever changing conditions warrant a new ATIS. A letter designates each broadcast: Alpha, Bravo, Charlie…Zulu, Alpha….

The pilot listens to the ATIS, gleans the information and notes the letter. When making the initial call you inform ATC that you have the current ATIS by saying the letter. Like this: "Omaha Approach, Cherokee Seven One Six Two Zulu, 25 west, 5500, *Lima…*" That Lima doesn't mean you're over Lima, Peru or full of beans but, instead, means you've listened to the ATIS that is designated L or Lima. The previous broadcast was K, Kilo, and the next will be M or Mike. Given the letter, the controller instantly knows what information the pilot has. If, meanwhile, the ATIS has been changed to M, the controller mutters to himself, "Ah, beans," and then says, "Cherokee Six Two Zulu, roger, information Mike now current…(and issues the new info)." Controllers are required to make certain that pilots have the current information, so if the pilot doesn't say that she has the ATIS, then the controller has to ask, "Verify you have Lima," or give the current information. All of this wastes time on the air. Radio airtime is precious. Consider each on-air word to be gold and expend your fortune economically. Pilots who talk too much thoroughly irritate controllers, and service suffers for everyone.

If it's a nice VFR day and the ceiling is above 5000 feet and the visibility is greater than 5 miles (SM or Statute Miles), then the ceiling and visibility may be omitted from the ATIS. The phrase "The weather is better than five thousand and five" might be included on the broadcast.

---

[66] Also called Automated Terminal Information System. The FAA can't decide.

Meet Air Traffic Control

I used to be an Air Traffic Controller (1979-97) and worked for the FAA in Center, Tower and Approach Control. I assure you, despite the rumors, most controllers are human. Many even smile. Some have been known to break into song, *"Puttin' on the Ritz...."*

Don't fear ATC. You own ATC. You pay for it. You should feel free (unless Congress implements user fees) to use ATC to its fullest. Airlines do not have ATC priority over GA. ATC services are dispensed on a *first come, first served basis*. In theory, anyhow. Controllers are paid according to the amount and complexity of their facility's traffic, and since controllers like money, they like pilots. Or should. In short, most controllers are nice people doing a fine job. Some are even pilots.

ATC is divided into two options: En Route and Terminal. An **En Route** facility is called **Air Route Traffic Control Center** (ARTCC) or "Center" on the radio. **Terminal** is the **Air Traffic Control Tower** (ATCT). Control positions within the tower are: **Local** (called "Tower" on the radio), **Ground Control** (called "Ground") and in busier facilities there's a **Clearance Delivery** (called "Clearance").

Additionally, the terminal option has **Approach** and **Departure Controls** called "Approach" and "Departure." These are the radar controllers who work traffic within a relatively short distance of a particular terminal or airport. Des Moines Approach, for instance, works traffic within 60 miles of the Des Moines Airport. Generally, Approach works the arrivals and over-flights, while Departure handles the departing aircraft. Often the same controller handles both. And it really doesn't matter if you accidentally call Approach "Departure" or vice versa. The controllers don't care; they've been called worse.

ATC subdivides the sky into fiefdoms. About 20 Centers "own" all the air over the country—Boston, New York, Washington, Chicago, Minneapolis, Denver, Salt Lake, Los Angeles and on and on. These Centers are vast industrial buildings usually located far from airports behind barbed wire fences. Inside, hundreds of Center controllers "work" IFR and VFR en route traffic.

Because traffic gets busiest around terminals, Center gives away smaller chunks of air space to Terminal Approach Controls, such as: Boston Approach, New York, Washington, Chicago, Des Moines and so forth. Traffic flows smoothly from Center to Approach, from one radar display to another miles away. As your target is handed off from one controller to another, you'll be told who to contact and on what radio frequency: "Contact Phoenix Approach, 123.45," or "Contact Chicago Center 118.15 (pronounced, 'One one eight point one five')." You simply acknowledge the change (it's wise to read back the frequency) and change frequencies. When you call or "check onto" the new frequency that controller

123

already knows you're coming. You simply announce, "Chicago Center, Cessna 2881L, 5000 (altitude)." Always give your altitude on initial call, so the controller can verify your transponder's altitude readout. Your GPS might have all the frequencies in memory but always use whatever frequency ATC assigns.

Tip: Never say "With you" when checking onto an ATC frequency. It's pointless slang and controllers hate it. Plus it sounds as though you have ATIS information Uniform — "With U."

As a VFR Private Pilot or Sport Pilot you're free to travel from coast to coast in visual conditions. While you are not required to contact ATC unless entering Class B, C or D airspace, you may wish to take advantage of ATC's VFR radar service called "Flight Following." I highly recommend it.

Workload permitting, a radar Approach controller or Center controller will provide radar traffic advisories. You simply call: "Oakland Center, Cherokee One Five Eight One November, over Livermore 12,500 (your altitude, pronounced 'one-two thousand five hundred'), request VFR flight following to Monterey." The Center controller enters your call sign and type aircraft into the computer, which generates a transponder code (squawk). If the controller sees your target exactly where you said your were (over Livermore in this case), the controller says, "Radar contact" and issues a transponder code such as, "Squawk 7414." Once the radar antenna interrogates your transponder and reads the assigned squawk it will correlate that code with the call sign, and your call sign appears on the controller's display as a data tag.

"Radar Contact" means "I see you." It does not mean the controller will necessarily separate you from anything—traffic, terrain, migratory fowl or foul weather. That's pilot responsibility.

On January 1, 2020, ADS-B will replace the old school Mode A and C transponder systems we've used for the past half-century.

A Typical VFR Cross-Country

Imagine you're on the ground at an airport inside Class C airspace. You want to fly 150 miles to an uncontrolled airport located inside Class G airspace. Your trip might go something like this:

You call Flight Service (1-800-WX-BRIEF)[67]. A briefer tells you about the weather reports and forecasts as well as any NOTAMs en route. No need to file a flight plan so you hang up

---

[67] I can also brief online at several sites including 800WXBRIEF.com or DUATS.com

and go outside to preflight the airplane. With that complete you strap in, fire up the engine and turn on the radios.

You listen to the ATIS (let's say letter D is current) and get the local winds, weather, altimeter setting and the runway in use. Next, call Clearance Delivery. Not every tower has a Clearance Delivery frequency. Some combine Ground Control and Clearance. Either way, you say: "Des Moines Clearance, Cherokee 55884, Delta, VFR to Moose Lake, Minnesota, heading 030 (don't say 'degrees'), request 5500 (don't say 'feet,' that's understood)." Clearance Delivery might ask for Moose Lake's airport ID code; in this case MZH. Feel free to toss that in on your initial call, "...VFR to Moose Lake, Minnesota, Mike Zulu Hotel..."

As you speak the Clearance Delivery controller enters pertinent data into the computer, which generates a transponder squawk. In the old days, when I worked traffic, we hand-wrote the information onto paper flight progress strips. Yeah, it was hell, kids...*the horror...the horror....* By now (it's hoped) ATC has gone paperless. The pilot won't know either way, and it really doesn't matter because the process is the same. The controller then answers something like this (write it down as it's read): "Cherokee 55884, Des Moines Clearance Delivery, after departure fly runway heading, climb and maintain 5000, expect 5500 ten minutes after departure, Departure Control frequency will be 123.9, squawk 0334."

Lots of information.

These are your initial departure instructions. By having a Clearance Delivery issue this, the tower controller doesn't have to issue it to each pilot. It saves airtime.

You read back the instructions and then switch to **Ground Control**. "Des Moines Ground, Cherokee 55884, transient parking (or wherever you're parked), taxi." You already told Clearance Delivery that you had the ATIS (Delta) so there's no need to tell the next controller. And Ground Control has all the information you gave to Clearance, so everyone knows where you're headed.

Ground says: "Cherokee 55884, Des Moines Ground, Runway Two Three, taxi via Bravo, Romeo." Read it back and taxi on Taxiways B and R. Remember, this clearance allows you to cross other taxiways but not other runways en route to the assigned runway. You must have an ATC clearance to cross any runway.

Once at Runway 23, you perform the run-up and pre-takeoff checklist in the run-up area and contact the tower. "Local" is an in-house term used by controllers to identify the person controlling the runways and the local airspace. You call this person "Tower." Often there's no obvious run-up area, so ask Ground, "Where can I do a run-up?"

When ready to depart call the tower: "Des Moines Tower, Cherokee 55884, ready Runway Two Three."[68]

The tower has all of your information provided to Clearance Delivery and, if there's no conflicting traffic, the tower controller says, "Cherokee 55884, Des Moines Tower, Runway Two Three, cleared for takeoff." Notice that no other instructions (headings, turns, altitude) were issued, so you're expected to fly the last instructions ("...runway heading...") issued by Clearance Delivery.

You acknowledge, depart and fly runway heading. You remain on runway heading and remain on tower frequency until the tower says, "Cherokee 884, contact Departure."[69] Tower will not issue a frequency because Clearance issued that earlier (123.9). When assigned a heading, even "runway heading," do not correct for wind. ATC takes the wind drift into consideration.

You acknowledge the change, "Contact Departure, Cherokee 884," and switch to 123.9: "Des Moines Departure, Cherokee 55884, 1500 (your current altitude in the climb to 5000 feet)." Departure sees your target off the end of Runway 23, which is marked on the radar display, and says, "Cherokee 55884, Des Moines Departure, radar contact, turn right on course, climb and maintain 5500." Read that back and turn.

Because you went through Clearance Delivery, all of your flight information is passed from controller to controller. When you reach the edge of the radar display the departure controller will say, "Cherokee 884, radar service terminated, squawk VFR." The VFR transponder squawk is 1200. You're on your own. If you want radar service all the way to your destination, ask for "flight following." You're encouraged to request that on the initial call to Clearance Delivery. Workload permitting, the departure controller will hand off your target and data to the neighboring Center controller and tell you to "Contact Minneapolis Center, 134.0." IFR traffic automatically gets ATC service to the destination, although not always radar service, because there are places where radar cannot see. ADS-B should, one day, eliminate those gaps.

While in "radar contact" and receiving flight following, handoffs from controller to controller will be repeated as you cross subsequent radar displays until approaching your destination. Since, in our scenario, it's inside class G airspace and has no tower and no approach control, you'll be told: "Cherokee 884, radar service terminated, squawk VFR."

Now, You're the Controller

---

[68] If departing from an intersection inform the tower, "...at intersection (and name the intersection)"

[69] After initial contact, call signs are shortened to the last three digits.

As you approach an uncontrolled airport (Class G or E) airspace, you'll listen to the AWOS or ASOS (if available) as soon as possible to get the weather and winds. Armed with that you'll decide which runway you prefer. Ten miles from the airport—if possible—call on CTAF: "Moose Lake Traffic, Cherokee 55884, ten southwest landing Runway 22."

If there are any other pilots in the pattern, and if they have radios, they *might* answer, saying what runway they're using. It may not be the same runway you intend to use. Avoid using the phrase, "active runway," on CTAF. Only ATC determines the active runway; at airports without an operating control tower the pilots decide, and your active might not be my active, so give the runway number: "departing runway Two Two," or "back-taxiing Runway Two Two." Yes, management at some uncontrolled airports will designate an active runway. You're still PIC, so you decide.

Note: Never say, "Traffic in the area, please advise." This amateurish, unapproved phraseology clogs up the CTAF. Additionally, AIM 4-1-9(g) reminds pilots never to use it. It just sounds stupid.

Once you determine your runway, enter the pattern and announce downwind, base and final—*if* you have time. Your first duty is to *fly the airplane*. Radio calls are last duty. Bernoulli's Principles, not Marconi's, produce lift.

Five Steps To Contact ATC. You state:

1. *Who you're calling*: "Des Moines Approach…"
2. *Who you are*: "Cherokee 55884…"
3. *Where you are* (in 3-D): "Two-five (25) south at 3500 (feet MSL; never say "feet" because it's understood)…"
4. *What you know*: The ATIS code, "Bravo (or whatever)."
5. *What you want*: "Transition north." Or "Landing Minneapolis." Or "Request touch-and-go's at Des Moines." Or whatever you want. If you say the ATIS code it's assumed you're landing at that airport.

This chapter has been a general overview of ATC and Airspace. There are many more particulars in the *AIM* and FARs. You're always learning, so always be digging into the books to learn more and don't believe everything you hear in the pilots lounge.

Test Questions:

Question 1. When a control tower, located on an airport within Class D airspace, ceases operation for the day, what happens to the airspace designation?

a. The airspace designation normally will not change
b. The airspace remains Class D airspace as long as a weather observer or automated weather system is available
c. The airspace reverts to Class E or a combination of Class E and G airspace during the hours the tower is not in operation

Question 2. The lateral dimensions of Class D airspace are based on (complete the sentence):

a. the number of airports located within that airspace
b. 4 statute miles from the geographical center of the primary airport
c. the instrument procedures for which the controlled airspace is established

Question 3. Under what condition may an aircraft operate from a satellite airport within Class C airspace?

a. The pilot must file a flight plan prior to departure
b. The pilot must monitor ATC until clear of the Class C airspace
c. The pilot must contact ATC as soon as practicable after takeoff

Answers:

1. **c.** The airspace reverts to Class E or a combination of Class E and G airspace during the hours the tower is not in operation (check *A/FD*)

2. **c.** "the instrument procedures for which the controlled airspace is established." Trick question here. Normally Class D airspace is 4 Nautical Miles in radius. But not always. It will always be adjusted for whatever instrument approach serves the airport.

3. **c.** The pilot must contact ATC as soon as practicable after takeoff

Chapter 7

Federal Aviation Regulations - It's the Law!

Remember these two numbers: 61 and 91. Most of your Private and Sport Pilot GA flying is regulated by small portions of Federal Aviation Regulations (FAR) Parts 61 and 91. FARs are also known as CFRs (Code of Federal Regulations). We'll use the acronym FAR because it's pronounceable. Trying to say "CFR" sounds like your stifling a sneeze.

Memorizing regulations and being able to spew them back on an exam proves little, other than you can pass a test—which, of course, is necessary to become a pilot. The way regulations are truly learned is by either violating them (not recommended) or by working them into every aspect of flight. Your flight instructor should do that; the ACS requires it. Still, you'll need a good handle on the basics before attempting to follow any rules, so let's jump into the Federal Aviation Regulations (FAR).

Part 61 spells out who can fly, what it takes to become a pilot or add on a rating or privilege, plus what is required to keep current.

Part 91 lists the rules of the road.

This chapter highlights the important, workaday regulations for VFR Sport and Private Pilots. At the end we'll introduce a few other rules that will appear on the FAA written knowledge test but may not be found on the tips of active pilot tongues. Some of this has already been explored in earlier chapters, but as we like to say in education: *Nothing succeeds like repetition.*

Part 61

61.3
Requirements For Certificates, Ratings and Authorizations

Several key things to take away from 61.3:

- You may not act as PIC, or a required crewmember, unless you have a valid **Pilot Certificate** in your possession (meaning in your wallet or readily available, such as in your flight bag).

- If required, you shall have, in your possession, a current **Medical Certificate** (except Sport Pilot[70]).

- You must have a **Photo ID** (driver's license, military ID, passport or other approved government photo ID).

- Not only must you carry these papers, but you must also present them to the FAA Administrator or his/her representative, or the NTSB, or *any* federal, state or local law enforcement officer, if asked.

61.15
Offenses Involving Alcohol or Drugs

When you apply for your medical certificate you must report any motor vehicle violations involving alcohol or drugs. Any. Going back forever. *Any...*
This includes Sport Pilots. Even though a medical certificate is not required for Sport Pilot, any alcohol or drug related violations must be reported. The FAA checks databanks on this one.

61.16
Refusal To Submit to Alcohol Testing

Not to dwell too long on the booze angle, but refusal to submit to an alcohol test adminsiterd by a law enforcement officer could result in loss of pilot certificate.

61.23
Medical Certificates: Requirement and Duration

Great news for Sport Pilots—you don't need a medical certificate to operate as a Sport Pilot. If you've ever been denied a medical certificate, though, you'll need to work with the FAA on this. Even when flying under Sport Pilot, the PIC cannot have any medical issues that might preclude safe flight. Example: You can't discover that you have diabetes, not tell the FAA and fly legally using your state driver's license as a Sport Pilot medical certificate.[71]

---

[70] Sport pilots must carry a valid driver's license and their pilot logbooks
[71] AOPA has a wonderful service to advise pilots with medical questions before contacting the FAA.

More great news: At the time of this second edition rewrite a Private Pilot needs at least a current third-class medical certificate to be PIC. That's not the great news. This is: Thanks to the efforts of AOPA, EAA and a slug of GA-friendly US senators and representatives, third-class medical certificates will not be required for most private pilots who have held a medical certificate within 10 years prior to July 15, 2016. New pilot's who've never held a medical certificate will need to take a one-time medical exam from a designated AME (Aviation Medical Examiner) who will issue the medical certificate.

A Pilot's Bill of Rights was passed on July 15, 2016 and subsequently signed into law by President Obama, giving the FAA up to one year to implement the changes. As of this writing, the changes are pending. Even if the FAA drags its administrative feet writing the new rules, the law will take effect—at the latest—on July 15, 2017. Check with AOPA or your AME (Aviation Medical Examiner) for details, of which there are way too many.

Paper and Plastic

The paper third-class medical certificate once doubled as the student pilot certificate. No longer. Now, a student pilot must apply online at faa.gov/iacra for a plastic student pilot certificate before being eligible for solo privileges. The student will also need the paper third-class medical certificate.

These are the three classes of medical certificates:

A **First-class medical** certificate (airline pilots) is good for 6 months. First-class medical certificates for pilots under age 40 are good for 1 year. When the first-class certificate expires it becomes a second-class medical.
A **Second-class medical** certificate (commercial) is good for 1 year. At the end of 1 year it becomes a third-class medical.
A **Third-class medical** certificate is good for 5 years after the exam date if the pilot has not reached his 40th birthday or 2 years for over-40 pilots.

61.31
Type Rating Requirements, Additional Training and Authorization Requirements

Tired of pedaling around in your Cessna 150? Want to strap on some more horsepower, maybe, pull the wheels up to go faster and raise your insurance rates? Well, you'll need more training and more endorsements.

To act as PIC of a Complex or High Performance airplane, you must receive and log ground and flight training and receive a logbook endorsement from an authorized flight instructor.

Complex means: An airplane with retractable landing gear, flaps and a controllable pitch propeller.

High Performance means: An Airplane with an engine of more than 200 horsepower.

Tailwheel: You'll need additional flight instruction and a one-time logbook endorsement to act as PIC of a tailwheel airplane.

Pressurized: You'll need additional flight instruction and a one-time logbook endorsement to act as PIC of a pressurized airplane.

You'll need a **Type Rating** to operate the following:
1. Large aircraft (over 12,500 pounds gross weight)
2. Turbojet-powered airplane
3. Other aircraft specified by the FAA (long list of neat stuff)

61.56
Flight Review

After you earn your Private Pilot certificate you'll need to defend it every two years. It doesn't expire, but in order to act as PIC you must have successfully completed a **Flight Review** with a CFI within the past 24 calendar months, giving it the nickname: *Biennial Flight Review* or *BFR*. Or have completed a Proficiency Check or Flight Test for a pilot certificate, rating or other operating privileges.

The reviewer (instructor) must endorse your logbook.

The expiration date of the 24 months falls on the last day of the 24th month.

61.57
Recent Flight Experience

Are you Current?
To carry passengers the pilot must have made and logged three takeoffs and three landings within the past 90 days.
All three landings must've been in the same category and class (plus type, if required) aircraft as the one in which passengers are to be carried.
Tailwheel landings must be to a full stop. Likewise, to be current for night in either tailwheel or tricycle airplanes, those landings must be to a full stop. Night, for currency purposes, is defined as 1 hour after sunset to 1 hour before sunrise.

> Reminder: The categories are: airplane, rotorcraft, glider, lighter-than-air. The classes are: single-engine land, single-engine sea, multi-engine land, multi-engine sea.

61.60
Change of Address

Doesn't seem like a big issue, but it is. You *shall* notify the FAA of a change in permanent mailing address. And you have 30 days to do it or your pilot certificate is invalid. That's the law. www.FAA.gov has links to make the change.

61.69
Glider Towing: Experience and Training Requirements

This one's fun. If you want to tow gliders you must have at least a Private Pilot Certificate (no Sport), plus 100 hours of PIC time in same category, class and type (if required) that's being used to tow. And within the past 12 months you must have made at least 3 actual (or simulated) glider tows while accompanied by a qualified pilot or 3 flights as PIC of a glider being towed.

61.113
Private Pilot Privileges and Limitations

May a Private Pilot fly for hire?
No, mostly.
May a Private Pilot share operating costs with friends?
Sure. Here's the rule:
"A private pilot may not pay less than the pro rata share of the operating expenses of a flight with passengers, provided the expenses involve only fuel, oil, airport expenditures, or rental fees." In other words, if you rent a Cessna 172 and take three non-pilot friends flying, you may share the rental expense with each person paying ¼.

Some business flight expenses can be recaptured. "A private pilot may, for compensation or hire, act as pilot in command of an aircraft in connection with any business or employment if:
(1) The flight is **only incidental** to that business or employment; and
(2) The aircraft does not carry passengers or property for compensation or hire.
If you're flying the company Cessna 172 to company business and not charging passengers to ride with you, then you may be paid by your employer.

Some charitable flights are reimbursable. "A private pilot may act as pilot in command of a charitable, nonprofit, or community event flight if:
1. FSDO is notified 7 days in advance

2. The flight is conducted from an adequate airport
3. The PIC has logged at least 200 hours
4. No acrobatic or formation flights
5. The aircraft has had a 100-hour inspection
6. The flight is day-VFR[72] "

Got a loud sport jacket, bad haircut and pair of white shoes? You could become an airplane salesman. Private Pilots may be reimbursed for expenses associated with sale of an aircraft provided the Private Pilot is an aircraft salesman and has at least 200 hours of logged flight time before demonstrating an aircraft in flight to a prospective buyer.

A Sport Pilot may only share the pro rata share of the operating expenses (1/2) with the passenger. No other reimbursements may be accepted, even for business that's incidental to the flight.

Part 91

91.3
Responsibility and Authority of the Pilot In Command

"With great power comes great responsibility."[73]

Here's your awesome pilot responsibility power: "The pilot in command of an aircraft is directly responsible for, and is the final authority as to, the operation of that aircraft." Or: No one flies the airplane but you.

If something goes wrong, FAR 91.3 gives you the power to do anything to save the flight: "In an in-flight emergency requiring immediate action, the pilot in command may deviate from *any* rule of this part to the extent required to meet that emergency."

Now the flipside. If you deviate from a rule the FAA might want a report: "Each pilot in command who deviates from a rule … shall, upon the request of the Administrator (FSDO), send a written report of that deviation to the Administrator."

91.7
Civil Aircraft Airworthiness

Who determines if an aircraft is airworthy before a flight? Is it the mechanic? No…
The FBO? Nope.

---

[72] See 91.146
[73] Spiderman

How about the FAA, the manufacturer or, I know, it's my mother who determines if the aircraft is airworthy. Right?

No, no, and no.

"The pilot in command (PIC) of a civil aircraft is responsible for determining whether that aircraft is in condition for safe flight."

91.9
Civil Aircraft Flight Manual, Marking and Placard Requirement

We discussed ARROW in chapter 1. You shall have the following paperwork on board for flight: **A**irworthiness Certificate, **R**egistration, **R**adio License (international flights only), **O**perating Limitations, **W**eight and Balance.*

If the aircraft has an approved flight manual, make sure it's onboard. Without a manual, required placards and markings must be displayed. The colored airspeed markings are an example of required placards and markings.

* While weight and balance paperwork is not specifically mentioned in 91.9, be sure it's on board.

91.13
Careless or Reckless Operation

This one's a bit of a catchall: "No person may operate an aircraft in a careless or reckless manner so as to endanger the life or property of another." Seems reasonable. *Don't do nuthin' dumb in flight.*

The second part of 91.13 says you can't be reckless or careless on the ground, either: "No person may operate an aircraft, other than for the purpose of air navigation, on any part of the surface of an airport used by aircraft for air commerce (including areas used by those aircraft for receiving or discharging persons or cargo), in a careless or reckless manner so as to endanger the life or property of another."

Bottom line: Don't fly or taxi like a knucklehead; it reflects poorly on the aviation community.

91.15
Dropping Objects

Each autumn, the *Great Pumpkin Bombing Contest* is held at an undisclosed location in southern Iowa. It's legal (mostly) under 91.15, provided the PIC does not create a hazard to persons or property (below or onboard).

To read more about this on AVWeb go to: http://www.avweb.com/news/skywrite/188626-1.html

91.17
Alcohol or Drugs

That's not a choice. Neither is welcome in or around an aircraft. Here's the reg: "No person may act or attempt to act as a crewmember of a civil aircraft -
(1) <u>Within8hours</u> after the consumption of any alcoholic beverage;
(2) <u>Whileundertheinfluence</u> of alcohol;
(3) <u>Whileusinganydrugthataffectstheperson'sfaculties</u> in any way contrary to safety; or (4) While having an alcohol concentration of <u>0.04 or greater</u>[74] in a blood or breath specimen."

Are you permitted to carry a drunken passenger? Normally, no. "Except in an emergency, no pilot … may allow a person who appears to be intoxicated or who demonstrates by manner or physical indications that the individual is under the influence of drugs (except a medical patient under proper care) to be carried in that aircraft." Plus, drunks usually get airsick. Not worth it.

91.103
Preflight Action

This is an important regulation to grasp and apply to every flight, beginning with your first lesson. It's the one that says you have to know everything. We pilots may be full of it, but is that *it* enough? Here's what the reg says you need: "Each pilot in command shall, before beginning a flight, become familiar with all available information concerning that flight." Phew, that's a tall order, so the FAA expands that concept into usable terms.

For a VFR flight not in the vicinity of the airport: "…weather reports and forecasts, fuel requirements, alternatives available if the planned flight cannot be completed, and any known traffic delays."

For any flight (VFR or IFR, local or cross-country): "…runway lengths at airports of intended use" plus you must know the aircraft's takeoff and landing distance requirements. In other words, you should know how much runway you'll need before departing or landing.

91.105
Flight Crewmembers at Stations

---

[74] You will see this on the FAA test. It is missed more often than any other item. Remember: 0.04

In flight, during takeoff or landing and en route, the pilot and required crewmembers must fasten their seatbelts while at their stations. Shoulder harnesses (if equipped) shall be worn during takeoff and landing.

91.107
Use of Safety Belts, Shoulder Harnesses and Child Restraint Systems

Okay, the pilot is strapped in, but what about the kids? The pilot shall ensure that each passenger has a belt and, if installed, a shoulder harness. Plus, the pilot must inform passengers how to use the belts. The pilot must tell passengers to put them on — "Hey, Granny! Strap in" — before taxi, takeoff or landing. Just like the airlines.

Passengers under age 2 may be held by an adult—totally unsafe but legal.

Sport parachutists need not be seated in proper seats. Sit on the floor for all anyone cares.

91.111
Operating Near Other Aircraft

Formation flying is fun and takes a relatively high skill level. Bumped wingtips can ruin your flight. Still, it's legal if you have prior agreement between all pilots in the formation aircraft. You're not allowed to join up with an airborne stranger just because you think it looks cool.

91.113
Right-of-Way Rules: Except Water Operations

The most important rule is: Aircraft in distress have right-of-way over all other aircraft. Head

On: When aircraft are approaching each other head-on, or nearly so, each pilot of each aircraft shall alter course to the right—whatever category, doesn't matter, turn right.

Converging: When aircraft of the same category are converging at approximately the same altitude (except head-on, or nearly so), the aircraft to the other's right has the right-of-way.

DifferentCategoriesConverging (you won't need a lawyer for this one, just memorize the list):
(1) A balloon has the right-of-way over any other category of aircraft (Why? It can't maneuver very well.)
(2) A glider has the right-of-way over an airship, powered parachute, weight-shift-control aircraft, airplane, or rotorcraft. (Why? Because a glider has no power, the others do.)

(3) An airship has the right-of-way over a powered parachute, weight-shift-control aircraft, airplane, or rotorcraft.

However, an aircraft towing or refueling other aircraft has the right-of-way over all other engine driven aircraft except those in distress.

And rock breaks scissors, which cuts paper, which covers rock…Got it? Good, on we go.

Right-of-way in the traffic pattern: "When two or more aircraft are approaching an airport for the purpose of landing, the aircraft at the lower altitude has the right-of-way." This doesn't mean you can cut off or overtake a higher airplane simply because you're lower. Courtesy and common sense still applies.

91.115
Right-of-Way Rules Water Operation

Yeah, water. If your Private or Sport Pilot certificate includes "Sea" then you need to know that "When an aircraft, or an aircraft and a vessel, are on crossing courses, the aircraft or vessel to the other's right has the right-of-way."

91.117

Aircraft Speed

Frankly, these speed limits won't apply to the average Sport, Private or Student pilot because most trainer airplanes don't go terribly fast. LSA (Light-Sport Aircraft) are limited by FAR 1.1 definition to: "A maximum airspeed in level flight with maximum continuous power (V_H) of not more than 120 knots CAS[75] under standard atmospheric conditions at sea level.

A maximum never-exceed speed (V_{NE}) of not more than 120 knots CAS for a glider.

A maximum stalling speed or minimum steady flight speed without the use of lift-enhancing devices (V_{S1}) of not more than 45 knots CAS at the aircraft's maximum certificated takeoff weight and most critical center of gravity."

For the private pilot, one day you may own a P-51 Mustang (keep the dream alive), so here are some speed rules:

Below 10,000 feet MSL, the indicated air speed (KIAS) limit is 250 knots (288 MPH). The same applies inside Class B airspace at any altitude.

---

[75] CAS Calibrated Airspeed

If you're flying your P-51 Mustang below a Class B shelf, the max indicated speed is 200 knots (230 MPH).

Approaching Class C or D airports, the indicated airspeed limit is 200 knots (230 MPH) when operating below 2500 feet AGL and within 4 NM of the primary airport.

All of us Cherokee drivers just keep dreaming….

91.119
Minimum Safe Altitudes: General

You need to know this for everyday flight.

When operating over congested areas (cities, towns, open-air assemblies), you must maintain an altitude of at least 1000 feet above the highest altitude within a horizontal radius of 2000 feet.

Over other than a congested area, the minimum altitude is 500 feet AGL. However, over open water or "sparsely populated" areas (think: Bonneville Salt Flats) you can go lower at your own peril. But you may not operate closer than 500 feet to any person, vessel, vehicle or structure. In short—no buzzing your buddies on the boat in the middle of Veronica Lake, Minnesota.[76]

Now, here's the catchall do-nuthin'-dumb clause: Pilots must always be at an altitude in all areas to permit an emergency landing without undue hazard to persons or property on the surface if the power unit fails.

91.121
Altimeter Settings

To ensure that all pilots are reading their altimeters based on the same barometric pressure, prior to takeoff set your altimeter (the number inside the Kollsman window) to the local altimeter setting. If that's not available (uncontrolled airport) set your altimeter's altitude readout to the departure airport's field elevation.

Should you venture at or above 18,000 feet (IFR only) you'll set your altimeter to 29.92.

91.123
Compliance with ATC Clearances and Instructions

---

[76] Near Frostbite Falls, courtesy of Rocky and Bullwinkle

You must do what air traffic control says...unless you don't want to. It's not quite that simple, but the PIC is not helpless in the ATC relationship.

"When an ATC clearance has been obtained, no pilot in command may deviate from that clearance unless an amended clearance is obtained, an emergency exists, or the deviation is in response to a traffic alert and collision avoidance system resolution advisory." In other words: Obey unless the clearance poses a threat. Likewise if an ATC clearance will cause you to violate some other rule, decline it. For instance, if a radar controller assigns a heading that will put you inside a cloud, you—the VFR pilot—must decline the heading.

If you disagree with ATC get a clarification: "When a pilot is uncertain of an ATC clearance, that pilot shall immediately request clarification from ATC." Don't be shy. It's not only your right but also your responsibility—by law—to get the clearance or instruction clarified.

If you declare an emergency and ATC gives you priority service, you may be asked to file a detailed report within 48 hours, even if no rule was broken.

Remember, you may deviate from any rule to the extent necessary to handle the emergency. Who can declare an emergency? Anyone, even ATC. A pilot might hint at a problem— "Um, Approach, don't want to bother you, but I seem to have, um, *cough*, smoke in the cockpit...over." The controller will skip the formality of asking, "Do you wish to declare an emergency?" and sound the alarm for you.

There is no shame or penalty for declaring an emergency. There can be a severe penalty for not requesting help until it's too late.

91.129
Operations In Class D Airspace

Don't let the title fool you. Much of what's in 91.129 applies to Classes C and B airspace even though the title refers to Class D. here's the kernel of 91.129:
"(i) Takeoff, landing, taxi clearance. No person may, at any airport with an operating control tower, operate an aircraft on a runway or taxiway, or take off or land an aircraft, unless an appropriate clearance is received from ATC." That means, talk to the tower—two-way communication—and get a clearance before using the runways or taxiways: "Cleared to land," "Cleared for takeoff," or "Taxi via."

The old ATC phraseology, "Taxi to," disappeared after June 30, 2010, replaced by instructions to "taxi via" a route and a clearance to cross any runway en route.

91.130
Operations in Class C Airspace

Keep in mind what you learned about 91.129 and add these items:

To operate within Class C airspace you must not only have two-way communication (as per 91.129), but you must also have an operating transponder with altitude reporting.

91.131
Operations in Class B Airspace

Builds on 91.130 and 91.129. Class B is controlled airspace around the busiest airports— Chicago and New York to name two.

The pilot must hold at least a Private Pilot certificate to operate inside Class B airspace. Technically, a student pilot may operate in class B with proper instructor training and endorsements, but you can pretty much forget about a student pilot operating inside Class B at the busiest airports.

Sport pilots cannot operate inside Classes B, C or D airspace unless they've received additional training and logbook endorsements from an authorized instructor.[77]

You must have a clearance to operate inside Class B airspace. That is the big difference between B and C airspace. You must hear: "Cleared to enter Bravo airspace." Or: "Cleared to enter New York Bravo airspace." Plus, you need the usual two-way radio communications (or how else would you hear the clearance? *Sheeshh…*). And the airplane needs a transponder with altitude reporting.

91.133
Restricted and Prohibited Areas
Feel like landing at Camp David to visit the President? Feel like getting shot down? Same thing. Prohibited Areas prohibit you from entering. *Fuggetaboutit.*

Restricted Areas, on the other hand, merely restrict your entry. Again, you might get shot down, but it'd be more of an accident than an intentional kill. Restricted Areas have many hidden dangers ranging from tethered balloons near the Mexican Border trailing miles of steel cable, to artillery ranges. Stay out when they're active or "hot."

91.135
Operations in Class A Airspace

---

[77] FAR 61.325

IFR only up there, 18,000 feet MSL to FL600 (60,000 feet). ATC positively controls and separates all traffic inside Class A.

91.151
Fuel Requirements for Flight in VFR Conditions

Old pilots lounge saying: "Unless you're on fire, you can never have too much fuel." We should probably add, "unless you're over gross weight," to that but you get the gist. Fuel is good. No fuel is usually bad. But how much fuel is a pilot required to carry? Glad you asked.

For daytime VFR flight an airplane must carry enough fuel "to fly to the first point of intended landing and, assuming normal cruising speed, to fly after that for at least 30 minutes." At night, you need at least 45 minutes reserve. These calculations are based upon known and forecast winds and weather.

Helicopters only need a 20-minute reserve.

91.155
Basic VFR Weather Minimums

At a controlled airport (B, C, D and E Surface Area), basic VFR weather requires a minimum of ceiling 1000 feet AGL and visibility 3 SM. Notice that visibility is given in statute miles while most other mileages are in nautical miles.

In-flight VFR limits are based on visibility and cloud clearance. Beginning with the uncontrolled G airspace and working our way up to highly controlled Class B, it looks like this:

Class G 1200 ft. or less AGL, regardless of MSL altitude:

Daytime the VFR pilot needs a minimum of 1-mile visibility and must remain clear of clouds. Sport and student pilots need 3 miles vis.*Nighttime* the VFR pilot needs a minimum of 3 miles visibility and must remain at least 1000 feet above any clouds, 500 feet below or 2000 feet horizontally from the clouds.

Class G more than 1200 ft. AGL, but less than 10,000 ft. MSL:

Daytime the VFR pilot needs a minimum of 1 mile visibility but must remain at least 1000 feet above any clouds, 500 feet below or 2000 feet horizontally from the clouds. Sport and student pilots need 3 miles vis.

Nighttime the VFR pilot needs a minimum of 3 miles visibility and must remain at least 1000 feet above any clouds, 500 feet below or 2000 feet horizontally from the clouds. Sport pilots can't fly at night.

Nighttime in the Class G Local Traffic Pattern: If you're staying in the pattern (within ½-mile of the runway) at night, VFR, you may operate with less than 3 SM visibility but not less than 1 SM.

Class G more than 1200 ft. AGL, and at or above 10,000 ft. MSL:

Day or Night you'll need 5 miles visibility and must remain at least 1000 feet above any clouds, 1000 feet below or 1 SM horizontally from the clouds.

Class E less than 10,000 ft. MSL:

Day or Night VFR needs 3 SM visibility and must remain at least 1000 feet above any clouds, 500 feet below or 2000 feet horizontally from the clouds.

Class E at or above 10,000 ft. MSL:

Day or Night VFR needs 5 SM visibility and must remain at least 1000 feet above any clouds, 1000 feet below or 1 SM horizontally from the clouds.

Class D:

Day or Night VFR needs 3 SM visibility and must remain at least 1000 feet above any clouds, 500 feet below or 2000 feet horizontally from the clouds.

Class C:

Day or Night VFR needs 3 SM visibility and must remain at least 1000 feet above any clouds, 500 feet below or 2000 feet horizontally from the clouds.

> **Class B:**
>
> Day or Night VFR needs 3 SM visibility and, oddly enough, the VFR pilot need only remain clear of clouds inside this highly controlled airspace. Why? Because ATC radar separates all aircraft inside Class B from each other (IFR and VFR), so the VFR pilots need not worry (theoretically) about other flights getting too close.

But wait, there's more to 91.155:

Except when operating Special VFR (SVFR) you may not operate, under VFR, within the lateral boundaries of the surface areas of Class B, Class C, Class D, or Class E airspace, beneath the ceiling (clouds broken or overcast, not scattered or few) under VFR when the ceiling is less than 1000 feet.[78] And unless ground visibility at that airport is at least 3 statute miles; or, if ground visibility is not reported at that airport, unless flight visibility during landing or takeoff, or while operating in the traffic pattern is at least 3 statute miles.

91.157
Special VFR (SVFR) weather minimums

When I was an air traffic controller in the tower at Monterey, California (MRY), a VFR pilot in a Grumman requested a Special VFR clearance to depart the airport and eventually head north along the shoreline. This was a common request, because Monterey was on the Pacific Ocean, and fog would routinely reduce the ceiling below 1000 feet and shut off VFR operations. Special VFR (SVFR) allowed VFR pilots to depart, get around the fog in less than VFR conditions and then proceed VFR on course in the California sunshine away from the shoreline.

Normally, the SVFR pilots would lift off and scud run beneath the marine deck for a few miles along the beach and then announce, "Cancel Special VFR" when in the clear. This Grumman pilot received his SVFR clearance, departed and climbed straight into the clouds—just like an IFR departure. "That was odd," I thought. And a few seconds later the Grumman pilot happily announced "I'm on top of the clouds now, so cancel my Special VFR." He sounded so pleased, so special.

Misconception: SVFR is not IFR. You can't fly through clouds on a SVFR clearance. (If the Grumman pilot is reading this, I picture a hand slapping a forehead right now. *Doh!*)

Benefit: VFR airplane pilots may operate using SVFR in Class D, C, and E Surface Areas (usually not Class B) with 1-mile flight visibility and clear of clouds.

---

[78] All ceiling heights are AGL

Pilots must request SVFR; ATC cannot initiate the procedure. To operate SVFR at night the pilot must be instrument-rated and the aircraft instrument-equipped. (Memorize that last statement.)

Student or Sport pilots may not receive SVFR.

SVFR does not have priority over IFR traffic. In fact, it's the other way 'round.

SVFR is normally received from a control tower. Inside Class E Surface Area there is no operating control tower, so the pilot contacts the appropriate ATC facility such as the Center or through FSS. The FSS then contacts the appropriate ATC facility for the clearance and relays it to the pilot.

91.159
VFR Cruising Altitude or Flight Level

When in cruise flight (going somewhere, not just maneuvering) at more than 3000 feet AGL and below 18,000 feet MSL, VFR pilots shall maintain specified altitudes based on the aircraft's magnetic course (not heading). Magnetic course is a line across the ground referenced to Magnetic North without wind correction. All altitudes are in feet MSL.

VFR cruising altitudes are:

When on a magnetic course between 0 (360) degrees and 179 degrees (roughly eastbound) use an odd altitude plus 500 feet: 3500, 5500 through 17,500 feet. *East is Odd Plus Five.*

When on a magnetic course of 180 degrees through 359 degrees (roughly westbound), use an even altitude plus 500 feet: 4500, 6500, 8500 through 16,500 feet. *West is Even Plus Five.*

My first instructor taught me to remember this VFR hemispheric rule with this mnemonic: "All the *odd*balls are on the East Coast, so eastbound altitudes get *odd* altitudes (plus 500 ft.)." Being from the East Coast I found that understandable, insulting, but understandable.

No VFR or SVFR is allowed above 18,000 feet MSL in class A airspace.

91.203
Civil Aircraft: Certifications required

ARROW:

- ✓ **A**irworthiness Certificate
- ✓ **R**egistration
- ✓ **R**adio License (if flying internationally)
- ✓ **O**perating Limitations
- ✓ **W**eight and Balance (although not specifically mentioned in 91.203, carry it anyhow)

91.207
Emergency Locator Transmitter (ELT)

ELT batteries shall be replaced or recharged (if able) after 1 cumulative hour of use or after 50% of their useful life expires.

You may only test an ELT (on 121.5) during the first 5 minutes after the hour (probably the most violated FAR in the book). No airborne ELT checks are allowed. All ATC facilities monitor the emergency frequency 121.5, so if a pilot tests an ELT while airborne it blares in all the ATC facilities for miles. Very annoying.

91.209
Aircraft Lights

When operating on the ground or in the air between sunset and sunrise position (navigation) lights must be displayed. In Alaska, where the sun never sets or never rises (seemingly), lights need to be on during the period a prominent unlighted object cannot be seen from a distance of 3 statute miles or the sun is more than 6 degrees below the horizon.

91.211
Supplemental Oxygen

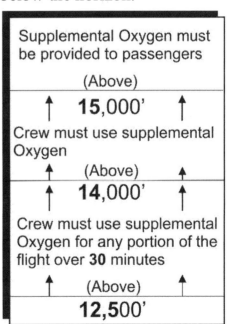

Remember these numbers:
12,500
30
14,000
15,000

Putting some sense to this reg:
12,500-14,000 30 minutes. When operating at cabin pressure altitudes above **12,500** feet MSL up to and including **14,000** feet MSL for more than **30** minutes, pilot and crewmembers shall use supplemental oxygen.

Above 14,000: Pilots and crewmembers shall use oxygen. Forget the 30-minute clause.

Above 15,000 feet cabin pressure altitude MSL: All occupants must be *provided with* oxygen. Passengers don't have to use it, but it must be provided for them.

91.215
ATC Transponder and Altitude Reporting Equipment Use

All aircraft shall have (and use) altitude-encoding transponders when operating:

➢ In Class A airspace
➢ Within the lateral limits *or above* Class B airspace
➢ Within 30 NM of a Class B primary airport
➢ Within the lateral limits *or above* Class C airspace
➢ Above 10,000 feet MSL, except at or below 2500 feet AGL (over mountains)

91.303
Aerobatic Flight

When referring to aircraft certification, the FAA refers to an "acrobatic" category, but when regulating flight it uses the term "aerobatic."

For this regulation's purpose aerobatic means: "An intentional maneuver involving an abrupt change in an aircraft's attitude, an abnormal attitude, or abnormal acceleration, not necessary for normal flight." In other words, fun stuff.

Aerobatic Fun is prohibited:

- When visibility is less than 3 SM
- At altitudes less than 1500 feet AGL (air show pilots get waivers from the FAA to fly lower).
- Within the lateral boundaries of Class B, C, D or E airspace designated for an airport.
- Within 4 NM of a federal airway's centerline
- Over a congested area or over an open-air assembly of people.

91.307
Parachutes and Parachuting

Normally, when intentionally executing a maneuver that exceeds 60 degrees of bank or a nose-up or nose-down attitude of 30 degrees, each occupant shall wear a parachute. Exceptions include single-seat aircraft and spin training for flight instructor certification.

Parachutes need to be repacked periodically. Chair type (canopy in back) must have been packed by a certificated and appropriately rated parachute rigger within the preceding 180 days (used to be 120 days; rule changed on 12/19/08).

91.313
Restricted Category Civil Aircraft: Operating Limitations

Feel like crop-dusting, dumping water on California wild fires or racing your 3000-hp Bearcat at Reno? Well, those aircraft might be in the Restricted category to which this reg applies. You may not fly your Restricted Category aircraft:
- Over densely populated areas
- In congested airways
- Near a busy airport where passenger transport is conducted.

91.319
Aircraft Having Experimental Certificates: Operating Limitations

Homebuilt or Kitbuilt aircraft are a strong segment of the GA fleet. There are advantages to homebuilts and a few restrictions. Here's a restriction that might appear on your written exam: "No person may operate an aircraft that has an experimental certificate over a densely populated area or in a congested airway."

91.403
General

This regulation is in the Maintenance, Preventive Maintenance, and Alterations section of Part 91.

"The owner or operator of an aircraft is primarily responsible for maintaining that aircraft in an airworthy condition, including compliance with Part 39 (Airworthiness Directives section)."

An operator is someone who uses or causes to use an aircraft with or without actually owning it—a lessee or renter for instance. So, even if you don't own the aircraft, if you operate it, you're responsible for making sure it's maintained properly and that all the ADs are complied with.

91.405
Maintenance Required

As with 91.403, the owner or operator shall not only ensure that all required maintenance is performed but that the mechanics make the proper logbook entries indicating that the aircraft was approved for return to service.

91.407
Operation After Maintenance, Preventive Maintenance, Rebuilding or Alteration

Whenever an aircraft has been maintained, rebuilt, or altered in a manner that may have appreciably changed its flight characteristics or substantially affected its operation in flight that aircraft may not be used to carry passengers until an appropriately rated pilot with at least a private pilot certificate flies the aircraft, makes an operational check of the maintenance performed or alteration made, and logs the flight in the aircraft records.

91.409
Inspections

Every aircraft must have an annual inspection, often called "the annual." That inspection expires on the last day of the 12th month after the previous inspection. So, if your Bonanza was "annual'd" on June 2, then that annual expires at midnight on June 30 a year later.

If an aircraft is used for compensation or hire it must be inspected on a 100-hour basis in addition to the annual inspection. Likewise if the aircraft is provided for flight instruction for hire. That 100 hours is based on the recording tachometer and indicates aircraft time in use.

An annual inspection "resets" the 100-hour inspection clock to 0.

An A&P mechanic may perform a 100-hour inspection. An A&P mechanic with Inspection Authorization (IA) must sign off the annual inspection.

The 100-hour limit may be exceeded if it's necessary to fly the aircraft to a place where the inspection can be performed. However, you don't "get free time." Here's the exception: *"The 100-hour limitation may be exceeded by not more than 10 hours while en route to reach a place where the inspection can be done. The excess time used to reach a place where the inspection can be done must be included in computing the next 100 hours of time in service."*

91.413
ATC Transponder Test and Inspections

The ATC transponder may not be used unless it has been tested and inspected (by a certified inspector) within the past 24 calendar months.

91.417
Maintenance Records

This is a follow-up to 91.409. More paperwork:
Records (logbooks) of the maintenance, preventive maintenance, and alteration and records of the 100-hour, annual, progressive (used by airlines mostly), and other inspections, as appropriate, for each aircraft (including the airframe) and each engine, propeller or rotor. The records must include:
- ✓ A description ...of the work performed; and
- ✓ The date of completion of the work performed; and
- ✓ The signature, and certificate number of the person approving the aircraft for return to service.
- ✓ Current AD status and method of compliance.

Maintenance logs should include the following information:
- ✓ The total time in service of the airframe, each engine, each propeller, and each rotor.
- ✓ The current status of life-limited parts of each airframe, engine, propeller, rotor, and appliance.
- ✓ The time since last overhaul of all items installed on the aircraft which are required to be overhauled on a specified time basis.

The owner shall make the logbooks available to the FAA or NTSB upon request, but aircraft logbooks need not/should not be carried in the aircraft.

Obscure FARs

FAR Part 39 says that compliance with ADs (Airworthiness Directives or FAA issued maintenance orders) is mandatory. An AD doesn't necessarily "ground" an aircraft until the AD is complied with. The AD might limit its use but still allow some flight. The AD text, which can be extremely confusing to interpret, holds the details.

Preventive Maintenance[79]

FAR Part 43 Appendix A lists a string of items that are considered Preventive Maintenance and may be performed by the non-A&P mechanic who is a private pilot and owns the airplane. This list includes, but is not limited to: Servicing landing gear and wheel bearings and replenishing hydraulic fluid.

---

[79] Note: It's "Preventive" and not "Preventative"

According to **FAR 43.3** the person who performs the preventive maintenance must make an entry in the aircraft maintenance records (logbook) stating the work done, the person's certificate number and type certificate and then sign the entry.

Test Questions:

Question 1. What regulation allows a Private Pilot to perform preventive maintenance?

a. 14 CFR Part 91.403
b. 14 CFR Part 43.3
c. 14 CFR Part 61.113

Question 2. Who may perform preventive maintenance on an aircraft and approve it for return to service?

a. Student or Recreational pilot
b. Private or Commercial pilot
c. None of the above

Answers:

1. **b.** 14 CFR Part 43.3
2. **b.** Private or Commercial pilot

Beyond FARs

NTSB Part 830
830.5
Immediate Notification

The National Transportation Safety Board (NTSB) investigates accidents and analyzes aviation safety matters. NTSB likes to know when something breaks, quits or crashes. But they don't want to know about every minor incident. Here's the NTSB Immediate Notification requirement:

The PIC shall notify the NTSB (through the FAA, usually) of any airplane accident in which substantial damage has occurred, even if there were no injuries.

Also, these listed incidents must be reported immediately to NTSB:

- Flight control system malfunction or failure
- Inability of any required flight crewmember to perform normal flight duties as a result of injury or illness
- Failure of structural components of a turbine engine excluding compressor and turbine blades and vanes

- In-flight fire
- Aircraft collide in flight
- Damage to property, other than the aircraft, estimated to exceed $25,000 for repair (including materials and labor) or fair market value in the event of total loss, whichever is less
- An overdue aircraft that is believed to be involved in an accident

830.10
Preservation of Aircraft Wreckage, Mail, Cargo and Records

If it crashes, don't move it except to remove victims injured or trapped, or to protect the wreckage from further destruction or to protect the public from injury.

830.15
Reports and Statements to be Filed

The operator shall report on form 6120.1/2 within 10 days after an accident or within 7 days of an overdue aircraft. [80]
Incident reports are filed only when the NTSB asks.

"Incident" means an occurrence other than an accident, associated with the operation of an aircraft, which affects or could affect the safety of operations.
"Aircraft accident" means an occurrence associated with the operation of an aircraft, which takes place between the time any person boards the aircraft with the intention of flight and all such persons have disembarked, and in which any person suffers death or serious injury, or in which the aircraft receives substantial damage.

NTSB death or **"fatal injury"** is: any injury, which results in death within 30 days of the accident.

Enough with the NTSB: Don't crash, it requires way too much paperwork.

Advisory Circulars:

Want something free from the FAA? Go to faa.gov and search for Advisory Circulars (AC). There you can download a slug of them on all sorts of nonregulatory aviation topics, issued in a numbered subject system corresponding to the subject areas of the FARs. AC subject 60 pertains to Airman, 70 to Airspace, and 90 covers Air Traffic and General Operating Rules. Yeah, that 60-70-90 could appear in an FAA test....just saying.

---

[80] I can hear Radar O'Reilly saying something like that on *M.A.S.H.*

Chapter 8
Aircraft Performance

Critical to any flight is the need to estimate performance: How much fuel will the engine use climbing to cruise altitude? After leveling off, how much less will it burn in flight and what speed—True Airspeed and Groundspeed—will result?

If we know how much fuel is in the tanks, and we estimate (fairly accurately) how much we'll burn per hour, we can easily figure out how long we can stay aloft. By understanding how the winds aloft affect our True Airspeed (TAS) we can estimate Groundspeed (GS) and know how far we can go across the ground before the gas gauge nudges E. So, fuel tanks hold more than fuel; they also hold time.

Are We There Yet?

Remember FAR 91.103? That rule says that before arriving at the destination the pilot must know if there'll be a long enough runway to handle the landing. The airplane's flight manual should have landing data that tell how much runway the airplane requires at various field elevations and how headwind, tailwind and nonstandard temperatures affect those numbers.

This manual cannot teach you how to fly your airplane. It can't and won't attempt to teach you everything about every flight—that's impossible. This textbook gives a broad overview of the process and focuses on the skills needed to tackle the FAA written knowledge exam, although not the specific test questions. Your personal flight instructor—and a lot of personal study, plus a lifetime of flying—will make you into a good pilot. Make that a great pilot. This book is simply one leg along that flight path.

You'll want to carry a few simple tools along that journey. Your flight bag should have a plotter, flight computer (E6B), pencil, sectional charts, A/FD, a jar of air and a Baby Ruth candy bar. Lindbergh flew the Atlantic with less. Keep your E6B handy for this first section as we explore aircraft performance. Keep the candy bar handy for all the time you'll spend stuck in some terminal waiting for weather to clear. Yes, ForeFlight or other satnav device will point you in the correct direction and offer a slug of invaluable information en route. I highly recommend using the latest and greatest navigation devices (*pause for dramatic effect*), once you've mastered the basics. We're not all destined to be drone pilots.

Air: The Stuff of the Atmosphere

As mentioned in chapter 2, without air aviation would never get off the ground. No air means no lift, no drag and no thrust. Gravity wins. Luckily, there's air. But what is it? Mostly Nitrogen and Oxygen, but more importantly, how does it change? Two important factors are pressure and temperature.

Water covers two-thirds of the Earth's surface. For centuries sailors used that fact to impress women in bars. The sky, however, covers 100% of the planet, thus making pilots 33% cooler than sailors.

Sea, sky and land affect each other, as you'll discover in more detail in the weather chapter. Airplanes fly through the atmosphere, which shrouds the entire planet. It has mass, and gravity attracts mass giving it weight. Air (the atmosphere) has an indefinite shape. Don't believe me? Look inside that jar of air in your flight kit. That air takes the shape of its container. Now, remove the lid and shake out the contents. *Whoa*...the air flows about, almost like water. In fact, air and water share many attributes. Yeah, the air is invisible (except in Beijing) so we have to imagine its shape shifting.

Let's chill that unit of air. (Hours later) Now, pour it out. Assuming room temperature is higher than the colder air, that cold air will sink. If it were warmer than the surrounding air, it would rise the way a hot-air balloon rises on a chilly morning. So, obviously, temperature affects how air moves, at least vertically.

Air shifts to fill a void, it wraps itself around objects, it moves and—as we learned in the aerodynamics chapter (Ch. 2)—it exerts and changes pressure. Consider that the atmosphere in which we fly has weight and crushes down on all of us. It's thickest (densest) at sea level where it weighs about 14.7 pounds per inch. But who flies at sea level? I mean other than pelicans and banner-towing pilots.

As your airplane climbs it does so into less dense air. As air density decreases—air molecules get further apart—the engine produces less power (that's why some are turbocharged, to compress the less dense air), the propeller produces less thrust, and the wings (airfoils) create less lift.

The atmosphere varies in pressure and temperature; one location is unlike another. So, for the sake of establishing a baseline atmosphere, a **Standard Atmosphere** was declared to be: At sea level the surface temperature is 59 degrees Fahrenheit (15 C), and the surface pressure is 29.92 inches of mercury (or 1013.2 millibars).

Remember: Standard Atmosphere at Sea Level: 59F (15 C), 29.92 inches.

That standard atmosphere exists at sea level, so to predict what happens as altitude increases a Standard Lapse Rate was developed. In a **Standard Lapse Rate** the temperature decreases by 3.5 degrees Fahrenheit (2 degrees C) per thousand feet up to 36,000 feet. Above that to 80,000 feet the temperature levels off. Above that your Cherokee's heater fails.

Pressure changes, too, with altitude. In a **Standard Pressure Lapse Rate** the pressure drops by 1 inch per thousand feet of altitude gain to 10,000 feet. There's less air above, so less pressure as you climb. [81]

Since the airplane manufacturer can't know in which atmosphere (pressure and temperature) you'll be operating at any given moment, the performance data are given in terms of standard atmosphere. It's up to the pilot to correct the POH/AFM performance figures to reflect actual conditions. For example, if your POH/AFM says that your 180-hp Spamcan XP will require 1500 feet of runway to depart from an airport at a 4000-foot elevation, that estimate is based on a standard day. At 4000 feet a standard day is roughly 45 degrees F. If the Outside Air Temperature (OAT) is 59 degrees (standard at sea level), that's not standard for your current altitude of 4000 feet; it's warmer than standard. You'll need to adjust the performance expectations. You'll need to figure out what altitude the airplane *thinks* it's at given the non-standard temperature. You need to figure the Density Altitude.

Defining **Density Altitude** begins with an understanding of **Pressure Altitude**, which is the height above a Standard Datum Plane (SDP). This is easily determined with the altimeter. The altimeter is a sensitive barometer. It's calibrated to display altitude in the standard atmosphere. Standard barometric pressure at sea level is 29.92 inches of mercury (Hg), so if the altimeter's barometric scale (Kollsman window) is set to 29.92 inches, the altimeter will display Pressure Altitude. At Flight Levels 180 (18,000 feet MSL) and above, IFR pilots set their altimeters to SDP (29.92 inches). Below that, pilots use the local altimeter setting, which usually ranges from 28.00 through 31.00 inches of mercury[82]. For the VFR pilot Pressure Altitude is used to determine Density Altitude.

Density Altitude is pressure altitude corrected for non-standard temperature (memorize that). As air density decreases, density altitude increases—the airplane "thinks" it's higher. As air density increases, density altitude decreases—the airplane "thinks" it's lower. Performance is based on density altitude. A 150-hp airplane on a standard day might be able to lift off a 3000-foot runway at an airport with a field elevation of 4000 feet. But if the

[81] Lapse rates are approximates.
[82] 28.00 and 31.00" are rare extreme settings

temperature increases, air density will decrease (air gets thinner), so the Density Altitude increases, dramatically enough in some cases that the airplane can no longer produce enough power, thrust and lift to get airborne.

Under standard conditions Pressure Altitude and Density Altitude are the same. Rarely is a day standard. Density varies directly with pressure and inversely with temperature.

How To Compute Density Altitude

First, find Pressure Altitude. The easiest way to do this is set the altimeter's barometric correction window (Kollsman) to 29.92 inches. Read the altimeter and write down that altitude. Reset the altimeter to whatever ATC (or AWOS, ASOS, ATIS, AFSS) gave you.

> **Note:** Air density is affected by pressure, temperature and humidity. A more humid day means a higher density altitude, but for testing purposes humidity is not factored in. For practical purposes on an extremely humid day (80% relative humidity or higher) add 2000 feet to your final Density Altitude computation. *High, Hot and Humid*—All bad = High Density Altitude.

On an electronic flight computer enter Pressure Altitude and OAT. Input an altitude, and the computer will give the Density Altitude.

Using a mechanical E6B (*whiz wheel*) circular flight computer set the pressure altitude (taken from the altimeter set to 29.92) opposite to the OAT. Caution: Use Celsius. Convert Fahrenheit to Celsius before entering the temperature or you'll get screwy answers. With Temperature and Pressure Altitude matched, read the result in the Density Altitude window.

Here's a teaser: Density Altitude changes with pressure and/or temperature. Aircraft efficiency suffers with increased Density Altitude. So, you'll need more runway length for takeoff and landing, and the airplane won't climb as well. But you still use the same Indicated Airspeeds on landing regardless of Density Altitude. In other words, if you fly the final approach at 70 Knots Indicated Airspeed (KIAS) at sea level on a cold day, you'll use the same Indicated Airspeed on a warm day approach to an airport at 4000 feet elevation. Use the same indicated airspeeds regardless of Density Altitude.[83] The problem is when the air becomes thin (high, hot, humid) your airplane may not be able to achieve the necessary Indicated Airspeed to produce lift and climb. You might be unable to climb up to Leadville, Colorado's traffic pattern.

---

[83] Assuming similar wind and load conditions

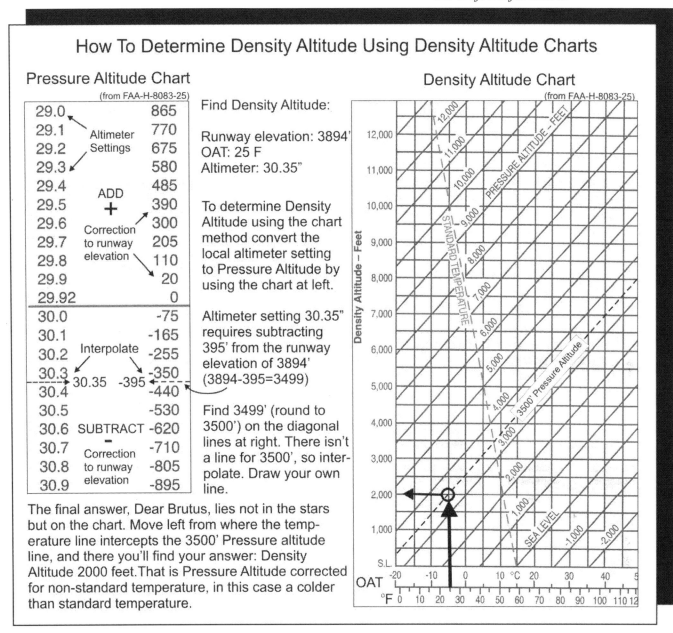

How To Determine Density Altitude Using Density Altitude Charts

Pressure Altitude Chart (from FAA-H-8083-25)

Altimeter Settings	
29.0	865
29.1	770
29.2	675
29.3	580
29.4	485
29.5	390
29.6	300
29.7	205
29.8	110
29.9	20
29.92	0
30.0	-75
30.1	-165
30.2	-255
30.3	-350
30.35	-395
30.4	-440
30.5	-530
30.6	-620
30.7	-710
30.8	-805
30.9	-895

ADD + Correction to runway elevation

Interpolate

SUBTRACT − Correction to runway elevation

Density Altitude Chart (from FAA-H-8083-25)

Find Density Altitude:

Runway elevation: 3894'
OAT: 25 F
Altimeter: 30.35"

To determine Density Altitude using the chart method convert the local altimeter setting to Pressure Altitude by using the chart at left.

Altimeter setting 30.35" requires subtracting 395' from the runway elevation of 3894' (3894-395=3499)

Find 3499' (round to 3500') on the diagonal lines at right. There isn't a line for 3500', so interpolate. Draw your own line.

The final answer, Dear Brutus, lies not in the stars but on the chart. Move left from where the temperature line intercepts the 3500' Pressure altitude line, and there you'll find your answer: Density Altitude 2000 feet. That is Pressure Altitude corrected for non-standard temperature, in this case a colder than standard temperature.

Takeoff Performance

Over the years, aircraft manufacturers have produced a wide variety of performance charts. Any chart allows the pilot to plug in known values, such as wind, temperature, altitude and airplane weight in order to estimate performance. There's another rub. A 40-year-old airplane with a run-out engine might not deliver performance promised by a performance chart. Still, it's important to understand how these performance figures are found.

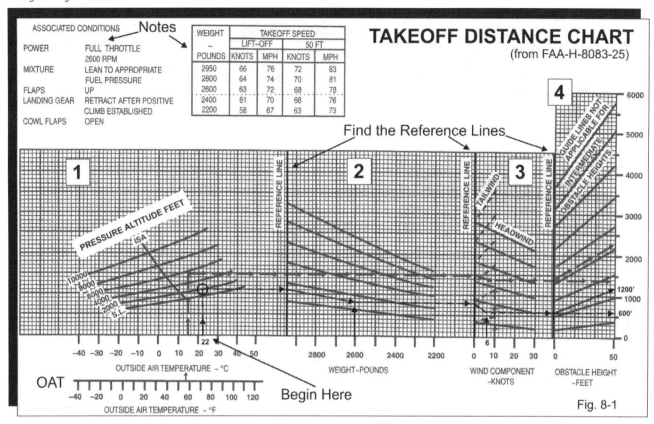

Fig. 8-1

Figure 8-1 is a typical four-panel "combined takeoff distance graph" from the FAA's *Handbook of Aeronautical Knowledge*. Each panel allows you to introduce a variable. Using the FAA's example of 2600-pound airplane departing into a six-knot headwind from an airport with a pressure altitude of 2000 feet at 22 degrees Celsius, let's see how many feet we'll need for the ground roll and how many to clear a 50-foot obstacle. (This same format is also used in some landing charts.)

Begin in Panel 1. Move vertically from 22C until intercepting the 2000' Pressure altitude line. Turn right and move directly to the Reference Line to exit Panel 1 and then enter Panel 2. From the Reference Line follow the sloping diagonal line down (run parallel to them) until intercepting a vertical line from the aircraft's weight, 2600 pounds. From that intersection move right again in a straight line to the next Reference Line to exit Panel 2 and enter Panel 3. As with the previous panel, follow the diagonal line downward until you intercept your wind component (headwind or tailwind) speed. In this case it's a six-knot headwind. Again, where your diagonal line meets the vertical factor (6 knots), stop and go straight to the right again until hitting the next Reference Line. You're leaving Panel 3 and entering the final Panel 4. We want to know two things: Ground roll and distance to clear a 50-foot obstacle, so draw two lines, one straight across to the end of the graph. That line is your ground roll, or how far you'll roll before the wheels lift. It's 600 feet. We also want to know how much total distance we'll need to clear that 50-foot Baobab tree off the end of the runway (getting a chainsaw to solve the problem is not an option). So, your second line parallels as closely as possible the diagonal line to the end of the graph. Note that it goes up, meaning you'll need more room to clear the obstacle. In fact, you'll need 1200 feet.

The trick with these multi-panel graphs is to carefully work your way through each panel. Enter the known data, such as temperature and altitude. Where the two lines meet, stop and move directly in straight line to the nearest Reference Line and stop. From there, enter your next two bits of data and repeat until you reach the conclusion at the far right of the chart. Practice a few, and it'll seem easy.

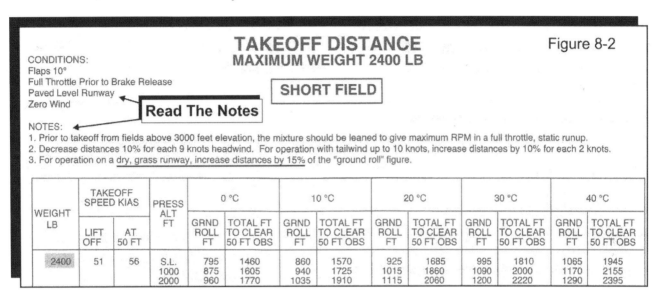

Figure 8-2 shows a slice of another type of performance chart for determining takeoff distance. As with any chart it's important to read and apply the notes. This chart applies to a "Paved, Level Runway." NOTES # 3 says to add 15% to the ground roll if the runway is dry grass. Makes sense. Grass will drag at the wheels requiring more distance to get moving fast enough to produce lift and break free of the ground. But how tall is that grass? Short putting-green grass offers little resistance while ten inches of hay might prevent liftoff. Some pilot sense is required to evaluate and apply these notes. Being a good pilot is all about analyzing available data in order to make good aeronautical decisions.

Here's an anomaly about grass. It'll impede takeoff performance, but it can shorten a landing roll, again, because the grass grabs the wheels to slow the airplane. Unless the pilot applies brakes. Wheels can skid on grass—wet or dry—causing a longer rollout. Mud and snow have the same effect. Either will slow you down, but when you apply brakes, the mud or snow will reduce friction, which reduces braking effectiveness. Wet grass can act like ice. Standing water on a paved runway can also act like ice causing the tires to hydroplane. In Dynamic Hydroplaning the tires are separated from the pavement by a thin layer of water. Braking action while water skiing is practically nil.

Side Note: Braking action, as measured by airport management vehicles or pilots slipping and sliding off a slick runway is reported in four official levels: *Good, Fair, Poor* and *Nil*. If the control tower receives a report of Braking Action Poor or Nil, a warning will broadcast on the ATIS: "Braking Action Advisories Are In Effect."

Runway slope or gradient is another element to consider when evaluating the takeoff and landing rolls. Many unimproved mountain or farm runways are on hillsides. Some are humpbacked with either end lower than the middle. The pilot should aim (wind and obstacles permitting) to land uphill and depart downhill. Many paved municipal airport runways are sloped. The gradient is published in the A/FD and expressed as a percentage, such as 3%, which means that for every 100 feet of runway length its height changes by 3 feet.

Pilot Induced Performance Restrictions (PIPR): Your POH/AFM chart data assume the airplane is properly flown and maintained. Low tire pressure or a wheezy engine will significantly reduce performance as will an improperly rigged airframe. If you don't know what correct tire pressure should be, or at least what shape a properly inflated tire should approximate, then ask a mechanic. A bug-encrusted, dirty, chipped, worn or bent propeller will reduce performance. Mud-caked wings will alter the airfoil so that performance suffers. A dirty air filter starves the engine of air and reduces performance. Most of these items should be spotted and corrected in the preflight inspection. Poor pilot technique can severely hamper aircraft performance.

Keep the Weight Off. As you pile in luggage and invite passengers to board, the airplane's gross weight increases. We learned in the weight and balance chapter (ch. 4) that each airplane has a certified Maximum Gross Weight for Takeoff. Overload the airplane and it won't perform as intended. Increased gross weight requires increased speed to produce enough lift to fly. More weight means more runway needed for takeoff and landing. More weight means slower cruise speeds and lower climb rates. More weight means higher stall speeds.

Wind. As a pilot ya gotta learn to love and respect the wind. It's our friend. Oh sure, it'll bounce you around until your passengers turn green, and it'll try to force you off a runway that's not aligned with its force. But the wind is simply air in motion. And what do wings need to create lift? Air in motion. Most of that moving air is produced by engine thrust, but Nature also provides air in motion—wind. Take advantage of it. Land and take off into the wind or at least as closely aligned with the headwind as possible.

Wind has a big effect on takeoff or landing performance. A headwind makes for a shorter ground roll. It allows the airplane to touch down at a slower groundspeed (same Indicated Airspeed for a given aircraft weight) and to reach flying speed on takeoff sooner and at a lower groundspeed than in a no-wind condition. Tailwinds have the opposite and a more profound effect than headwinds to the extent that a tailwind landing could lead to overshooting the touchdown point.

A headwind equal to 10% of the takeoff airspeed will shorten the takeoff roll by 19%. But a tailwind of the same speed will increase the takeoff ground roll by 21%.

Crosswind Component

The winds are rarely calm or pointed directly down the runway. Crosswinds are an aviation reality, and pilots need to learn how to handle them and how to figure what effect crosswinds have on performance, particularly takeoff and landing performance.

Certificated airplanes are tested for, and must demonstrate, a certain level of crosswind capability. The goal is to certify the airplane so that a pilot with "average piloting skills" can handle a 90-degree crosswind with a velocity up to 0.2 Vso (20% stall speed landing configuration). If your airplane stalls at 45 knots, then the average pilot (Yes, you're well above average) should be capable of handling a 9-knot direct crosswind in that airplane.

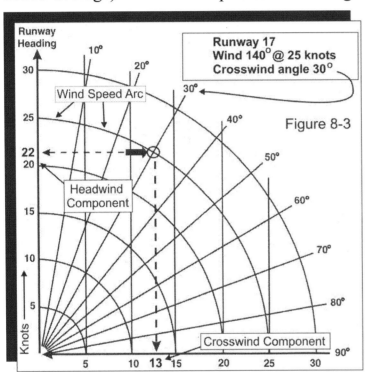

Figure 8-3

This is the **Maximum Demonstrated Crosswind Component**. It's fixed by the manufacturer for FAA certification purposes. It does not mean that the airplane cannot handle stronger crosswinds. It means that the "average pilot" should do fine at this demonstrated limit.

But life isn't all right angles, so how does the "average pilot" figure how a less-than-90-degree crosswind will affect the airplane? For that there's the **Crosswind Component Chart**. It takes the actual wind and divides it into its **Headwind Component** and **Crosswind Component**.

Example: (Refer to Figure 8-3)
Scenario: You're using Runway 17. The wind is from 140 degrees at 25 knots. Immediately, we see that there's a 30-degree spread between Runway 17 (170 degrees), and the wind iscoming from 140 degrees.

Note: All runways are referenced to magnetic north, so all surface winds issued by the tower, ATIS, AWOS, or ASOS are also magnetic. Yes, the runway's actual magnetic heading might be, say, 174 degrees and the winds might be closer to 143 degrees than 140. Round off. Plus, winds rarely blow in straight textbook lines. They swirl and change directions in short distances and get ripped apart by trees and hangars. In short, the neat wind report on the AWOS might not match your touchdown reality, so be ready for anything. Still, you want to figure roughly what's happening so keep reading.

The wind angle here is 30 degrees (170-140 = 30). Find the 30-degree line outside the outer arc (the arcs represent wind speeds). Follow the line until it intercepts the arc for 25 knots.

For wind speeds between the plotted speeds (5 – 30 knot increments) you'll need to interpolate.

Where the 30-degree line intercepts the 25-knot arc draw a line straight to the vertical axis and one straight to the horizontal axis. Read those two numbers. Your Headwind Component, in this example, should be 22 knots, meaning that's how much of that crosswind should act as a headwind. Your Crosswind Component is 13 knots, or how much of that 25-knot wind will act as a crosswind (from the left) pushing you to the right as you land or take off. If the POH/AFM lists the Demonstrated Crosswind Component as 17 knots, this situation should be easily handled by "average piloting skills." If the Demonstrated Crosswind Component is less than 13 knots then the average pilot should seek a runway more closely aligned with the wind…or develop better-than-average skills.

Landing Distances—Go Figure

Landing Distance: "The number of takeoffs must always equal the number of landings. It's the law." — Anonymous

In that spirit, when you take off and clear the 50-foot obstacle, you'll eventually need to land. And knowing the FAA testers, there will probably be another 50-foot obstacle at the approach end of the runway. Here's a sample problem, again from the FAA's *Pilots Handbook of Aeronautical Knowledge* (*PHAK*):

GROSS WEIGHT LB	APPROACH SPEED IAS, MPH	AT SEA LEVEL & 59°F		AT 2500 FT & 50°F		AT 5000 FT & 41°F		AT 7500 FT & 32°F	
		GROUND ROLL	TOTAL TO CLEAR 50 FT OBS	GROUND ROLL	TOTAL TO CLEAR 50 FT OBS	GROUND ROLL	TOTAL TO CLEAR 50 FT OBS	GROUND ROLL	TOTAL TO CLEAR 50 FT OBS
1600	60	445	1075	470	1135	495	1195	520	1255

LANDING DISTANCE — FLAPS LOWERED TO 40° - POWER OFF HARD SURFACE RUNWAY - ZERO WIND

NOTES: 1. Decrease the distances shown by 10% for each 4 knots of headwind.
2. Increase the distance by 10% for each 60°F temperature increase above standard.
3. For operation on a dry, grass runway, increase distances (both "ground roll" and "total to clear 50 ft obstacle") by 20% of the "total to clear 50 ft obstacle" figure.

Figure 8-4

Problem (*other than the table being too small to read without a microscope*):
Pressure Altitude: 1250 feet
Temperature: Standard

Using the table in Figure 8-4 find the ground roll distance and the total distance to clear a 50-foot obstacle.

First, read all the notes; you may come back to them. Now, decide what you can ignore. Since we're at 1250 feet MSL, we can ignore the panels beneath 5000 FT and 7500 FT. But there is no 1250-FT panel, so we must interpolate between sea level (0 FT) and 2500 FT.

Since 1250 FT is halfway between 0-2500, our answer will be halfway between what's shown in the tables.

The Ground Roll at 2500 FT is 470. At Sea level it's 445. Interpolate: Add the two values together (470 + 445 = 915). Divide the sum in half (915/2 = 457.5) The ground roll will be 457.5 feet. Do the same with the distances to clear the 50-foot obstacle: 1075 + 1135 = 2210 feet. Now divide in half: 2210/2 = 1105 feet to clear the obstacle at an airport with a 1250-foot elevation.

Now, rest your eyes.

CRUISE POWER SETTINGS

(from FAA-H-8083-25)

65% MAXIMUM CONTINUOUS POWER (OR FULL THROTTLE)
2800 POUNDS

PRESS ALT.	IOAT		ENGINE SPEED	MAN. PRESS	FUEL FLOW PER ENGINE		TAS		IOAT		ENGINE SPEED	MAN. PRESS	FUEL FLOW PER ENGINE		TAS		IOAT		ENGINE SPEED	MAN. PRESS	FUEL FLOW PER ENGINE		TAS	
	°F	°C	RPM	IN HG	PSI	GPH	KTS	MPH	°F	°C	RPM	IN HG	PSI	GPH	KTS	MPH	°F	°C	RPM	IN HG	PSI	GPH	KTS	MPH
SL	27	-3	2450	20.7	6.6	11.5	147	169	63	17	2450	21.2	6.6	11.5	150	173	99	37	2450	21.8	6.6	11.5	153	176
2000	19	-7	2450	20.4	6.6	11.5	149	171	55	13	2450	21.0	6.6	11.5	153	176	91	33	2450	21.5	6.6	11.5	156	180
4000	12	-11	2450	20.1	6.6	11.5	152	175	48	9	2450	20.7	6.6	11.5	156	180	84	29	2450	21.3	6.6	11.5	159	183
6000	5	-15	2450	19.8	6.6	11.5	155	178	41	5	2450	20.4	6.6	11.5	158	182	79	26	2450	21.0	6.6	11.5	161	185
8000	-2	-19	2450	19.5	6.6	11.5	157	181	36	2	2450	20.2	6.6	11.5	161	185	72	22	2450	20.8	6.6	11.5	164	189
10000	-8	-22	2450	19.2	6.6	11.5	160	184	28	-2	2450	19.9	6.6	11.5	163	188	64	18	2450	20.3	6.5	11.4	166	191
12000	-15	-26	2450	18.8	6.4	11.3	162	186	21	-6	2450	18.8	6.4	10.9	163	188	57	14	2450	18.8	5.9	10.6	163	188
14000	-22	-30	2450	17.4	5.8	10.5	159	183	14	-10	2450	17.4	5.6	10.1	160	184	50	10	2450	17.4	5.4	9.8	160	184
16000	-29	-34	2450	16.1	5.3	9.7	156	180	7	-14	2450	16.1	5.1	9.4	156	180	43	6	2450	16.1	4.9	9.1	155	178

Data for 11,000 feet aren't shown, so interpolate between information at 10,000 feet and 12,000 feet. 11.5 - 10.9 = 0.6. Divide 0.6 by 2 = 0.3. Now, add 0.3 + 10.9 = 11.2 GPH.

Figure 8-5

En Route Performance: Between takeoff and landing is cruise. Many performance charts are available, but the FAA likes the one in Figure 8-5. This table sets cruise power at 65%. It's a three-panel chart with Standard temperature in the middle and ISA (Pressure Altitude) –20 C on the left end and ISA +20 on the right.

Be sure to note if the test questions ask for RPMs or Manifold Pressure. It may use C or F temperatures. And watch for tricks confusing knots with MPH or GPH (Gallons per Hour) versus PSI (Fuel flow in Pounds per Square Inch).

That said; using CRUISE POWER SETTINGS (Figure 8-5), find the RPM setting to maintain 65% power at 6000 feet ISA with an OAT of 36 F above standard.

Step 1: Start on the left side: PRES ALT. Find 6000.
Step 2: Decide which of the three panels you'll need and discard the other two. The temp is 36 degrees above standard so use the third panel.
Step 3: Read across from 6000 feet. 2450 RPMs or 21.0 inches manifold pressure will burn 11.5 GPH (6.6 PSI) resulting in a cruise speed of 161 knots.

Test Question:

(Refer to Figure 8-5 CRUISE POWER SETTINGS, FAA-H-8083-25)[84]
What fuel flow should you expect at 11,000 feet on a standard day with 65% maximum continuous power?

a. 106 gallons per hour
b. 11.2 gallons per hour
c. 11.8 gallons per hour

Answer: [85] (See footnote)

Use the center panel, because the temperature is standard. You must interpolate between figures at 10,000 feet and 12,000 feet. 11,000 is halfway between. Fuel flow at 10,000 feet is 11.5 GPH. At 12,000 feet it's 10.9 GPH.
11.5 − 10.9 = 0.6
Divide 0.6 in half = 0.3.
Add 0.3 to 10.9 (or subtract it from 11.5) = 11.2 GPH.

Try another:

Question 2. High humidity has what effect on aircraft performance?

a. It increases performance
b. It decreases performance
c. It has no effect on performance

Question 3. When the outside air temperature (OAT) at a given altitude is warmer than standard, the density altitude will be (complete the sentence)

a. equal to pressure altitude
b. lower than pressure altitude
c. higher than pressure altitude

Answers:

2. **b.** It decreases performance
3. **c.** higher than pressure altitude

In the next chapter we apply performance with FARs to plan a cross-country trip. You'll need your sectional charts, plotter, E6B computer, pencil, paper, calculator and a toothbrush. Always bring a toothbrush when you fly to help you make that no-go decision when the weather turns sour.

---

[84] Whenever you see FAA-H-(number), the H means Handbook, something the FAA produces and is in public domain.
[85] answer: **b.** 11.2 gallons per hour (from FAA-H-8083-25)

Chapter 9

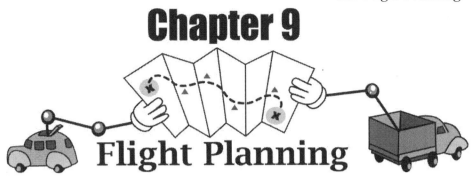

Flight Planning

The primary purpose of flight: To have fun.

The secondary purpose of flight: To get somewhere.

Antique Airplane Association's motto: "Almost getting there is half the fun."[86]

If you're taking up flying solely to get from Point A to Point Barrow in the quickest time, well, I can't help you. That's transportation. It has no soul. Buses and airlines move people-cargo, while general aviation airplanes move souls. In fact, until it was considered politically insensitive, the FAA flight plan forms would ask for the number of *Souls On Board*.[87] Back then, even the FAA recognized that leaving the planet to fly to another place on it took a leap of faith, and that airplanes moved spirits not just bodies.

Be that as it may, let's get somewhere in a single-engine airplane by planning a cross-country trip. Along the way we'll use dead reckoning, radio navaids, maybe a little GPS, and incorporating the ancient art of pilotage we'll select a few checkpoints on the ground to make sure all the electronic wizardry isn't leading us astray.

Pilotage

How do you get from the kitchen to the garage? Or from the garage to school? GPS? Celestial navigation? Do you contact the federal government and file a travel request for a routing: "Ah, I'd like to go to my car, and I'm in the bathroom, how do I, like, ya know, get there?"

Of course not, none of the above. You simply go. Navigation is performed by guiding yourself past familiar landmarks—the refrigerator, the sink, through the garage door, down the driveway—watch for the neighbor kid who always leaves his dang bike in the way—onto the street and then along a string of familiar routes past known landmarks until you reach your destination.

---

[86] Unofficial; go to antiqueairfield.com for more
[87] Yes, the abbreviation was "SOB"

In unfamiliar territory some of us older travelers will consult paper maps, while more tech-savvy types tune in a GPS (Global Positioning System) and trust an orbiting computer to point the way. Some women—never men[88]—will ask for directions. But the primary method to human navigation is simply to open our eyes and go. Likewise in aviation.

The first powered (controlled) flight was on December 17, 1903 at Kitty Hawk, North Carolina. As Orville climbed onto the Wright Flyer he said, "I've never flown this route before, Wil, what if I get lost?" Wilbur promised he'd walk down the beach and pick him up, thus not only did the Wrights inaugurate flight they also discovered the primary flaw in air travel: How do you get to your destination after landing? That will never be solved, but, as a Private Pilot, you can go just about anywhere in the world and get within walking distance (if you like to walk[89]) of where you really want to be.

Remember: It's the flight that matters, not the travel.

Okay, enough hangar philosophy. Let's get somewhere using **Pilotage**, which is defined as "navigation by visual reference to landmarks."[90] The primary tool for pilotage is the VFR Sectional Chart (aka a Sectional) produced by the FAA's National Aeronautical Charting Office (NACO) and sold through some FBOs or online distributors.

Sectionals are the pretty charts full of color (sadly reproduced here in B&W). The terrain changes from deep green at lower elevation to dusty browns in the western high country. Small towns are depicted with little dots or in massive yellow blobs where suburban sprawl has spread fungus-like across the landscape. Obstacles are depicted with sharp triangles to denote smokestacks and most of the thousands of radio towers that have popped up across the landscape like so many deadly weeds, there to satisfy texting lust.

In short, sectionals paint a graphic image of the world below, and there's never a cloud over that landscape…on the map, anyhow. VFR sectionals are, as you'd expect, primarily for the VFR pilot operating in VFR weather conditions (IFR pilots are wise to carry them, too, or the digital equivalent). With a chart open on your lap, you fly across the country following a course line and checking off landmarks or "checkpoints" along the way. It's easy. It's fun.

VFR sectional charts, for the conterminous United States, are updated every six months and, even though no FAR says that thou "shall" have a sectional chart on board or that the sectional chart be current, you are highly advised to travel only with current sectionals in order to begin to satisfy FAR 91.103, the rule that says you must have "all information available." If you're caught with an out-of-date sectional—or no sectional—it'd be tough to

---

[88] "It is better to be lost than to admit to being lost." –*Arthur Azzetti*
[89] "Anything's within walking distance if you have enough time." –Artie Azzetti
[90] FAR 1.1

convince anyone that you flew prepared. I recommend that you subscribe to a sectional service, so you'll always have current charts. [91]

The sectional chart has a scale of 1 inch = 6.86 nm or 1:500,000. **World Aeronautical Charts** (WAC) are similar to sectionals but at twice the scale 1 inch = 13.7 nm or 1:1,000,000 and are revised annually. Sectionals are ideal for slow and medium speed VFR aircraft, while the faster VFR traffic might be more suited to the less detailed WAC that covers a wider area. Your choice, but we'll stick with the sectionals here.

Note: All chart samples in this manual are out-of-date and are not to be used for navigation.

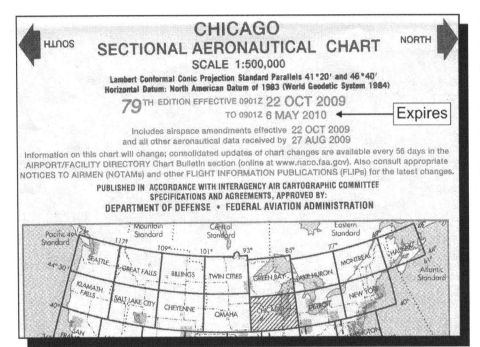

When preplanning any trip verify that you have current chart information. Before opening the sectional check the valid dates printed on the cover. Next, decide if you have the correct chart. The lower 48 states are divided into 37 sections, each with a sectional chart, and each named for a major city on that chart. We're using the *Chicago* sectional here. There is a wad of aeronautical information on the sectional chart, too much to detail in this short chapter. On a rainy IFR day spread a chart on the hangar floor and crawl your way across. Learn to identify every symbol and how to interpret the airport and navaid information. Expire charts make for cheap gift wrapping paper.

Sectional charts depict terrain contours, obstacles, military routes, special use airspace (SUA) plus Classes G through B airspace, although some of that is implied rather than boldly painted. Class A airspace is at and above 18,000 feet MSL so of no value on a VFR sectional. Although sectionals alone do not provide all available information for flight, I dare say that a VFR pilot could navigate from Atlantic to Pacific using only current sectionals and do quite nicely. Figure 9-1 is a portion of the Chicago sectional east of Waterloo, Iowa (ALO). We'll plan a short VFR cross-country trip from Oelwein, Iowa (OLZ) to Vinton Memorial Airport (VTI) 28 miles south, using pilotage as our primary means of navigation.

---

[91] A current GPS or ForeFlight database, in lieu of paper charts, goes a long way toward satisfying this regulation.

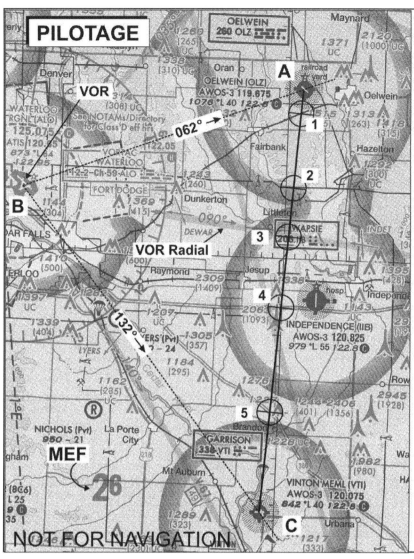

Pilotage means navigating via landmarks along your course. Select checkpoints that will be easy to spot from thousands of feet up. Bodies of water aren't always reliable. A prolonged drought can eliminate what you thought would be an easy-to-see river crossing.

After departing Oelwein (Area A) the first checkpoint (#1) is only 2nm away, where the route crosses a railroad track. Six miles later (#2) it crosses a power line.

Four miles later the route passes the town of Littleton (#3), which might be difficult to see, so set our VOR receiver to the Waterloo VOR's (Area B) 090° radial. Your VOR CDI needle will center as you cross this radial.

Six miles after Littleton, is four-lane Highway 20 southwest of Independence airport (#4). Seven miles later you'll cross Highway 380 (#5).

Seven more miles and you'll land at the destination, Vinton Memorial Airport. Additionally, draw a line from the Waterloo VOR (Area B) across Vinton airport. That defines the 132° radial. Set 132° in your VOR receiver, and when the CDI needle centers you'll cross Vinton, home of *Iowa Flight Training*.

Figure 9-1

A Pilotage Trip: First, draw a line between the two airports. Accent with a yellow highlighter if that helps you keep things in focus.

Next, using your plotter, measure the distance between the two points: 28 nm.

Now, do a quick fuel calculation: Assuming full fuel, say 40 gallons, a fuel burn of 8 GPH and a 90-knot airspeed we can broadly estimate that, barring strong winds, we should be able to make the 28-mile trip in about 18 minutes. Burning 8 GPH we should use roughly 3 gallons on the trip. In short, we have plenty of fuel. This WAG[92] estimate is based on the fact that 90 knots = 1.5 miles/minute (60 knots = 1 mile/minute). Later, we'll use the E6B flight computer and actual winds aloft to figure more accurate times.

Orient your direction. The course (no wind) from Oelwein to Vinton looks to be roughly south, maybe a little southwest, say 190 degrees. Again, WAG estimates used simply to get

---

[92] WAG: Wild Ass Guess (old, non-PC ATC slang)

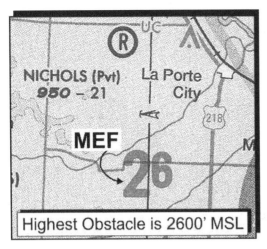

NICHOLS (Pvt) La Porte
950 – 21 City

MEF

Highest Obstacle is 2600' MSL

your head thinking in the correct direction. I was an air traffic controller for many years, and have seen pilots get totally confused immediately after departure when the controller says, "Resume own navigation." Even though the compass isn't needed for pilotage, it's best to know roughly what direction you should be pointed. Tip: Look at the VOR compass rose around Waterloo. Those numbers, 0 through 33, indicate magnetic radials (aligned to magnetic north) radiating from the VOR. No, you won't see the radials on the ground, so they, too, don't count for pilotage, but when looking at the chart, you can use VOR radials for orientation, even when navigating without radios. VOR radials make great cross-reference checkpoints en route. Sadly, they're being phased out.

We know the distance and direction, so let's decide how high we need to fly to avoid disrupting cell phone service. West of Vinton is the (blue) number pair **26**. That is the **Maximum Elevation Figure** (MEF) within the quadrangle marked by Lat/Long (Latitude/Longitude) ticked lines on the chart. It indicates in thousands and hundreds of feet, the height of the highest known obstacle (mountain peak, TV tower, tall immovable Swede, whatever) within that large quadrangle. In this case, the highest obstacle is roughly 2600 feet MSL.

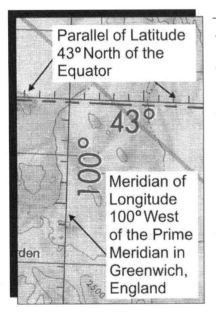

Parallel of Latitude
43° North of the
Equator

43°

100°

Meridian of
Longitude
100° West
of the Prime
Meridian in
Greenwich,
England

Latitude and Longitude or "Lat/Long"

The earth is a sphere, which makes it tough to fly a straight line. Luckily, it's really big so you don't notice the curvature when flying in a Cessna 150. The planet is mapped in a grid formed by **Meridians of Longitude**, which are lines drawn from north to south poles and cross the equator at right angles. These meridians indicate the number of degrees East or West of the 0-degree **Prime Meridian, which runs** through Greenwich, England. Coordinated Universal Time (UTC)— also called Zulu Time or Greenwich Time—is based on this Prime Meridian. Degrees are divided into minutes with 60 minutes between each degree.

Parallels of Latitude run east/west but do not converge. They parallel the equator. Measurements are referenced North or South of the Equator. Any location can be defined by where the lines of latitude and longitude cross. For instance: Des Moines, Iowa is 41 degrees and 32 minutes North (of the Equator) and 93 degrees and 39 minutes West (of the

Prime Meridian). Each minute of latitude arc is a nautical mile. Rarely will VFR pilots ever use this method, but you need to know it for the test and just to sound smart should you join the 18th Century Royal Navy.

Plan to fly at least 500 feet above the MEF. Given the MEF of 2600 feet MSL, let's use 3500 feet MSL as our cruising altitude.

Pick out landmarks or checkpoints. If we're traveling at a mile-and-a-half per minute, checkpoints 10 miles apart will pass roughly every seven minutes. So, select checkpoints located along the route, spaced 10 to 20NM apart. The trick is to pick landmarks that will be easy to identify. The checkpoints we've selected on this trip are too close together for practical use but show what's available on the charts.

NORDO: The contraction means No Radio. This entire trip can be made without a radio...unless you get within 5NM of Waterloo airport (blue dashed circle around the blue airport symbol).

Pilotage is a navigation method normally used in conjunction with dead reckoning and radio or GPS navigation. Pilotage does not relieve the pilot of following ATC rules. The next step in cross-country planning is to review the airspace en route.

Airspace En Route

Let's begin at Oelwein (Figure 9-2). The airport symbol is magenta, and there's a magenta shaded circle with

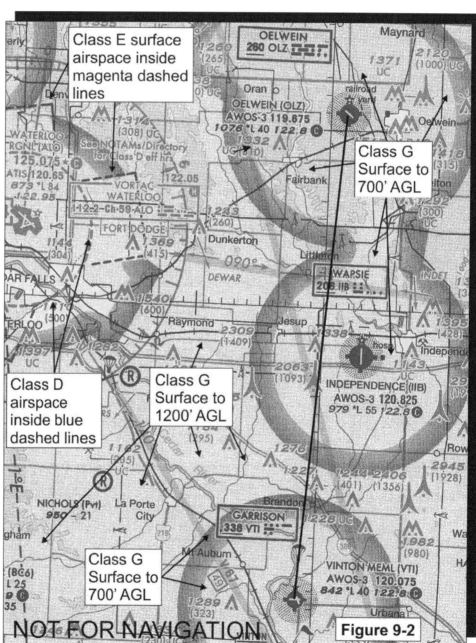

Figure 9-2

170

extension around the field. This is Class G airspace from the surface to 700 feet AGL. No radio needed. Leaving 700 feet AGL you'll enter Class E airspace. Still, no radio required, but greater visibility and cloud clearance minima apply. You can make this 28-mile trip VFR without ever talking to ATC, but if you turn west of course you'll encounter Waterloo's Class D airspace. Two-way radio communication with Waterloo ATCT (tower) is required before crossing the blue dashed lines encircling the airport. No transponder is required unless you want radar service from Waterloo Approach Control.

Quiz: What is the ATCT frequency for ALO?

Answer: (See footnote [93])

Airport data are printed near the airport symbol. Blue airports (controlled) use blue print and magenta (uncontrolled) airports use magenta.

A/FD

More detailed airport data are located in the Airport/Facility Directory (A/FD; see Figure 9-3). It's recommended to have a current A/FD, or electronic equivalent, onboard the aircraft.

When departing an airport served by a control tower inside Class D, C or B airspace, you must get permission to use

The FAA's **Airport/Facilty Directory** (A/FD) is printed on cheap paper and in a clunky code, but it holds a wealth of valuable information about your destination airport (Excerpts are reproduced here):

Time conversion from UTC to local
Airport is located 4 miles NW of the city
Fuel availability (100 LL and Jet A)
Airfield Elevation
Airport Beacon
VASI lights

Runway Numbers

Pilot Controlled
Approach Lighting

Runway Dimensions

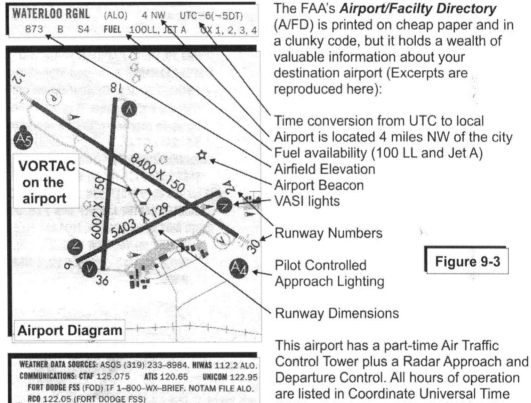

Figure 9-3

This airport has a part-time Air Traffic Control Tower plus a Radar Approach and Departure Control. All hours of operation are listed in Coordinate Universal Time (UTC or Z-time; see conversion in upper box. UTC -6 means subtract 6 hours from UTC to get local standard time. UTC; -5DT means subtract 5 hours for Daylight Saving Time). The symbol ‡ means that in Daylight Saving Time the effective hours are one hour earlier than shown.

Where Land And Hold Short Operations (LAHSO) are in use, the Hold Short Point and Distance Available data are listed.

---

[93] ALO tower 125.075

any runway or taxiway. But let's say you've just departed Oelwein, which has no control tower. (See Figure 9-2) Oelwein is inside Class G airspace from the surface to 700 feet AGL, so you don't need two-way communication or a transponder. You're VFR, headed for Vinton, when you decide to change your destination to Waterloo, which is inside Class D airspace. No problem. Turn toward Waterloo, tune in the ATIS (Automatic Terminal Information Service) and listen to the wind, weather, runway in use and any pertinent NOTAMs or ATC messages. Get the current ATIS letter code (A, B, C…Z). Then, call Waterloo Tower on 127.07 (drop that last digit 5; most GA radios can't tune that). "Waterloo Tower, Cessna 150KN[94], ten east, Echo (or whatever ATIS code is current), landing Waterloo" (if you omit "landing Waterloo" ATC should assume that's your plan). The tower controller will answer with something like, "Cessna 150KN, Waterloo Tower (that establishes two-way communication and you may enter the Class D airspace), make straight in runway 24 (or whatever)…" Now wait for either a sequence, "…number two, follow a Twin Beech on final…" or "…cleared to land."

Later, when you depart Waterloo ("Cleared for takeoff.") and turn on course for Vinton, again, you'll leave Class D airspace 4 miles from the airport (or vertically when leaving the upper limit). You do not need permission to change frequencies, nor do you need to announce "Clear southeast" when leaving the Class D airspace, unless, ATC requests the report.

Quiz: What does the star beside the Waterloo ATCT frequency (125.075*) mean?

Answer: (See footnote [95])

Arrival at Vinton: Monitor AWOS frequency 120.07 to listen to the winds, altimeter and weather.

Vinton CTAF is 122.8. Make your first position report about ten miles out, "Vinton traffic, Cessna 150KN, ten northwest landing runway 34 (or whatever runway you choose). There is no control tower here, no ATC. The PIC selects the runway based on wind conditions, pilot ability and NOTAMs (if a runway is NOTAM'd closed, don't use it).

Quiz: Vinton's Class G airspace reaches to what altitude AGL?

Answer (See footnote [96]): Notice the shaded magenta transition circle around the entire airport.

---

[94] Spoke as: "One Five Zero Kilo November"

[95] Tower operates part-time; see A/FD for hours of operation. 125.075 becomes Class E CTAF when the tower is closed. Drop the last 5 in 125.075 and use 125.07. No radio required when the tower's closed, but it's safer to use one.

[96] 700 feet AGL

Do The Math

So much for pilotage. Time to break out the plotter and E6B flight computer to plan a cross-country flight using Dead Reckoning.

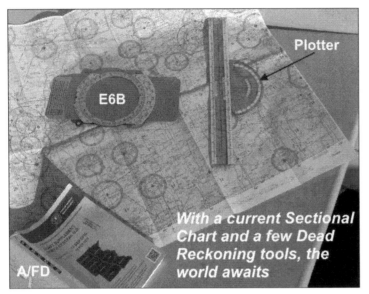

With a current Sectional Chart and a few Dead Reckoning tools, the world awaits

Dead Reckoning is "the navigation of an airplane solely by means of computations based on airspeed, course, heading, wind direction, and speed, groundspeed, and elapsed time."[97] Think of it as reckoning a course that's dead on.[98] Let's plot a course from Osceola, Iowa to Ames, Iowa, add winds and figure a heading.

Open your Omaha sectional chart to the South side and look for Osceola Airport (I75) located approximately 30NM south of Des Moines Airport (see Figure 9-4, page 185). Our destination is Todd Field, a private strip, near Ankeny, Iowa, approximately 14NM north of Des Moines.

With a straight edge, or plotter, draw a line from Osceola to Todd. Now measure the distance along the plotter's edge. Be sure you have the correct scale. Plotters may show nautical or statute miles or both. They may show a scale for sectional charts and one for WAC. We want nautical miles on the sectional chart scale.

The distance is 43 NM.

A quick glance at the airspace en route shows that we'll depart from Osceola's Class G airspace, climb into Class E at 700 feet AGL (within 5 NM), and then 19 miles north of Osceola encounter a magenta ring signifying Class C airspace around Des Moines. Prior to that ring we need to call Des Moines Approach Control on 135.2. That frequency is shown in a magenta box with the white interior southwest of Des Moines (we've reproduced it southeast of DSM to save space): "CTC DES MOINES APP WITHIN 20NM ON 135.2" This information is also in the A/FD.

We could overfly the Class C airspace and talk to no one if we had an altitude encoding transponder and flew above 5000 feet MSL. Or fly beneath the 2200-foot Class C shelf.

---

[97] AIM
[98] Sometimes called "Ded Reckoning" short for "Deduced Reckoning"; we'll use "Dead Reckoning," which sounds like the title to a 1940s Warner Brothers film.

> **50**
>
> **22**
>
> The upper (normally magenta) number indicates the top of the Class C airspace 50 = 5000 feet MSL. The lower number, 22, indicates the base of the outer shelf: 22 = 2200 feet MSL.

Let's plan to fly below 5000 feet MSL. But what would the proper altitude be for our direction of flight? To determine that we refer to FAR 91.159, which says that when cruising VFR *above 3000 feet AGL*, the pilot shall fly odd altitudes plus 500 feet for easterly magnetic courses (0 through 179 degrees) and even altitudes plus 500 feet for westerly magnetic courses (180 degrees through 359).

Determine Magnetic Course: Take True Course (TC), add or subtract Magnetic Variation (VAR) to achieve Magnetic Course (MC). No wind is factored in this process. Compass Deviation is not factored either.

$$TC +/- VAR = MC$$

Back to our course line to find our proper altitude. Using a plotter we learn that the True Course (TC) from Osceola to Ames (uncorrected for magnetic variation) is 008 degrees. If the Magnetic Pole and True North Pole were collocated, that would be our course. But they're not, so we subtract 2 degrees of magnetic variation (VAR) as indicated by the dashed magenta isogonic line 12 miles east of Osceola. It reads "2E" or 2 degrees between Magnetic North and True North. The "E" means an easterly variation, so we subtract (*East is least; West is best*) from our True Course (TC). The result:

$$008 \text{ (TC)} - 002 \text{ (VAR)} = 006 \text{ degrees (MC)}$$

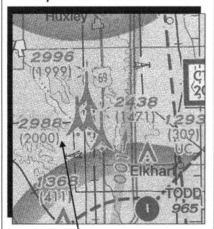

Airplane Pickle Forks

A cluster of four threatening towers stands north of Todd Field. Tallest: 2000' AGL.

Note: Course is not the same as Heading. More on that later.

What altitude do we fly for a magnetic course of 006 degrees? Answer: 0 through 179 degrees fly odd altitudes plus 500 feet, so if cruising above 3000 feet AGL we'd fly an odd altitude plus 500 feet MSL: 5500, 7500, 9500…17,500 feet MSL.

Let's choose 3500 feet MSL as our cruise altitude. And let's see if that's a safe altitude. Look for the MEF (Maximum Elevation Figures).

North of Osceola, our departure point, is **19** (in blue). That means something sticks up to 1900 feet MSL or close to that (the MEF has a pad in it to protect from poor geometry). West of Osceola is a tower reaching 1775 feet MSL. That won't be on our route. Nothing along our initial route appears too threatening. A short distance north of Todd Field sits a cluster of TV towers poking up like airplane pickle forks between Ankeny and Ames. Deadly. The tallest tower touches 2988 feet MSL.

So far we have a line (the course), distance and a cruising altitude. We've scouted for obstacles en route, and we know what airspace we'll encounter and what ATC facility we need to call. Our flight weather is VFR—clear and unlimited visibility, so we don't have to be concerned about the Class E surface airspace around Ankeny (dashed magenta circle) restricting our VFR operation.

Next, we figure our headings, estimated times en route and estimated fuel requirement.

A **Course** is a line drawn across the map. It can be aligned to True North to achieve True Course or aligned to Magnetic North for Magnetic Course. **Heading** is the course corrected for wind and errors in the airplane's magnetic compass. Heading is where the pilot points or "heads" the airplane. (Perhaps it should be called "nosing" since the airplane's nose points the way. Perhaps not.)

Here's the Dead Reckoning formula (memorize):

TC +/- WCA = TH +/- VAR = MH +/- DEV = CH

The goal is to find the Compass Heading (CH), a number on the compass to follow that corrects for all the vagaries of magnetic variation (VAR), wind drift and compass deviation (DEV).

Winds aloft along our route are 020 degrees @ 10 knots. Our Cessna 172's TAS is 105 knots. Grab your E6B flight computer plus an erasable pencil to figure this out using this Step-By-Step E6B process:

1. Look at the wind side of the computer (side with the clear plastic).
2. Find **TRUE INDEX**. It's at the top of the dial.
3. Set the true wind direction (our case: 020 degrees) beneath the WIND INDEX pointer.
4. Find the **Grommet**. It's the tiny circle in the plastic.
5. Set (slide) the grommet over any number. Hint: "100" works best.
6. Mark the wind. How? The wind speed is 10 knots. Count up 10 from 100 (110) and make a small but legible dot or mark with the pencil. You now have the 10-knot wind marked along the 020-degree wind direction.
7. Place your TC beneath the TRUE INDEX (turn the dial until 008) lines up.
8. Slide the TAS (105) beneath the wind dot (pencil mark).

9. Read your Groundspeed (GS) beneath the Grommet (96 knots).
10. Read the Wind Correction Angle (WCA) beneath the penciled wind dot 2 degrees Right or +2.
11. To find TH (True Heading) add 008 (TC) + 002 (WCA) = 010 (TH)
12. Add or Subtract VAR. Ours is 2 degrees E so subtract 2 degrees from TH (010-002 = 008 So MH is 008).
13. Add or subtract Magnetic Deviation (from compass correction card in the airplane). We'll say + 002 degrees deviation. The result: 008 (MH) + 002 (DEV) = 010 (CH).

Lots of hoops just to get a tiny number, but that's the process. Theoretically, if the winds-aloft forecast holds correct, you should be able to fly the CH 010 degrees and arrive directly over your destination without the wind drifting you off course. Bottom line: Heading holds course.

An electronic E6B will do these calculations in a flash…assuming the batteries aren't dead. DUATS (Direct User Access Terminal Service) or other free online weather and flight planning programs will figure your courses and headings in an even faster flash…assuming you have computer access. One advantage to learning the E6B (and, honestly, most pilots toss it in the flight bag never to be used again after the check ride) is you can see on the plastic face just how the winds affect your course or any course. It gets you thinking about the winds—a vital aviation skill.

Speeds, Go Figure

Flip the E6B over to the circular slide-ruler side. It's 1957 all over again. Let's use the GS 96 knots to estimate times and fuel requirements.

Notice how the inner plate rotates. Find the SPEED INDEX. That's the black triangle pointer at 60. It's also called the ONE-HOUR INDEX, because 60 can represent 60 minutes (one hour). This index is used for rates such as knots, miles-per-hour or gallons-per-hour. Turn the dial until the SPEED INDEX points to your groundspeed (GS) computed from the wind side of the computer. In our case, 96 knots.

CAUTION: Don't confuse terms. Use knots with nautical miles and MPH with statute miles.

Turn the dial until the SPEED INDEX points to 96 on the MILES/FUEL scale.

But there isn't a 96….

That's correct. The numbers can be changed to meet our needs simply by moving decimal points or adding zeros. Or, in this case, find 90 and count 6 ticks up to 96. Match the SPEED INDEX to 96.

We know we want to travel 43NM from Osceola to Todd Field. Leave everything set and read around the outer MILES scale until you see 43. Again, it's 40 plus count three tick marks to represent 43. The outer ring represents miles, and the scale beneath it represents time. Beneath 43 is 26.8, round up to 27. It will take us 27 minutes to travel 43NM at 96 knots groundspeed in our Cessna 172. About as long as it takes to calculate the answer. You'll get faster with experience. And then you'll use GPS, which does all this for you.

Try a few:

1. At groundspeed 245 knots how long will it take to travel 78 NM?

Answer: [99] (See footnote) remember 245 won't appear on the mile scale, so look between 24 and 25, add zeros (240 and 250). Halfway between is 245. Set the SPEED INDEX there and find 78 on the outer MILES scale. Read the number directly below 78. Round off.

2. At groundspeed 135 MPH how long will it take to cover 135 nautical miles?

Answer: [100] (see footnote) Remember to convert MPH to Knots first. Compare apples and apples, not apples and pomegranates. To change from MPH (or statute) to knots (nautical), look at the outer scale until you see 70. Arching over 70 is a box with **naut** on one end and **stat** on the other. This is the conversion chart for statute to nautical. Put 135 MPH under **stat** and read 117 under **naut.** Now, put the SPEED INDEX beneath 117 and read the time beneath the mileage.

Notice that time can be read as minutes or on the scale below minutes as *hours: minutes.*

Fuel usage can be estimated using the same technique for finding time en route. The airplane's POH will give you the burn rates, or how many gallons-per-hour you'll use at specific power settings. Generally, you burn more in climb, less in cruise and far less in descent. For simplicity here, let's say that our Cessna 172 burns 8.3 gallons per hour, and we want to know how long we can stay aloft with 35 gallons of usable fuel on board.

We have two knowns: Amount of fuel and the burn rate. Start with the rate and that means go to the PER HOUR INDEX (60). Set the 60 INDEX beneath 8.3. Again, interpolate. Find 80 and 90. Move the decimals to 8.0 and 9.0; halfway between is 8.5 and two ticks left of that is 8.3. Match the INDEX to 8.3 (gallons per hour).

---

[99] about 19 minutes
[100] 69 minutes

Look at the MILES/FUEL scale. Find 35 (gallons). Read the number below. Burning 8.3 GPH we can expect to fly for 25 minutes until we're out of gas, right? No, it doesn't make sense. That 25 needs a zero. Make it 250 minutes or 4:10 hours. We can expect to stay aloft for 250 minutes on 35 gallons, burning 8.3 GPH. Always ask yourself if the answer makes sense.

Take it another step further. If we can go 250 minutes at 96 knots groundspeed, how far down the road will we need to look for an emergency landing field when the tanks run dry?

Answer: Set the SPEED INDEX to 96 knots and read the inner TIME scale at 250 minutes. Look above it and we should make it 400NM until the last drop burns.

Math makes airplanes fly.

As pilots we try to keep the math simple and logical.

Flight Plans and Flight Logs

These terms are often used interchangeably. Here, we'll use **Flight Plan** to indicate the VFR Flight Plan filed with Flight Service, whether by phone or online. **Flight Log** is the list of checkpoints over which we'll fly (See sample logs on pages 186-187). It includes Estimated Times En Route (ETE), mileage, estimate fuel, and notes. While the FAA publishes an official Flight Plan Form (FAA Form 7233-1, see page 188), there is no single style flight log. You get to design your own to meet your evolving pilot needs.

A flight log is not required for any flight. However, the student pilot should master this procedure and be able demonstrate proficiency during a practical exam, even if you have the slickest computerized flight planning app on your i-thingie ™. These crude flight-planning skills are the foundations for any electronic flight planning. So, ya need ta know this stuff.

That said every good pilot uses some form of a flight log. It may be a scribbled set of notes on a napkin or a detailed flight log clamped to a kneeboard. Nowadays, the flight log may be in your GPS and presented on a video screen. Your flight instructor should teach you how to build and use a flight log. What's presented in this chapter is one version.

The purpose of any flight log is simple: To get and keep you on course and out of trouble. The flight log is a step-by-step trip plan. We'll use our Osceola to Ankeny (Todd Field) route for an example. We drew the course line, studied the terrain and airspace and figured our fuel and time estimates. Now, that graphic plan transfers to a form.

For this flight, we'll combine Pilotage and Dead Reckoning, a common VFR practice. Radio navigation (VORs mainly, although the FAA continues decommissioning VORs as GPS is the better choice) can also be used, and a detailed discussion on VOR orientation is in the Chapter 9 Appendix.

Using the Visual Flight Log write the departure airport name in the top left box. Beneath that, list visual checkpoints along the route. You decide how far apart they should be, but less than 10NM gets rather crowded.

Using groundspeed and fuel use estimates, complete the boxes to the right of each checkpoint.

A Navigation Aid (navaid) or a crossing radial from the navaid (think VOR) can be a checkpoint. In fact, they make great checkpoints, especially when there's an easily defined visual checkpoint at that location. The vertical column below the NAVIGATION AID box allows you to write the name, ident and frequency for a particular navaid. If there is no navaid, leave it blank. In the TO/FROM box write the course *to* or the radial *from* the navaid.

Based on your estimated groundspeed you can estimate how long it will take you to fly from checkpoint to checkpoint. Write these estimates under the columns labeled DISTANCE and ELAPSED TIME. Once airborne, you'll note the actual times en route. This will allow you to analyze the actual winds aloft versus the forecast winds and figure more accurate estimates to your destination. Your instructor will teach this skill in flight. (You can't get everything from a book or a flight simulator.) This same procedure applies to the GS (Groundspeed) and CH (Compass Heading) columns.

RMKS means Remarks and is straightforward. Write anything you want in there: Weather, PIREPS, NOTAMs, recipes, phone numbers, Lotto numbers....

Cross-country flying includes a fair amount of preplanning. As you gain experience this process will streamline and become more efficient. You'll learn what to discard and what to include. You'll learn safe shortcuts that make flying trips more enjoyable and less like a school project. But, first, learn the procedures. Streamline later.

File a Flight Plan

Most VFR flights are conducted safely without them. News reporters go bananas when they discover that not every airplane is on a flight plan. They're not pilots. You are, you decide whether or not to use the free (so far) service. Filing a flight plan is required for IFR and international operations and is highly recommended for flights over remote terrain and large bodies of water.

Your instructor should walk you through the steps and have you actually file, open and (real important) close a flight plan on a dual cross-country trip. You do not need the official FAA flight plan form, because most flight plans are filed over the phone, radio or on line (DUATS or 1800WXBRIEF.com). But you must use the official flight plan format (see page 188[101]) and follow these steps to file a VFR Flight Plan (we'll assume you've already figured your times, fuel requirements and such):

1. Complete a blank Flight Plan Form, filling in each box. Boxes left empty label "None."

2. Contact Flight Service (800-WX-BRIEF) and say, "I'd like to file a VFR flight plan." When the briefer says, "Go ahead," read the information from Box #1 through #16. The briefer has a flight plan form mask on the computer screen and does not need for you to say the names of the boxes. Simply give the information in the order it appears. If a box does not apply, such as #11 "Remarks" or #13 "Alternate Airport," say: "None."

Bits of Confusing Info: Box #3 requests the **Aircraft Type/Equipment Suffix.** The *AIM* lists all the proper suffixes that pertain to the navigation and transponder equipment on board. An aircraft without a transponder, for instance, is /X, pronounced "Slant Xray." Slant Tango, "C150/T,"for example, means you have a Cessna 150 with a transponder but no Mode C altitude reporting. Slant Uniform: "C150/U" is a Cessna 150 with transponder and altitude encoding. Slant Golf (C150/G) means the Cessna 150 has a transponder, Mode C (altitude encoder) and GPS.

TAS: All speeds on the flight plan form are in True Airspeed (TAS) and in knots (KTAS).

Airport Identifiers: Ideally, you should know the airport ICAO[102] identifier. If not, say the full name: "Osceola, Iowa airport." Chances are you'll be talking to a briefer many miles from your departure or destination, so it's best to have the identifier handy. It can be found on the sectional chart or A/FD.

Hint: If you get confused while filing over the radio or phone, ask the briefer what's needed. They're usually helpful.

Time: Think Universal. All times are UTC (Coordinated Universal Time) or Zulu (Z) Time[103]. If you don't know the conversion, ask the briefer.

---

[101] The FAA will eventually require the International Flight Plan Form; here we'll stick with the old one
[102] ICAO: International Civil Aviation Organization
[103] Called "Zulu Time" because the time has a Z suffix, e.g.: 2145Z

Altitude: All MSL. No need to say "feet."

Fuel On Board: Flight Service wants to know how much time your fuel will last, so—should you fail to show up at your destination—rescuers can estimate how far you could fly before running out. "Gallons" means nothing to the briefer. "Liters" means nothing to most Americans.

Color of Aircraft: Stick to the board color scheme, "Red and white." Skip: "…with the faintest gold pinstripe accenting a beige background above a feathered wash of mauve that highlights the eggshell interior and my blue eyes."

After you file (radio or phone) the briefer might read you the latest weather and ask you to call back with PIREPs en route.

Open/Close Your Flight Plan

Once you file a VFR Flight Plan, it sits, inactive, in the FSS computer until you activate it. It does not go to any ATC computer. Only IFR flight plans do that. The Class C radar controller ahead knows nothing about your VFR flight plan and cares nothing about it. A VFR flight plan is mostly for search and rescue (SAR) purposes—not for ATC. Once airborne you must call FSS (AFSS) to activate your flight plan. Say, "Please open my VFR flight plan for Cessna 1408Y, off Osceola (I75) at 1545 (UTC is implied)."

Upon arrival at the destination call Flight Service to close your VFR flight plan: "Princeton Radio, Cessna 1408Y at Ames, please close my VFR flight plan." You can do this in the air before entering the traffic pattern or on the ground (if you can reach FSS on the radio). Or you may have to call on the telephone (1-800-WXBRIEF). Either way, close within 30 minutes of your estimated arrival time or a search begins. Usually, the first step in locating an overdue aircraft is for FSS to call the airport: "Hey, you see a red and white Cessna 172, N1408Y on the ramp?" If the airport manager (or gas kid) says, "yes," the search ends. If the answer is no, the search widens, until hours later, the Civil Air Patrol (CAP) has airplanes scouring your filed route. Comforting but potentially expensive in the case of a false alarm.

If you file a VFR flight plan but never open it, the flight plan disappears from the FSS computer after about two hours. No harm, no foul.

Is it proper to ask ATC (the control tower at your destination airport) to close your VFR flight plan? No. The controllers have other duties and unless you can't reach Flight Service, make the call yourself. ATC will pass along the information, if you can't reach FSS. Don't make it a practice. Don't ask UNICOM to close your flight plan either. It's your responsibility.

Why file VFR? For local flight around relatively civilized areas, a VFR flight plan is mostly pointless. If your engine quits and you land on the San Diego Freeway, the news copters will find you before CAP, FSS or CHP can mount a search. However, stray a few miles from civilization and the terrain—particularly out west—can get rugged and remote. Lose an engine five miles south of Interstate 10 in Arizona and you're down in the desert with a nasty walk through 120-degree heat with no company but a few rattlesnakes. File, open, close. Repeat PRN.

Thinking Ahead: When you go for your instrument rating you'll learn the procedures for filing IFR flight plans. Same format, but a whole different spin. At the time of this rewrite, the FAA is planning to switch over to the International Flight Plan Form, so the old form will go the way of NDBs, Flight Watch (EFAS) and CFIs smoking unfiltered Luckies in your airplane.

RNAV Navigation

RNAV means "Area Navigation." This includes GPS and, at one time, LORAN. GPS means Global Positioning System, and LORAN means Long Range Navigation. LORAN was around long before GPS but has been decommissioned. You may encounter old LORAN receivers in an airplane, and if a passenger asks, "Grandma, what's LORAN?" just say it's a Dr. Seuss character. GPS is the darling of modern navigation and rightfully so. It revolutionized IFR and VFR navigation, to say nothing of street directions and pizza delivery.

GPS

This manual does not teach RNAV operation, because it changes too quickly and many functions are specific to the unit you're using. Plus, high-tech navigation devices demand serious study and should be worked into your instrument scan and cockpit resource management (CRM) without overloading you. But, GPS is a vital part of the National Airspace System (NAS) so let's consider the basics.

The **GPS** (Global Positioning System) receiver in the aircraft gets position information from a constellation of 24 satellites, five of which should always be observable anywhere on or above the planet. Your GPS receiver needs to acquire at least four satellites to establish a three-dimensional position that includes latitude, longitude and altitude.

Most GPS receivers, even a cheap handheld, come with extensive databases that include just about anything a user could want. For pilots, an aviation database—depending on the brand—includes all known public use airports, airport information such as CTAF and runway lengths. A GPS database can also identify conventional navaids such as VORs plus all of the intersections along federal airways and on published instrument approaches. In short, the GPS has just about every bit of information a pilot could want to fly just about anywhere.

Databases, like paper charts, have a shelf life and must be updated periodically to ensure that the pilot has the current information. That's usually done online or by replacing a data card in the unit.

GPS units vary in presentation but most offer some sort of screen where the pilot can view a moving map, displaying the flight's progress as well as constantly computing groundspeed as well as time, distance and bearing to the destination or other fix. GPS, if used correctly greatly reduces workload. If used incorrectly, it can be as frustrating as trying to program TiVo.

VOR and VORTAC
The VOR has been around for decades and will be with us for many more years, although in dwindling numbers of VOR stations. You'll need to master the VFR VOR functions so refer to the Chapter 9 Appendix on page 273.

Time Zones

All ATC and weather times are in *Coordinated Universal Time* (UTC) or *Zulu Time*, so named because the time has a Z after it. Example: 2145Z. Zulu Time is based on the Prime Meridian that passes through Greenwich, England, so you may hear Zulu time referred to as Greenwich Time. Whatever the name, there is a one-hour difference between time zones. When moving west, subtract an hour from the previous time zone: Central is one hour earlier than Eastern, for example. Reverse the process and add an hour when going from west to east. Daylight Saving (not Savings) thoroughly screws this up, and that's one reason UTC (Zulu Time) is so convenient. It never changes for the political whims of various "Saving" times.

In the summertime USA remember 4-5-6-7; as in add 4 hours in summer to Eastern Time to get UTC. Add 5 hours to Central Time to get UTC and so forth until you reach the West Coast. In winter, think 5-6-7-8. Add five hours to wintry Eastern Time to get UTC and so forth. Hint: The gap from local time to UTC is bigger during standard time than during Daylight Saving Time.

Some tests try to trick you by asking for your UTC ETA (Estimated Time of Arrival). First figure the time en route and then convert to Zulu (UTC).

Test Question:

How should a VFR flight plan be closed when landing at a tower-controlled airport (inside Class B, C or D airspace)?

a. The tower controller will automatically close the flight plan when the aircraft clears the runway
b. The pilot must close the flight plan with FSS upon landing
c. The tower will relay the instructions to the nearest FSS when the aircraft contacts the tower for a landing clearance

Answer:

b. The pilot must close the flight plan with FSS upon landing. This is not the tower controller's responsibility.

Dead Reckoning begins with a line drawn across the sectional chart from Osceola, the departure airport (Area A), to the destination, Todd Field (Area B).

Place the navigational plotter along the course line with the grommet (hole) over where the course intercepts either a meridian of longitude (ideally) or a parallel of latitude. Read True Course (TC) on the plotter (008 degrees).

Add or subtract the Wind Correction Angle (WCA) found on your E6B flight computer. Subtract 2 degrees easterly variation and you have the Magnetic Heading (MH) to fly. Add or subtract any Compass Deviation, and that's the Compass Heading that will take you to the destination. Assuming the forecast winds are accurate.

Note: Flying direct to the DSM VOR and then from there direct to Todd Field eliminates the math but does add mileage.

Call Des Moines Approach on 135.2 prior to crossing the 10-mile Class C airspace ring.

Choose easy-to-spot check points (1,2,3) for your flight log.

The VFR Checkpoint marked by a flag indicates a place that ATC can identify on its radar scopes. Reference your location from those checkpoints if possible: "...five east of New Virginia."

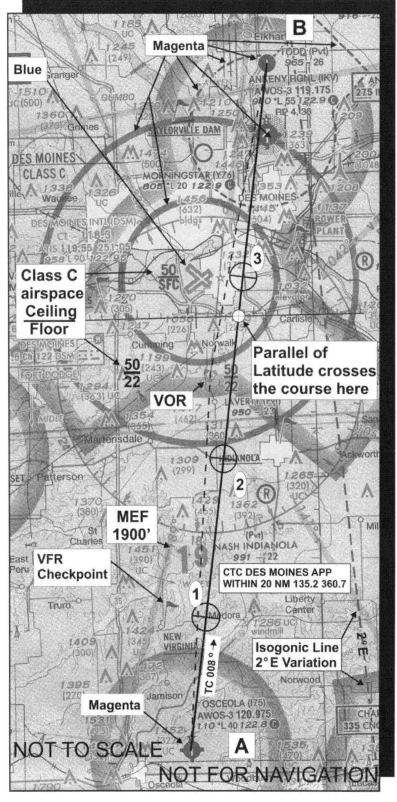

- - - - Dead Reckoning Course
- - - - VOR Routing
⊕ Flight Log Checkpoint

Figure 9-4

VFR Flight Log Osceola to Todd Field

Figure 9-5

CHECKPOINT	COURSE	DISTANCE LEG / TO GO	ETE / ATE	GS Estimated / Actual	FUEL GPH / Gal. Used	RMKS/NAVAIDS
175 (Departure Time) / TIME	010	0 / 43	0	0		Departure Point
1. MEDORA (Time Over Fix)	010	8 / 35	:06	85	10 / 0.6	(Climb speed is slower than cruise; fuel burn is higher)
2. Indianola (Time Over Fix)	010	10 / 25	:06	96	8 / 0.8	Checkpoint is over east-west highway. Class C starts near here.
3. DSM Airport (Time Over Fix)	010	11 / 14	:07	96	8 / 0.9	Abeam DSM
TODD Field (Landing Time)	010	14 / 0	:08	105	7 / 0.9	Descent speed is faster than cruise; fuel burn lower.) CTAF 122.9
TOTALS:			:27		3.2 gallons	

Sample VFR Flight Log (Clip 'n Save)

CHECKPOINT / TIME	COURSE	DISTANCE LEG / TO GO	ETE / ATE	GS Estimated/Actual	FUEL Estimated/Actual	RMKS/NAVAIDS

Open Flight Plan:_____   Close Flight Plan:_____

U.S. DEPARTMENT OF TRANSPORTATION FEDERAL AVIATION ADMINISTRATION FAA Form 7233-1 **FLIGHT PLAN**	(FAA USE ONLY)	☐ PILOT BRIEFING	☐ VNR	TIME STARTED	SPECIALIST INITIALS
		☐ STOPOVER			

1. TYPE		2. AIRCRAFT IDENTIFICATION	3. AIRCRAFT TYPE/ SPECIAL EQUIPMENT	4. TRUE AIRSPEED	5. DEPARTURE POINT	6. DEPARTURE TIME		7. CRUISING ALTITUDE
	VFR					PROPOSED (Z)	ACTUAL (Z)	
	IFR							
	DVFR			KTS				

8. ROUTE OF FLIGHT

9. DESTINATION (Name of airport and city)	10. EST. TIME ENROUTE		11. REMARKS
	HOURS	MINUTES	

12. FUEL ON BOARD		13. ALTERNATE AIRPORTS	14. PILOT'S NAME, ADDRESS & TELEPHONE NUMBER & AIRCRAFT HOME BASE	15. NUMBER ABOARD
HOURS	MINUTES			
			17. DESTINATION CONTACT/TELEPHONE (OPTIONAL)	

16. COLOR OF AIRCRAFT	CIVIL AIRCRAFT PILOTS. FAR Part 91 requires you file an IFR flight plan to operate under instrument flight rules in controlled airspace. Failure to file could result in a civil penalty not to exceed $1,000 for each violation (Section 901 of the Federal Aviation Act of 1958, as amended). Filing of a VFR flight plan is recommended as a good operating practice. See also part 99 for requirements concerning DVFR flight plans.

Chapter 10
Aviation Weather

"Everyone complains about the weather, but nobody does anything about it."
—*Mark Twain*[104]

Well, now's your chance. As a pilot, you can and must control the weather, or at least your relationship to it. This manual is designed for the VFR Private or Sport Pilot. The VFR pilot must, at all times, remain in VFR conditions. One of the deadliest mistakes a non-instrument rated pilot can make is to, as the NTSB accident reports put it: "continue VFR into (IFR) weather conditions."

Let's dispel one aviation myth: An instrument rating is not a license to seek out crappy weather, fly through it and scare the bejiminnies out of the passengers. The instrument rating allows the smart and proficient instrument pilot to navigate safely in less than VFR weather conditions. The object of instrument flight is to get through the low visibility and into the clear. It's not to be taken lightly. The small amount of "hood time" the student pilot receives while becoming a VFR private pilot merely exposes the pilot to poorly simulated instrument flight. It does not make the pilot instrument proficient. Forty, or more, hours of intense instrument training from a qualified instrument instructor (CFII) are needed to approach instrument proficiency. I hope I've made this point clear: Never attempt flight into less than VFR conditions as a VFR pilot.

Enough preaching. Let's examine aviation weather both from the point of what might limit VFR flight and what we can expect even on clear days.

The Atmosphere In Which We Fly

Some of this was mentioned earlier, but it's worth reviewing.

Gas

We fly through the air, which is a gas made up of about 78% nitrogen and 21% oxygen with trace gases making up the remaining 1%. These gases are layered from the earth's surface to

---

[104] Riverboat pilot

the brink of outer space. Of course that high up VFR flight is not recommended (VNR). Let's examine those layers:

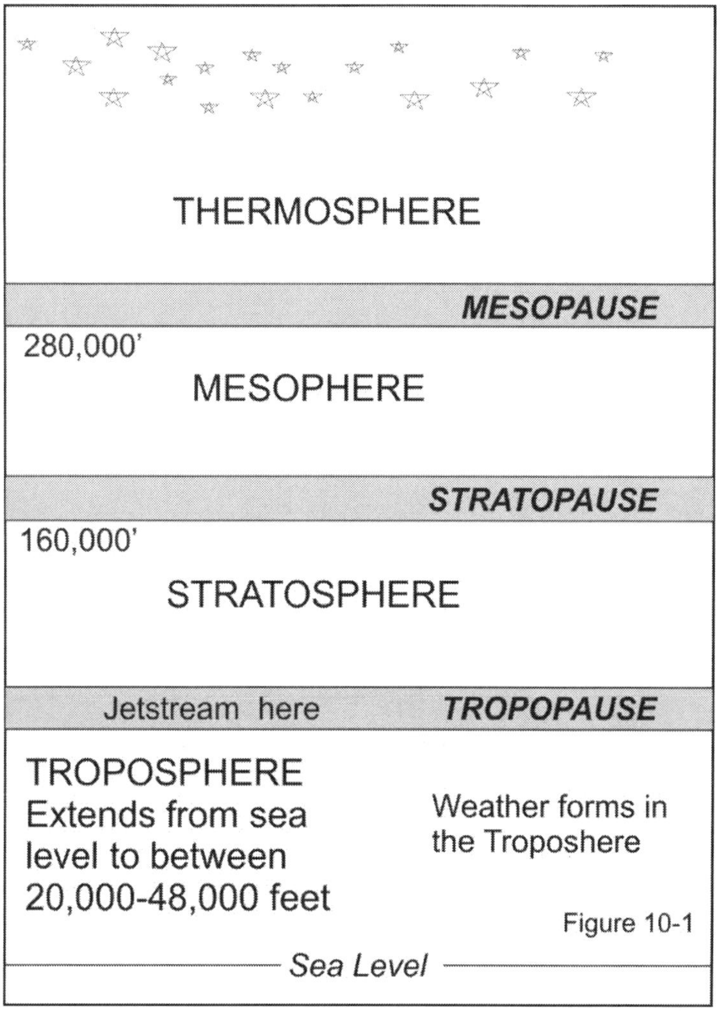

We live, walk, breathe and mow our lawns in the **Troposphere**. It extends from the surface to 48,000 feet over the equator and 20,000 feet over the two poles. Weather forms in the troposphere. All GA VFR flying is in the Troposphere.[105] Pretty crowded gasbag, the Troposphere, no wonder it gets polluted, dropping flight visibility to zero at times.

The troposphere has a notable characteristic: Temperatures decrease at a rate of roughly 2 degrees Celsius (3.5 Fahrenheit) for every 1000 feet of altitude increase. The air pressure decreases at about an inch of mercury per 1000 feet in altitude gain, as well. Go higher, get colder and breathe thinner air (Denver's motto).

Topping the Troposphere is the **Tropopause**. This boundary traps moisture—and weather—in the Troposphere below. The Tropopause changes height with the season and with location. The **Jetstream**—a river of high-speed, high-altitude air—is associated with the Tropopause. While your Cherokee probably won't operate routinely in the Tropopause or ride the 150-knot Jetstream to New Jersey, knowing its location may help with macro weather planning.

THERMOSPHERE

MESOPAUSE

280,000'
MESOPHERE

STRATOPAUSE

160,000'
STRATOSPHERE

Jetstream here **TROPOPAUSE**

TROPOSPHERE
Extends from sea level to between 20,000-48,000 feet

Weather forms in the Troposhere

Figure 10-1

— Sea Level —

Above the Tropopause is the **Stratosphere**, which reaches up to about 160,000 feet above the Earth. Some jets fly in the Stratosphere above the unpleasant weather we piston GA pilots must endure or avoid. Above the Stratosphere is the **Stratopause** and above that is the **Mesophere**, then above that the **Mesopause**, and finally the **Thermosphere** where you get a fairly good view of outer space, because it's right there.

Atmospheric Pressure and Air Flow

---

[105] Yes, many GA aircraft can fly above 20,000 feet but not VFR over the lower 48 states. Class A airspace starts at 18,000 feet.

At sea level the atmosphere squeezes down and around us at 14.7 pounds per square inch. Go higher and the pressure decreases. At sea level the standard pressure (ISA[106]) is **29.92** inches of mercury, meaning sea level air pressure will push a column of mercury 29.92 inches up a tube, also expressed as 1013.2 millibars (1 inch of mercury equals about 34 mbs). Here's what the airplane pilot needs to do with that information: Set your altimeter to whatever ATC or the automated weather observation (AWOS, ASOS, ATIS) gives as an altimeter setting. If Denver tower says, "Altimeter 29.92," then set 29.92 in the Kollsman window. When all pilots use a common pressure surface reference, provided by ATC or other observers, then all aircraft altimeters should work together correctly.

Yes, all other factors being equal, the air at Denver's 5000-foot elevation is less dense than Atlantic City's sea level elevation, but the altimeter settings, issued by ATC or weather observers, will factor in these geographic differences. The pilot simply uses the local altimeter setting. Atmospheric pressure changes with location, so the pilot is expected to update the altimeter setting every 100NM. [107]

It's the Heat

Air is always in motion, either vertically as ascending and descending currents or horizontally as wind. This air motion, called **atmospheric circulation**, changes the weather. The uneven heating of the Earth's surface causes our weather. That's a simple statement but is the bedrock of weather theory. Picture the planet exposed to the Sun. It doesn't shine evenly on all of us. Some parts of the world are hot, some cold. Some have water (most of the planet), and some parts are desert while others are ice-capped (although melting with climate change). Rotating on its tilted axis, some parts of the Earth get more sun exposure than others, those parts are hotter, and the air over those parts rises more than over the cooler regions. Uneven heating sets up

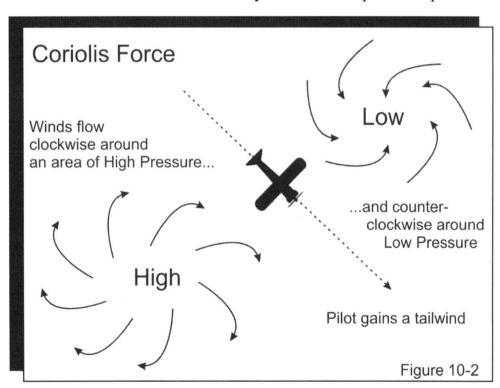

Coriolis Force

Winds flow clockwise around an area of High Pressure...

Low

...and counter-clockwise around Low Pressure

High

Pilot gains a tailwind

Figure 10-2

---

[106] ISA International Standard Atmosphere
[107] FAR 91.121

circulation patterns. The air rises over the warm Equator and sinks over the cold poles. This causes a circulation pattern. A funny thing happens to these patterns, though. They shift due to a phenomenon called Coriolis Force.

Coriolis Force is caused by the Earth's rotation. It deflects air masses (really big) to the right in the Northern Hemisphere, so the air that's cooling over the poles doesn't gush in a straight line toward the Equator. It, instead, follows a curved path. This phenomenon is greatest at the poles, and disappears at the equator.

As these air masses circulate and deflect, the wind closest to the earth's surface (within 2000 feet) is affected by the terrain—mountains, trees and goats. **Friction** slows the wind. Friction changes the way air moves closer to the ground, so that the surface winds will differ in speed and direction from winds aloft.

Air masses will have different densities and different pressures, labeled **High Pressure** or **Low Pressure**. Air moves from areas of high pressure to areas of low pressure. If you look at a weather map and spot the **H** and **L** labels (High and Low) you can visualize air moving from H to L.

Here's an important wind/weather travel tip: In the Northern Hemisphere[108] air flows clockwise around a High and counterclockwise around a Low-pressure area. This is important stuff when planning a cross-country route. You can take advantage of the Highs and Lows to slingshot your flight with higher groundspeeds.

Wait, There's More….

Think heat: As the Sun shines the Earth bakes. Actually, it radiates heat that makes everything walking or flying above it feel like it's baking, particularly in summer. Heat radiates from the surface at different rates depending upon what's down there. Rocks, plowed fields, casino parking lots all radiate much heat. Trees, shrubs, grass and lakes radiate smaller amounts of heat. As a result, these uneven radiation rates cause local circulating **convective currents (thermals)**.

The air is often turbulent in convective currents. This is especially noticeable where the terrain changes dramatically from hard, dry rock to cooler green or water, such as along a shoreline. Picture a beach. Throughout the day, the beach and attached land heats faster than the water. The hot air is less dense and rises over the land. Cool air from the water flows into the less dense area creating a refreshing **sea breeze**. At night the process reverses as the land cools and creates a **land breeze**. Uneven convective currents happen all over the planet. Localized convective currents, such as from the shopping mall built at the end of

---

[108] Yes, this book is northern-centric. When sales pick up in Brazil, I'll translate it into Portuguese and discuss Southern Hemispherical oddities

your runway, can make an otherwise stabilized approach bounce in turbulence. At low altitudes as you pass over pavement or dark plowed fields you'll feel the aircraft balloon upward, only to sink as it crosses the nearby lake or dark vegetation. The pilot needs to read the terrain surrounding the runway and be prepared to add or reduce power in turbulence.

Expect updrafts over the hot rising air from dry land and downdrafts over water. Expect wind shear where the two masses scrape past each other. Flying higher reduces exposure to convective turbulence.

> **Tip:** Climb above cumulus clouds to reach smooth air. Cumulus clouds with extensive vertical development, however, may out-climb anything you're flying, in which case the convective currents are intense and may indicate thunderstorm formation. In *Cherokee v. Thunderstorm* scenarios, Thunderstorm always wins. Avoid them.

Wind Shear

This one gets a lot of publicity particularly when airliners are involved. Here's the FAA definition of Wind Shear: "A sudden, drastic change in wind speed and/or direction over a very small area." All aircraft are exposed to **Low Level Wind Shear.** Many air traffic control towers have LLWAS (Low Level Wind Shear Alert Systems), which *might* alert the pilot to the presence of shifting winds near the surface. Wind shear, of any kind, can toss smaller airplanes around uncomfortably, but properly handled it's not to be feared so much as anticipated and respected. You will encounter wind shear on almost every flight. As a surface wind blows across nearby hangars part of the moving air mass shears off causing turbulent winds near the ground. As a front moves through winds can, and do, quickly shift, causing wind shear. Temperature inversions may hold wind shear. Mountaintops poking into strong upper winds will produce wind shear of particularly strong force. Your instructor will teach you the proper techniques for recognizing and coping with wind shear.

Microburst is another form of wind shear and is generally associated with thunderstorms. Microbursts are usually small in area, covering less than a mile and within 1000 feet vertically. They last about 15 seconds but in that short, evil life can produce downdrafts at a rate of 6000 feet per minute. Horizontal winds of 45 knots or more are possible. They can appear in seconds.

Microbursts may be invisible until they kick up dust, debris or airplanes, so the pilot needs to be aware of their potential existence and recognize telltale signs of flying into one. Here are the clues[109] during inadvertent takeoff or arrival in a microburst[110]:

---

[109] Taken directly from FAA-H-8083-25

[110] Inadvertent, because no smart pilot intentionally departs or lands when microbursts are present.

1. *The airplane experiences a performance-increasing headwind followed by...*
2. *Performance-decreasing downdrafts.*
3. *Then the wind rapidly shears to a tailwind...*
4. *And can result in terrain impact.*

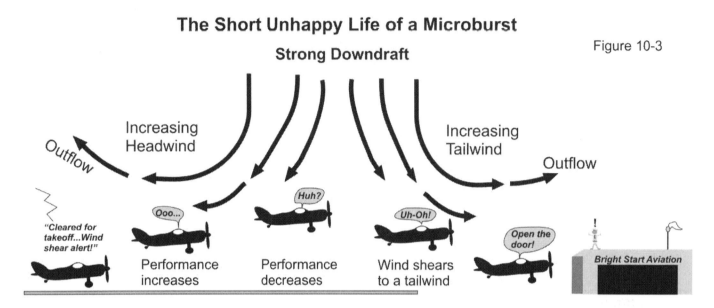

The Short Unhappy Life of a Microburst

Figure 10-3

Mountain Wave

While attending a Denver Broncos game, the crowd—excited by the fact that Denver even has a team—gets to its feet in a wave motion that rolls through the stadium. That's "The Wave." Should the spectators look skyward toward the Rockies they might notice almond-shaped **Lenticular Clouds** in the mountain's leeward sky. These lens-shaped clouds appear to be stationary as winds of 50 knots (or greater) blow through them. Mountain-savvy CFIs and glider pilots can tell you a lot more about avoiding or using these winds. As a new private pilot (or a student about to take the FAA test), you should know that turbulence is a distinct possibility in Mountain Waves when "winds of 40 knots or greater blow across the mountain ridge, and the air is stable."

Test Questions:

1. Convective circulation patterns associated with sea breezes are caused by

a. Warm, dense air moving inland from over the water
b. water absorbing and radiating heat faster than the land
c. cool, dense air moving inland from over the water

2. Thermal development depends upon

a. a counterclockwise circulation of air
b. temperature inversions
c. solar heating

3. Almond-shaped or lens-shaped clouds, which appear stationary, and may contain winds of 50 knots or greater, are referred to as _____ _____ clouds.

a. inactive frontal
b. standing lenticular
c. roll wash

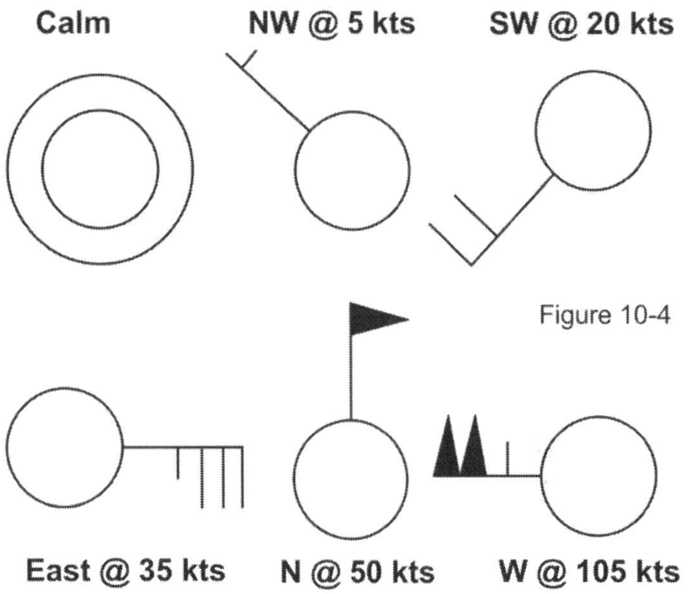

Answers:

1. **c.** cool, dense air moving inland from over the water
2. **c.** solar heating
3. **b.** standing lenticular

Put Wind on the Weather Maps

Wind is depicted on weather maps by a circle indicating the reporting station and an arrow (line) that points in the direction from which the wind is coming. Remember: The line points to where the wind is coming from. Winds are reported by the direction from which they blow. Examples: A southerly wind is from the south, blowing north. A northwest wind blows to the southeast from the northwest.

How wind direction and speed is depicted on surface weather charts. The arrow points into the wind. Each barb (——) indicates 10 knots. Half-barb (—) 5 knots. A flag (▶) 50 knots.

Figure 10-4

Placing barbs on the arrow shows wind speed. Each barb represents 10 knots. Half a barb is 5 knots. A tiny triangle, or flag, represents 50 knots of wind. By tallying up the barbs and pennants the viewer quickly sees the wind speeds.

Pressure is also recorded at reporting stations and expressed in millibars. Lines are drawn between all the stations

Tightly spaced isobars indicate a steep pressure gradient with strong winds.

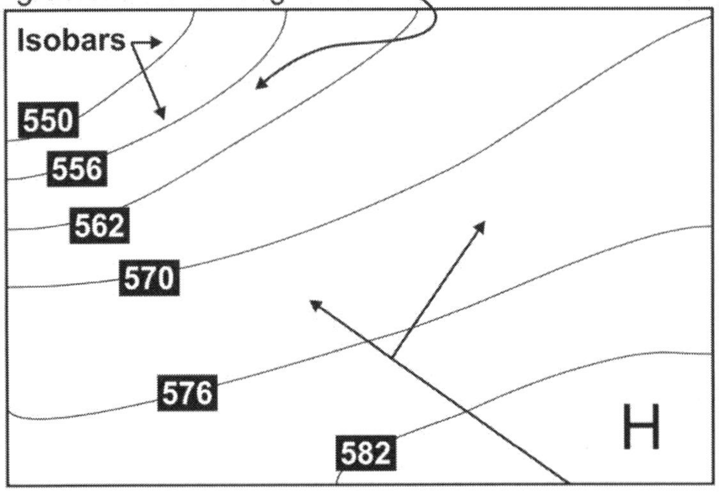

Isobars

550
556
562
570
576
582

H

Isobars spread out indicates a shallow pressure gradient and lighter winds.

Figure 10-5

reporting equal pressure. These lines of equal pressure are called **Isobars**. A casual glance at a surface chart will show many curving Isobars indicating the changing pressure gradients. This gives a visual image of the winds. Isobars that are close together have a steep gradient and indicate strong winds. Isobars spread far apart indicates shallow gradient and lighter winds.

Isobars also show High and Low Pressure areas, plus Ridge, Trough and Cols.

Weather Definitions:
A **High** is an area of high pressure surrounded by lower pressure.
A **Low** is an area of low pressure surrounded by higher pressure.
A **Ridge** is an elongated area of high pressure.
A **Trough (TROF)** is an elongated area of low pressure.
A **Col** is the intersection between a Ridge and a Trough, or an area of neutrality between two Highs and two Lows.

Stability

How well the atmosphere resists vertical motion determines its stability. A stable atmosphere has little vertical movement. Vertical disturbances are dampened before they become excessive. Stable air (generally) means smooth air. Conversely, in an unstable atmosphere vertical movements tend to increase. Turbulence, extensive vertical cloud development, and severe weather, such as thunderstorms, may result. Good visibility is characteristic of unstable air. Stratiform clouds are characteristic of stable air. Also, "moist, stable air flowing upslope can be expected to produce stratus-type clouds."

Air expands and cools as it rises due to decreased air pressure. In descending air the opposite is true. As pressure increases in descending air, temperature increases as it's compressed. These two conditions are called **adiabatic cooling** and **adiabatic heating.**

The rate at which air heats or cools as altitude changes is called the **lapse rate**. As air rises through the atmosphere it cools, *on average*, by 2 degrees C (3.5 F) per 1000 feet.

But…

Moist air is less dense than dry air. The moist air will rise and expand through the dryer air. Moist air tends to cool off more slowly than dry air (retains heat longer). Moist air, therefore, is considered less stable, because it must rise to higher altitudes in order to cool off to the temperature of surrounding dry air. Think of steam from a coffee cup. It's less dense than the dryer surrounding cool air, so it rises until it cools.

Two lapse rates describe this action: The **Dry Adiabatic Lapse Rate** of unsaturated air is 3 degrees C (5.4 F) temperature change for every 1000 feet of altitude change. The **Moist Adiabatic Lapse Rate** is lower and varies between 1.1 degree C to 2.8 degrees C (2 F to 5 F) per 1000 feet. Moist air is slower to lose its heat so climbs higher before cooling to equal the surrounding dry air.

The **Actual Lapse Rate** is a "measurement (that) can be used to determine the stability of the atmosphere."[111] Warm air rises into cooler air. Measuring the rate at which the temperature actually changes measures its stability.

Broadly speaking, dry cool air is stable. It resists vertical movement, so you get relatively smooth flying conditions. When air is warm and moist (tropical), it moves vertically.

Normally, as air rises it expands and cools. As you climb higher, the OAT normally reads lower. An **inversion** exists when temperature increases with altitude. Inversions are usually shallow layers above which the normal lapse rate resumes, and temperatures, again, drop with altitude. The inversion layer acts like a lid holding in pollutants and moisture below. Fog, smog (smoke and fog) and haze can result. Visibility is usually poor within an inversion layer and clearer above it. Cool clear nights can cause Inversions when cooler air near the ground is capped by warmer air aloft. Expect fog. When a warm front rolls over cooler ground, such as snow, fog can easily form within the resultant inversion layer.

Atmospheric moisture appears as liquid, solid or vapor. **Evaporation** changes liquid to vapor. **Sublimation** changes solid to vapor and **condensation** turns vapor back into liquid. In all cases, heat is exchanged. The warmer air becomes, the more moisture it can hold. Humidity is the term used to describe the amount of moisture in an air mass. **Relative humidity** is the amount of moisture in the air compared to the amount of moisture it *could* hold at that temperature. A relative humidity of 50 percent means that the air, at that temperature and pressure, holds half of the moisture it could hold. A 95 percent relative humidity means the air is close to saturation. When you hit 100 percent relative humidity the moisture precipitates out as rain, fog or something else visible. The air can't hold any more moisture at that temperature.

When you listen to the AWOS, ASOS, ATIS or other weather reports you'll hear Temperature and Dew point. Temperature is a heat measurement of the air. **Dew point** is the temperature to which the OAT must be lowered to reach saturation, or the temperature at which fog, rain, frost, snow or some other visible moisture will form, thus screwing up your VFR vacation plans. *Example*: The AWOS reports Temperature 17, Dew point 15. If the temperature drops by 2 more degrees Celsius, fog could form. At sunset this becomes a real issue because the air temperature is likely to drop, so fog, in this case, could be a threat.

---

[111] Oh, does that ever sound like a test question item…

Dew forms when surface temperatures cool to the dew point. Dew is pretty on a biplane's wings when you crawl out of your sleeping bag on a cool, clear summer morning in Blakesburg, Iowa.[112] Frost is like dew that freezes to those wings. It appears harmless but can adversely affect the airfoil's ability to produce lift. Remove all frost from the airplane before flight. All of it. No kidding, all of it.

Fog is a cloud that forms within 50 feet of the earth's surface when the air cools to the dew point. Several ways to classify fog based on how it forms:

- **Upslope fog** forms when moist unstable air is forced up a slope in the mountains.
- **Steam fog** (sea smoke) forms when cold, dry air flows over warm water.
- **Ice fog** forms in cold weather when water vapor slips directly into crystals. Mostly an Arctic (or Minnesota) phenomenon.
- **Radiation fog** forms on cool, clear nights with light winds. Common in low-lying areas, if it only reaches to 20 feet it's called ground fog.
- **Advection fog**, common along California's Monterey Bay, forms when wind (sea breeze) blows warm moist air over cooler bodies, such as the coastline near sunset. Advection fog needs wind.

Clouds—From Both Sides Now

As a non-pilot you viewed clouds mostly from the Earth, marveling, perhaps, at their shapes and movement. Well, keep marveling, only now, you get to poke around them. Once instrument-rated, you'll get to fly through them; truly, some of the most invigorating of human pursuits. As a VFR Private Pilot, though, stay clear of clouds. In fact, in Class E, D or C Airspace remain at least 1000 feet above, 500 feet below and 2000 feet horizontally from clouds. [113] (See how one topic blends with another? That's called ACS stream-of-consciousness.)

A cloud is visible moisture, water vapor in contact with condensation nuclei, such as a dust particle, in cool enough air for the vapor to become visible. Clouds are categorized by Height, Shape and Behavior.

Cloud Types:

Low Clouds: Form at or below 6500 feet AGL. Composed of water droplets mostly, but may include super-cooled water droplets that form aircraft icing. Low clouds include stratus, stratocumulus, nimbostratus and fog. Low clouds are the ones most likely to affect VFR flight. The lower they are, the less likely you'll fly VFR.

---

[112] Home to the Antique Airfield (IA27) and the Antique Airplane Association: www.antiqueairfield.com
[113] See Chapter 7 for FAR review of cloud rules

Middle Clouds: Extending from around 6500 feet to 20,000 feet are composed of water, ice crystals and possible super-cooled water droplets. In the Middle Cloud family are altocumulus and altostratus.

High Clouds: These reach above 20,000 feet and are composed of ice crystals. Types of High Clouds include cirrus, cirrostratus and cirrocumulus.

Clouds With Extensive Vertical Development: We're talking tall, here, folks. These clouds begin in the low to middle cloud range and grow into towering cumulus (TCU) and cumulonimbus (thunderstorms). High moisture content, turbulence, unstable air, shear, ice, tornadoes…not much to like about these monsters in flight. Avoid them.

Here are a few more cloud terms that are good to know:

Cumulus—Heaped or piled clouds
Stratus—Layered clouds
Cirrus—Ringlets. Fibrous clouds. High-level clouds above 20,000 feet
Castellanus—Common base with separate vertical development. Castle-like
Lenticularus—Lens shaped. Formed over mountains in strong winds
Nimbus—Rain clouds
Fracto—Ragged, broken clouds
Alto—Applies to Mid-level clouds

How To Estimate Cloud Bases (neat campfire trick)

Since clouds form when the temperature and dew point meet (0 degrees difference), a pilot can estimate the base of cumulus clouds using this formula:
Rising air in a convective current cools at 5.4 degrees Fahrenheit for every 1000 feet of altitude gain (approximately). The dew point decreases at 1 degree F for every 1000 feet gain. So, the temperature and dew points converge (on average) at 4.4 degrees F per thousand feet. Take the surface temperature/dew point spread as reported on the AWOS or ATIS and divide by 4.4. That gives the bases of the cumulus layer in feet AGL.

Test Question:

1. At approximately what altitude AGL would you expect the base of cumuliform clouds if the surface air temperature is 84 degrees F and the dew point is 40 degrees F?

a. 9000 feet AGL
b. 10,000 feet AGL
c. 11,000 feet AGL

2. At about what altitude MSL would you estimate the base of the cumulus clouds to be if the surface air temperature at 1000 feet MSL is 68 degrees F and the dew point is 46 degrees F?

a. 4000 feet MSL
b. 5000 feet MSL
c. 6000 feet MSL

Answer:

1. **b.** The temperature/dew point spread in this question is 44 degrees (84-40=44). Divide 44 by 4.4 = 10 or 10,000 feet AGL.

2. **c.** Find the temp/dew point spread (68-46=22). Divide 22 by 4.4 = 5 or 5000 feet. But, that's AGL. The airport is at 1000 feet MSL so add the 5000 feet to the airport elevation: 5000 + 1000 = 6000 feet MSL

Clouds as Ceiling and Visibility Restrictions

When looking into a cloud, even fog, visibility is reduced by the thickness of the moisture and associated airborne micro debris. Visibility is measured in statute miles and fractions thereof. For IFR purposes, visibility is also measured as RVR (Runway Visual Range). The VFR pilot may see this term in a briefing, but it applies mainly to instrument operations. Most VFR operations require at least 3 SM visibility, either ground visibility (reported by a ground observer) or flight visibility (reported by the pilot).

The bases of the clouds form the ceiling. By definition the **Ceiling** is "The lowest layer of clouds reported as broken or overcast[114] or the vertical visibility into an obscuration like fog or haze." Clouds classified as "scattered" or "few" would not by themselves constitute a ceiling. An observation may list several layers that by themselves might be only scattered or few but cumulatively block enough sky to constitute a broken or overcast ceiling. In controlled airspace, the VFR pilot needs at least 3 SM visibility and a ceiling of at least 1000 feet. All cloud heights are given in AGL.

A Brief Word About Thunderstorms:

Run away!

---

[114] Broken means between 5/8 and 7/8 of the sky is blocked. Overcast means more than 7/8 is blocked. An overcast can have holes in it.

Okay, don't panic at the sight of towering CUs spitting lightning, hail and frogs but remember this rule-of-thumb for departing in the face of an approaching thunderstorm: "Don't!"

Thunderstorms form in several ways and come in various levels of meanness. In order to form, all thunderstorms need three things: Moisture, unstable air and a lifting action.

Moisture—Lots of it. Thunderstorms, even small ones, can hold vast amounts of rain.

Unstable air—That moisture needs to precipitate out in cold air at high altitudes in order to fall several miles back to earth.

Lifting Action—That moisture needs to be lifted, somehow, into the colder air. Heat, wind forced up a slope or an approaching cold front are some of the means for lifting the moist air aloft.

Squall line: A continuous line of non-frontal or pre-frontal cumulonimbus. These "generally produce the most intense hazard to aircraft."

Thunderstorm Hazards Include: Extreme turbulence, heavy rain, hail, lightning (not a serious threat to in-flight aircraft but nasty when walking across the ramp, and – for test purposes – "is always associated with a thunderstorm"), updrafts and downdrafts exceeding 3000 feet-per-minute and tornadoes.

Thunderstorm Life Cycle:

Cumulus Stage—Mostly vertical development, continuous updrafts dominate and prohibit moisture from falling.
Mature Stage—Precipitation begins to fall, because raindrops and hail are too heavy for the updrafts to hold aloft. This is phase of "greatest intensity." The top of the cumulus cloud spreads out in an anvil shape and the storm begins the…
Dissipating Stage—Downdrafts dominate and the storm spreads out expending the last of its energy.

Test Questions:

1. If thunderstorms are reported near your destination airport, which hazardous atmospheric phenomenon might be expected on the landing approach?

a. Precipitation static
b. Wind shear turbulence
c. Steady rain

2. A non-frontal, narrow band of active thunderstorms that often develops ahead of a cold front is called a

a. pre-frontal system
b. squall line
c. dry line

3. What ingredients are needed for thunderstorms to form?

a. High humidity, lifting force, and unstable conditions
b. High humidity, high temperature, and cumulus clouds
c. Lifting force, moist air, and extensive cloud coverage

Answers

1. **b.** Wind shear turbulence. There are other hazards, such as hail, lightning and heavy rain, but those weren't options. Precipitation static, also known as "St. Elmo's Fire", creates static on the radios is not a real problem. Steady rain is not expected in thunderstorms, which produce rain showers.

2. **b.** squall line

3. **a.** High humidity, lifting force, and unstable conditions

Icing

As a VFR Private or Sport Pilot you must remain clear of clouds. This should keep you legal and free of most structural icing conditions. Except for deploying flaps or landing gear, the airplane is not designed to change shape in flight. The airfoil needs to retain its curves to produce lift. Other control surfaces need their original shapes as well. When an airplane becomes "iced up" the airfoil, propeller, empennage—everything changes shape and the airplane loses efficiency. It'll weigh more, too. The result is a decreased performance, possibly to the extent that the airplane no longer flies. So—avoid icing conditions. How do you avoid icing? By knowing something about it.

In order to get structural icing, the airplane must fly through visible moisture. This can be rain or smaller cloud droplets. The airframe structure's temperature must be below freezing (0 degrees C).

Freezing Rain often creates an environment that causes the highest rate of structural ice accumulation.

Nice To Know Info:
Ice Types: Ice is reported as Rime, Clear or Mixed.
Rime is opaque like the ice inside your college dorm freezer, the one you never cleaned during freshman year....
Clear is smooth and, well, clear.
Mixed ice isn't reserved for mixed drinks, but, instead, is a blend of Clear and Rime ice.

Test Question:

You encounter ice pellets at the surface, this is a hint that there

a. are thunderstorms in the area
b. has been cold front passage
c. is a temperature inversion with freezing rain at a higher altitude

Answer:

c. (there) is a temperature inversion with freezing rain at a higher altitude

Fronts

An **air mass** is a "widespread mass of air having similar characteristics (e.g. temperature), which usually helps to identify the source region of the air." **Fronts** are distinct boundaries between air masses, which takes on the characteristics of the surrounding area. So, a Continental Polar (cP) air mass is cold and dry, while a Maritime Tropical (mT) air mass is humid and warm. These air masses have different densities. Now, move that air mass like some marauding army. Where one air mass meets another is called a front. A change in weather occurs. Wind shifts and temperature changes are indicative of frontal passage. There are four types of fronts the Private Pilot should know:

1. Warm
2. Cold
3. Stationary
4. Occluded

Warm Fronts exist where warm air moves to replace a colder air mass. Warm fronts tend to move slowly (10-20 knots). A warm front's leading edge slides over the top of a cold air mass and gradually nudges it out of the way. Warm air holds more moisture than cold air, so warm fronts are usually humid. What happens as that warm humid air slides

Warm Front

A warm front is an advancing warm air mass replacing colder air. It's depicted on charts with this symbol, either in black or red.

over the cold air and rises? It cools, water condenses and falls as rain, snow or something else that thoroughly ruins a good VFR flight plan. Remember that. Warm fronts are slow, stupid, humid creatures that reduce visibility, although the ride might be smooth. Clouds are generally stratiform (flat, layered), and fog is a real possibility. In summer, cumulonimbus are commonly found along the warm front's leading edge where the two air masses collide. Barometric pressure falls with an approaching warm front. On weather charts warm fronts are depicted by a line with red (possibly black), round bumpers.

Cold Fronts move faster than warm fronts (25-30 knots but can top 55 knots). Cold, dense, stable air bulldozes under the stagnant warm, humid air shoving it aloft. What happens when warm, humid air is forced up (lifted) rapidly in to colder air? Cooling, water condenses and rain falls. Cumulus clouds are common in cold fronts. Visibility is usually good in a cold front. Turbulence is likely.

> **Cold Front**
>
> A cold front is an advancing cold air mass replacing warmer air. It's depicted on charts with this symbol in either black or blue.

Fast-moving cold fronts may produce squall lines as far as 200 miles ahead of a cold front. The fast-moving cold front can include rapidly formed, extremely violent thunderstorms, followed by clear skies with gusty winds, colder temperatures and turbulence.

Stationary Front is a stalemate. Think the Western Front across France 1916 with two forces blocking each other. When cold and warm fronts of equal strength meet, they stall. Weather along the stationary front is a mixed bag of cold and warm front characteristics.

> **Stationary Front**
>
> The boundary between air masses of relatively equal force is a stationary front and is depicted on charts with blue and red or black.

Occluded Fronts are identifiable when a fast-moving cold front hits or catches up with a slower moving warm front, like the hare overtaking the turtle in the same race. The warm front characteristics prevail until the colder weather intrudes.

Occluded fronts are subdivided into **cold front occlusion** and **warm front occlusion**. In a *cold front occlusion*, the fast-moving cold front is colder than the air ahead of the warm front it's overtaking. The result is a mixture of cold and warm front conditions. Nastier, is the *warm front occlusion* in which the rapidly approaching cold front is warmer than the air ahead of the warm front it's overtaking. Weather is often severe. Embedded thunderstorms, rain and fog are possible in warm front occlusions.

> **Occluded Front**
>
> Where a fast-moving cold front catches a slower warm front an occluded front occurs. It's depicted on charts black or purple.

Test Questions:

1. What do we call the boundary between two different air masses?

a.   frontolysis
b.   frontogenesis
c.   front

2. What weather phenomenon will always occur when flying across a front?

a.   A change in the wind direction
b.   A change in the type of precipitation
c.   A change in the stability of the air mass

3. One of the most easily recognized discontinuities across a front is

a.   a change in temperature
b.   an increase in cloud coverage
c.   an increase in relative humidity

Answers:

1. **c.** front. This is the transition zone or boundary between two air masses of different density

2. **a.** A change in the wind direction. The front is the boundary between two air masses of different density and air pressure. Air flows from High to Low pressure areas. As a front passes, air pressure changes (altimeter settings must change) and air flows as wind from a different direction.

3. **a.** a change in temperature. When a cold front replaces warmer air, the OAT drops. Warm front replaces cold air the OAT rises. You've probably crossed a front.

Get a Briefing Before You Fly

It can't be overemphasized how important it is to get a preflight briefing before any flight. The weather may be fine, but a briefing will alert you to navaid outages or hazards en route, such as airspace closures or volcanic eruptions. Of course, the latter you might notice on your own. Still, get a briefing before flying. Flight Service can brief over the phone (1-800-WXBRIEF; also 1800WXBRIEF.com) or over a radio frequency found on your sectional chart. DUATS is another good way to brief online.

Briefings come in three flavors: Standard, Abbreviated and Outlook. If you can't remember which you need, the AFSS briefer will probably give a standard briefing, which gives the most information. Standard briefings follow a set format.

The **Standard Briefing** sequence is:

1. *Adverse Conditions* to include thunderstorms and airport closures. Your flight planning might end at step #1.

2. *VFRNR or VFR Not Recommended.* Also known as *VNR*. It may seem as though FSS briefers begin most VFR standard briefing with that statement, but it's there to warn the VFR-only pilot that conditions may be less than VFR. This could be a real trip-stopper, still, the PIC decides the go/no-go. Some wag once suggested that AFSS change its toll-free number to: 1-800VFRNR. Wasn't me.

3. *Synopsis.* This is the overview or the big weather picture listing fronts and major weather systems affecting the wide area around your operation.

4. *Current Conditions.* What's happening now (or recently). If your departure time is more than two hours away, the briefer skips this part.

5. *En Route Forecast.* A summary of forecast weather en route.

6. *Destination Forecast.* The summary forecast for your destination at your ETA.

7. *Winds and Temperatures Aloft.* Usually, you'll receive only the winds aloft unless you request the temperatures.

8. *NOTAMs.* Notice to Airmen (and women). Tricky thing, NOTAMs, once they're published in a paper edition called the *Notice To Airman Publication* (*NTAP*[115]), to which few pilots subscribe, they're dropped from the briefer's list. Published NOTAMs are available on request. It's a faulty system at best.

9. *ATC Delays.* Mostly an IFR issue. However, if you're planning to fly to a popular destination such as Oshkosh, Wisconsin during the EAA blowout, you'll need to be aware of ATC delays, reservation and flow procedures.

10. *Other Information.* Like a Remarks section. The briefer might give you the frequency on which to open your VFR flight plan at this point.

---

[115] NTAP contains all currant NOTAMs and is published ever 28 days (Hint: possible test question)

Abbreviated Briefing

What it sounds like. You called earlier for a standard briefing, but the weather was marginal, so you have breakfast and call again, hoping, as all pilots do, that eating improves the weather. No need for a full Standard Briefing, so request an "Abbreviated Briefing." You'll get updated weather. Then, go have lunch and wait for the weather to improve.

Outlook Briefing

Excited about the big trip tomorrow? Can't sleep? Who ya gonna call? Flight Service! (Mentally insert *Ghostbusters* music here.) If your departure time is **more than 6 hours** in the future, you can call for an Outlook Briefing to begin formulating your plans. When the time comes to preplan and eventually depart, call for a standard briefing.

Test Questions:

1. What should pilots state initially when telephoning a weather briefing facility for preflight weather information?

a. Tell the number of occupants on board
b. State their total flight time
c. Identify themselves as pilots

2. What should pilots state initially when telephoning a weather briefing facility for preflight weather information? (Yup, it's the same as the above question but the FAA has two versions that are worded exactly with different answers, plus more questions about briefings with slightly different wording.)

a. The intended route of flight radio frequencies
b. The intended route of flight and destination
c. The address of the pilot in command

Answers:

1. **c.** Identify themselves as pilots
2. **b.** The intended route of flight and destination

Weather Charts, Forecasts and Observations

Decoding NWS (National Weather Service) weather symbology and chartology has driven more students away from aviation than Homeland Security and the high cost of avgas. And it need not be that way. Understanding weather is crucial to being a safe pilot. You won't learn everything about aviation weather from this chapter, which is meant as an introduction to weather.

Meteorologists with the NWS and other agencies do a marvelous job at tracking, analyzing and, to some extent, forecasting the weather. They provide the data and some analysis. The pilot must take all that and form the go/no-go decision. Most pilots nowadays get their weather from *The Weather Channel* and free apps. Good sources, those. Airline pilots knotting their ties in the hotel room before catching the morning crew bus will keep one ear cocked toward the TV set. Once at the airport, the airline crew checks into a briefing room to get a more detailed weather briefing, usually via computer. These professional pilots go through the same process that you, the Private (or Sport) Pilot, will follow. You may not have a crew briefer, but you have Flight Service at 1-800-WXBRIEF and 1800WXBRIEF.com. And you have DUATS.com (Direct User Access Terminal Service), a free computer service similar to what the airlines use. There's no excuse not to have the latest weather. And, unlike an airline pilot, you don't have wear a tie to get it.

Graphics on the FAA written exam may not match what you'll encounter with modern weather services, but they all follow common rules. A basic understanding of weather lingo and symbology forms a solid foundation to whatever weather service you later use.

> Hint: Memorizing the actual test questions and answers gets you through the written exam.[116]

Observations

Three weather observation types:
1. Surface
2. Upper Air
3. Radar

Surface Observation: Every flying day you'll use the **Aviation Routine Weather Report** called **METAR**.[117] Surface METARs report local weather. This is a METAR example:
METAR KMCW 171545Z AUTO 15021G26 3/4SM +TSRA BR BKN008 OVC012CB 18/17 A2970 RMK PRESFR

Huh?

---

[116] The FAA's written Knowledge Exam is undergoing much-needed rewrites and, it's hoped, many of the old, useless questions will vanish.

[117] Many weather terms, such as METAR, are French in origin and have no logical mnemonic link to English...or Portuguese. Sorry.

Don't worry, either the Flight Service agent reads you the weather in relatively plain English, or on DUATS you can select Plain Language translations. In short, you can go your entire Private Pilot flying life without ever knowing how to decode a raw METAR. That is, of course, after you pass the FAA written. (Keeps coming back to that rascal, doesn't it?) And should you travel outside the English-only USA you may need to decipher METARs yourself.

Intensity or Proximity	Descriptor	Precipitation	Obscuration	Misc.
- Light Moderate (no qualifier) + Heavy VC in the vicinity Figure 10-6	MI Shallow BC Patches DR Low Drifting BL Blowing SH Showers FZ Freezing PR Partial TS Thunderstorm	DZ Precipitation RA Rain SN Snow SG Snow grains IC Ice crystals (diamond dust) PL Ice Pellets GR Hail GS Small hail or snow pellets UP Unknown precipitation (automated station such as AWOS only)	BR Mist FG Fog FU Smoke DU Dust SA Sand PY Spray VA Volcanic ash HZ Haze	SQ Squalls PO Dust/ sand whirls FC Funnel cloud +FC Tornado or waterspout DS Dust storm

METAR weather is described using the above codes in order from left to right. For example: +SHRA means (starting from the left column): heavy rain showers.

Let's pick this METAR apart:
METAR KMCW 171545Z AUTO 15021G26 3/4SM +TSRA BR BKN008 OVC012CB 18/17 A2970 RMK PRESFR

Type of Report: <u>METAR</u> KMCW …. You'll find two types of METAR. One is the routine "METAR," which the above report is. The other is a SPECI or special report. METAR is reported hourly and SPECI is issued whenever the weather changes radically enough to warrant a special report.

Station Identifier: METAR <u>KMCW</u> … Each reporting station (worldwide) has an ICAO[118] four-letter code. KMCW is for Mason City, Iowa. Stations in the Lower 48 states begin with "K".

Date and Time of the Report: METAR KMCW <u>171545Z</u> … This six-digit code gives date and time. This is for the 17th day of the month at 1545Z. All times are UTC or Zulu so this report was issued at 1545 Universal Coordinated Time (Zulu or Greenwich Mean Time).

---

[118] ICAO International Civil Aviation Organization

Modifier: METAR KMCW 171545Z <u>AUTO</u> … AUTO doesn't mean that the observer noted the rain while driving an automobile to the airport. Instead, AUTO means that the observer isn't human. It's an *auto*mated observation station such as ASOS.

Wind: METAR KMCW 171545Z AUTO <u>15021G26</u> … Five-digit code, so this wind is coming from 150 degrees (True) at 21 knots Gusting to 26 knots (G26) or Peak Gust 26 knots. If winds are greater than 99 knots (hang onto your hat and bar the hangar door, Katie!), the wind will be given in six digits. Variable winds are reported as VRB. If the wind's direction varies by more than 60 degrees, and the speed is more than 6 knots a separate group of numbers separated by the letter "V" will note the extreme wind directions.

Visibility: METAR KMCW 171545Z AUTO 15021G26 <u>3/4SM</u> … Visibility is in Statute Miles (SM) and, as in this case, fractions of miles (3/4-mile). If RVR[119] is reported, it will look like this: R15L/1400FT, meaning Runway 15 Left visual range 1400 feet.

Weather: METAR KMCW 171545Z AUTO 15021G26 3/SM <u>+TSRA BR</u> …. Weather is subdivided into two groups—Qualifiers and Weather Phenomenon. Qualifiers include the intensity of whatever is present: Heavy (+), Light (-) or Moderate ( ).
TS is a descriptor for Thunderstorm.
RA is the Weather Phenomenon, in this case Rain.
BR is also a Weather Phenomenon, but it is an obscuration (limits visibility). BR means "Mist."
(See Figure 10-6 for the complete METAR Descriptor and Weather Phenomenon list)

Sky Condition: METAR KMCW 171545Z AUTO 15021G26 3/SM +TSRA BR <u>BKN008 OVC012CB</u> … BKN means Broken and OVC means Overcast. 008 means 800 feet, the base of the first layer (BKN). The overcast layer (OVC) begins at 1200 feet AGL (012). CB means Cumulonimbus.

Temperature and Dew Point: METAR KMCW 171545Z AUTO 15021G26 3/SM +TSRA BR BKN008 OVC012CB <u>18/17</u> … Always in Celsius, the left side is temperature 18, the right dew point 17. That's close together, so fog might be coming. The letter "M" would indicate temperatures below 0 degrees C.

Altimeter Setting: METAR KMCW 171545Z AUTO 15021G26 3/SM +TSRA BR BKN008 OVC012CB 18/17 <u>A2970</u> … Think "A for Altimeter" and then read the four digits, 2970 is 29.70 inches.

---

[119] RVR: Runway Visual Range, an IFR thing

Remarks: METAR KMCW 171545Z AUTO 15021G26 3/SM +TSRA BR BKN008 OVC012CB 18/17 A2970 <u>RMK PRESFR</u> RMK means "Remarks" and PRESFR means "Pressure is falling rapidly."

All in all, a thoroughly yucky day to fly, but that's the METAR format.

The Other Two Observation Types:

Upper Air Observation: Two methods to observe the upper atmosphere: Pilot Reports (PIREPs) and Radiosonde.
Pilot Reports are reports from, well, pilots about what they see aloft.
Radiosonde is usually a weather-measuring instrument that's carried aloft by weather balloons.

Radar Observations: There are three types of ground-based radar used to observe weather:

1. **NEXRAD** (Next Generation Weather Radar) aka "Doppler Radar," popular with TV weather personalities who like to say, "Doppler."
2. **TDWR** or Terminal Doppler Weather Radar, which is installed at major airports and warns of impending severe weather including wind shear, gust fronts and heavy precipitation.
3. **ASR** Airport Surveillance Radar. Primarily used by ATC for air traffic separation and sequencing, ASR can see precipitation and help with weather avoidance.

Pilot Reports

Pilots love to talk to other pilots about their flight, and Flight Service, NWS and ATC would love to get in on the gabfest. So, when you encounter good, bad or indifferent weather en route call FSS and give a Pilot Report (**PIREP**). As with everything in aviation weather, there's a specific format and list of official abbreviations, some of which you'll need to know for the written test. Again, all are translated into English when using DUATS or speaking with a briefer.
Here's a typical coded PIREP as it would appear tagged to a METAR:

UA/OV KOKC-KTUL/TM 1800/FL120/TP BE90//SK BKN018-TOP055/OVC072-TOP089/CLR ABV/TA M7/WV/080021/TB LGT 055-072/IC LGT-MOD RIME 072-089
Figure 10-7

Now dissect it.

"PIREP (UA) Over (OV) the route between Oklahoma City (KOKC) and Tulsa (KTUL) at 1800Z (TM) at 12,000 feet MSL (FL), the pilot of a BE90 (TP for type of aircraft) reports that the sky's (SK) cloud base was Broken (BKN018) at 1800 feet MSL with cloud Tops at 5500 feet MSL (TOP055), and the next cloud layer base formed the overcast (OVC072) at 7200 feet MSL, and its tops were at 8900 (TOP089) feet MSL, and it was clear above that (CLR ABV). The Air Temperature (TA) was Minus 7 Celsius (M7). The Winds (WV doesn't mean over West Virginia; it means Wind) were from 080 degrees (Magnetic) at 21 knots (080021). Turbulence (TB) was light (LGT) between 5500 feet MSL and 7200 (055-072) feet MSL. Icing (IC) was light to moderate (LGT-MOD) rime (RIME) from 7200 feet to 8900 feet MSL (072-089).

Now, using the above PIREP, answer these questions from the FAA's exam:

1. If the terrain elevation is 1295 feet MSL, what is the height above ground level of the base of the ceiling?
2. The reported base and tops of the overcast layer reported are?
3. The reported wind and temperature at 12,000 feet MSL are?
4. The intensity of the turbulence reported at a specific altitude is?
5. The reported intensity and type of icing is?

Answers:

1. 505 feet AGL. The reported base of the BKN layer is 1800 feet MSL BKN018). Subtract 1295 terrain elevation and you get 505 feet AGL.
2. 7200 feet MSL and 8900 feet MSL. Find OVC072-TOP089. 072 is the MSL base of the overcast (7200) and 089 is 8900 feet MSL, the Tops of that overcast.
3. 080 degrees @ 21 knots and –7 degrees Celsius. Find TA Temperature Aloft—M7 means –7 degrees C. 080021 means winds from 080 degrees @ 21 knots.
4. Light from 5500 feet to 7200 feet. TB means Turbulence. It was Light (LGT) from 055 (5500 feet) to 072 (7200 feet)
5. Light to Moderate RIME. LGT-MOD is easy to decipher and RIME means Rime.

PIREPS are fairly easy to interpret and are important to ATC and to forecasters, so don't be bashful giving a PIREP. And don't sweat the format, speak in plain English and FSS will encode it appropriately.

The Future in Aviation Forecasts

All of the previously discussed weather data observed by pilots, robots, NWS employees, balloons, radar, satellites, augurs—in short, anyone observing the weather—goes into creating a forecast, possibly the toughest and most thankless job in aviation. The Private Pilot should know about three types of forecasts: Terminal Aerodrome Forecast (TAF),

Aviation Area Forecast (FA) and Winds Aloft Forecast (FD), plus two in-flight weather advisories: SIGMET and AIRMET.

TAF

A Standard Briefing should include a TAF, if the airport has one. Most don't. Usually only the larger airports get a TAF, so you'll need to find a TAF near your route and apply it with some caution and educated interpolation.

The **TAF** (Terminal Aerodrome Forecast) covers a 5 statute-mile radius around the airport. It's usually valid for a 24-hour period, and a new one is issued four times daily at 0000Z, 0600Z, 1200Z and 1800Z.

TAF gives this information in this order:

Type of Report: The TAF can be routine (TAF) or an amended TAF (TAF AMD).

Station Identifier: The ICAO airport abbreviation, such as KOKC (Oklahoma City).

Date and Time of Origin: Given in six digits. Example: 051130Z means the 5th day of the month at 1130Z.

Valid Period Date and Time: Again, a six-digit number, such as 051212. First two digits are the day (the 5th), and next two digits are the beginning time (1200Z) followed by the ending time (1200Z).

Forecast Wind: Example 14008KT. Five digits, unless winds will top 99 knots, in which case a third digit is added. This wind is from 140 degrees (referenced to True North[120]) at 8 knots.

Forecast Visibility: Example 5SM means 5 Statue Miles. May be in fractions. When visibility is forecast to be greater than 6 miles, the code is P6SM (think of it as *Plus 6 Statute Miles*).

Forecast Significant Weather: Example, BR. This means Mist (Don't ask how they get BR from Mist). No Significant Weather is forecast as NSW.

Forecast Sky Condition: Example, BKN030 forecasts a broken ceiling at 3000 feet AGL.

Forecast Change Group: Example, TEMPO 1316 1 1/2SM BR indicates fluctuating weather anticipated between 1300Z and 1600Z with visibility temporarily 1 ½ Statute Miles

---

[120] TAF forecast winds are referenced to True North while broadcast surface winds are referenced to Magnetic North. METAR observed winds are referenced to True North.

in Mist (BR). Similarly FM means a change is forecast to begin at a certain time. FM 1600 18010KT means From, or beginning at 1600Z winds will be 180 degrees at 10 knots. FM is associated with rapid and significant forecast changes. Gradual forecast changes are noted with BECMG as in "Becoming..." Example: BECMG 2224 20013G20KT means Becoming between 2200Z and 2400Z winds from 200 degrees at 13 knots Gusting to 20 knots.

Probability Forecast: Excluding the first 6 hours of a 24-hour forecast, the Probability Forecast is the percentage likelihood of thunderstorms and precipitation occurring in the coming hours.

Test Questions:

Refer to this TAF (Figure 10-8):

KDSM   Figure 10-8
121720Z 121818 20012KT 5SM HZ BKN030 PROB40 2022 1 SM TSRA OVC008CB
FM2200 33015G20KT 6PSM BKN015 OVC025 PROB40 2202 3SM SHRA
FM 0200 35012KT OVC008 PROB40 0205 2SM –RASN BECMG 0608 02008KT
BKN012
 BECMG 1012 00000KT 3SM BR SKC TEMP 1214 1/2SM FG FM1600 VRB06KT P6SM
SKC

---

1. In the TAF for KDSM, what does "SHRA" mean?

2. What is the valid period for the TAF for KDSM?

3. Between 1000Z and 1200Z the visibility at KDSM is forecast to be?

4. What is the forecast wind for KDSM from 1600Z until the end of the forecast?

5. The only cloud type forecast in a TAF is?

Answers:

1. **Rain showers.** SH (showers) is the descriptor. RA is rain.

2. **1800Z to 1800Z.** First line in the TAF reads: "121720Z <u>121818</u> 20012KT..." The first number cluster, "121720Z" is the six-digit issuance date/time—the 12th at 1720Z. The

next six-digit cluster is the valid day and times: Valid on day 12 from 1800Z to day 13 (implied) 1800Z, a 24-hour period.[121]

3. **3 Statute Miles.** Near the bottom: BECMG 1012 00000KT 3SM BR... means: "Becoming between 1000Z and 1200Z wind calm, visibility 3 Statute Miles (3SM) in Mist..."

4. **Variable in direction at 6 knots.** Last line: FM1600 VRB06KT P6SM SKC Means: From 1600Z wind Variable at 6 knots, visibility greater than 6 Statute Miles, Sky Clear.

5. **Cumulonimbus.** Thunderstorm type clouds (cumulonimbus) are the only cloud types included in a TAF. Example: OVC008<u>CB</u>

Area Forecasts

Think big.
Iowa big?
Bigger.
Montana big?
Even bigger.

Area Forecasts (FA) cover large areas comprised of several states, and I don't mean adorable New England states, either. Montana, Idaho, Utah, Wyoming, Colorado, Nevada, Arizona and New Mexico constitute an area. The Lower 48 is divided into six such areas, each designated for a city within the area: San Francisco (SFO), Salt Lake City (SLC), Chicago (CHI), Dallas/Fort Worth (DFW), Miami (MIA) and Boston (BOS).

This is literally the big picture in aviation forecasting general weather conditions, clouds and VMC (Visual Meteorological Conditions). Since FAs make forecasts for smaller areas within the larger picture, they are used to interpolate what the weather might be like for an airport not served by a TAF.

<u>Test Question:</u>

From which primary source should information be obtained regarding expected weather at the estimated time of arrival (ETA) if your destination has no TAF?

a. Low-Level Prognostic Chart
b. Weather depiction Chart
c. Area Forecast

---

[121] TAF valid times are in the process of changing to 36 hours

The answer is **c.** Area Forecast. Not every airport has a Terminal Forecast (TAF), so the pilot uses the Area Forecast (FA).

FAs are issued three times daily and are valid for 18 hours.

An Area Forecast is disseminated in four sections: Header, Precautionary Statements, Synopsis, VFR Clouds and Weather.

Header:
The Header has the location identifier, issuance date and time, the valid forecast time plus the coverage area. (See Example 10-9 below.)

FA **Header** Example:[122]

DFWC FA 120945	Figure 10-9
SYNOPSIS AND VFR CLDS/WX	
SYNOPSIS VALID UNTIL 130400	
CLDS/WX VALID UNTIL 122200...OTLK VALID	
122200-130400	
OK TX AR LA MS AL AND CSTL WTRS	

This FA Header (above) was issued by Dallas/Fort Worth for the Oklahoma, Texas, Louisiana, Mississippi and Alabama plus portions of the Gulf Coastal Waters. The FA was issued on the 12th day of the month at 0945. The Synopsis is valid from issuance time until 0400 on the 13th. Clouds (VFR) and weather info is valid until 2200 on the 12th and the Outlook (OTLK) stretches until 0400 on the 13th.

Precautionary Statement:
What it sounds like—a warning. In the example below, the FA warns, in AIRMET SIERRA, of IFR conditions and Mountain Obscurations.

FA **Precautionary Statement** Example (See Figure 10-10): [123]

SEE AIRMET SIERRA FOR IFR CONDS AND MTN OBSCN.   Figure 10-10
TS IMPLY SEV OR GTR TURB SEV ICE LLWS AND IFR CONDS.
NON MSL HGTS DENOTED BY AGL OR CIG.

---

[122] FAA-H-8083-25 ch. 11
[123] FAA-H-8083-25 ch 11

TS means there's a possibility of thunderstorms, which, as the code continues, implies severe or greater turbulence, severe icing, low level wind shear and, again, IFR conditions.

The bottom line explains that any height that's not MSL is AGL.

Synopsis:
This is the big picture (Figure 10-11).

FA **Synopsis** Example:[124]

SYNOPSIS...LOW PRES TROF 10Z OK/TX PNHDL AREA FCST MOV EWD INTO CNTRL-SWRN OK BY 04Z. WRMFNT 10Z CNTRL OK-SRN AR-NRN MS FCST LIFT NWD INTO NERN OK-NRN AR EXTRM NRN MS BY 04Z.	Figure 10-11

At 1000Z a low-pressure trough (TROF) stretches across the Oklahoma and Texas Panhandle. It's forecast to move East into Central and Southwestern Oklahoma by 0400Z. AT 1000Z a Warm Front (WRMFNT) over Central Oklahoma, Southern Arkansas and Northern Mississippi will lift (LFT) into Northeastern Oklahoma and Northern Arkansas and Extreme (EXTRM) Northern Mississippi by 0400Z.

VFR Clouds and Weather:
The stuff VFR pilots want to know. Just how skuzzy will it be?

FA **VFR Clouds and Weather** Example (Figure 10-12):

S CNTRL AND SERN TX AGL SCT-BKN010. TOPS 030. VIS 3-5SM BR. 14-16Z BECMG AGL SCT030. 19Z AGL SCT050. OTLK...VFR OK PNDLAND NW...AGL SCT030 SCT-BKN100. TOPS FL200. 15Z AGL SCT040 SCT100. AFT 20Z SCT TSRA DVLPG..FEW POSS SEV. CB TOPS FL450. OTLK...VFR	Figure 10-12

Not great but not too bad and getting better. (See Figure 10-12.) In South central and Southeastern Texas clouds will be Scattered to Broken at 1000 feet AGL with 3 to 5 miles

---

[124] ibid

visibility in Mist (BR). That's skinny VFR. But between 1400Z and 1600Z things improve as clouds turn to Scattered at 3000 feet AGL (14-16Z BECMG AGL SCT030). At 1900Z the scattered layer (not a ceiling) raises to 5000 feet AGL and the outlook beyond that is for VFR.

In the Oklahoma Panhandle and Northwestern Oklahoma (PNDLAND NW), however, cloud heights may rise but notice the cloud Tops: TOPS FL200. A distinct sign that cumulous clouds will build. Sure enough after 2000Z (AFT 20Z) TSRA develops, meaning Thunderstorms (and) Rain. A few of these may be severe. CB (Cumulonimbus) Tops will be around 45,000 feet MSL (FL450).

The Outlook, despite all this convective horror, is for VFR conditions (OTLK...VFR). Note: VFR means decent ceilings and visibility, not necessarily a smooth ride.

In-Flight Weather Advisories

In-flight is a bit of a misnomer, because although these forecasts are designed to aid pilots en route, any pilot can access them for preflight planning. In-flight Advisories include: AIRMET, SIGMET and CONVECTIVE SIGMET.

AIRMETs (WA) are issued every 6 hours. Updates are issued as needed. While AIRMET information is considered of operational importance to all aircraft, it is of particular interest to pilots of smaller aircraft or aircraft of "limited operational capabilities."

AIRMETs contain forecasts of moderate icing, moderate turbulence, sustained winds of 30 knots or greater, widespread areas of ceilings less than 1000 feet and/or visibility less than 3 SM, and extensive mountain obscurement.

AIRMET Bulletins are coded with an S, T or Z to indicate a particular weather hazard.

AIRMET S (Sierra) to indicate IFR weather and mountain obscurations.
AIRMET T (Tango) indicates Turbulence, strong surface winds and low-level wind shear.
AIRMET Z (Zulu) is for icing and freezing levels.

SIGMET (WS) means Significant Meteorological Information. Pay attention to these in whatever you fly. While AIRMETS tend to be of interest to pilots in smaller aircraft, SIGMETs are for everyone.

SIGMETs are "In flight advisories concerning non-convective weather that is potentially hazardous to all aircraft." (Memorize that.)

SIGMETs include:

- Severe icing not associated with thunderstorms
- Severe, Extreme or Clear Air Turbulence (CAT) not associated with thunderstorms
- Dust storms or sandstorms that lower visibility to less than 3 miles
- Volcanic ash

SIGMETs are unscheduled, they appear when needed (It's tough to schedule a volcanic eruption). They're valid for 4 hours unless it's related to hurricanes in which case it's valid for 6 hours.

Urgent SIGMETs (UWS). When a SIGMET is first issued it's labeled Urgent, as in "Heads up, folks." If the weather problem persists, subsequent SIGMETs are numbered sequentially. SIGMETs are labeled N through Y (excluding S and T), as in SIGMET ROMEO2... the numeral 2 indicate that this is a reissuance of the original SIGMET Romeo. (And, yes, it's possibly the most complicated labeling system imaginable.)

Convective SIGMETS (WST) pertain to, as the name implies, significant weather that involves convective (lifting) forces. We're talking the nastiest stuff here:

- Severe thunderstorms with surface winds greater than 50 knots
- Hail at the surface greater than or equal to 3/4–inch diameter
- Tornadoes
- Embedded thunderstorms
- Lines of thunderstorms
- Thunderstorms with heavy or greater precipitation that affects 40 percent or more of a 3000 square-mile or greater region

Convective SIGMETs are not issued for Hawaii or Alaska. Convective SIGMETs for the lower 48 states are labeled according to the region:
- E for Eastern
- C for Central
- W for Western

Convective SIGMETs are issued at 55 minutes past the hour or whenever one is needed. Convective SIGMET forecasts are valid for 2 hours and are numbered 1 through 99, starting over again at 0000Z.

Test Question:

1. SIGMETs are issued as a warning of weather conditions hazardous to which aircraft?

a. Small aircraft only

b. Large aircraft only
c. All aircraft

2. AIRMETs are advisories of significant weather phenomena but of lower intensities than SIGMETs and are intended for dissemination to:

a. only IFR pilots
b. all pilots
c. only VFR pilots

Answers:

1. **c.** All aircraft
2. **b.** all pilots

Winds Aloft (FD) (and temperatures aloft) forecasts are made twice daily for the lower 48 states plus Hawaii and Alaska. Remember those radiosonde balloon samplings your read about some pages back? Well, data from those balloon rides are used to formulate the Winds Aloft forecast.

Here are some important things to know about FDs:

- Wind direction is referenced to True North and speed is in knots.
- Temperature is in Celsius.
- No wind forecast is made within 1500 feet of the station elevation.
- No temperature forecast is made within 2500 feet of the station elevation.
- When wind speed is forecast to be more than 100 knots but less than 199 knots, a 50 is added to the direction and 100 is subtracted from the speed. Confusing? You bet.
- Decode this example[125]: 731960
- There's no such direction as 730 degrees, so subtract 50 from 73 (73-50=23) Add a zero to the 23 and you get 230 degrees True. Now, add 100 to the next two digits, 19. 100+19 = 119 knots. The 60 is the temperature aloft, which since there's no + or − sign, it's assumed to be negative or –60 C.
- When wind speed forecast tops 200 knots you still subtract 50 from the direction and add 100 to speed which will be shown as 99. Example: 7799 = wind from 270 degrees True at 199 knots (or greater).
- Calm winds aloft forecasts (less than 5 knots) are written as 9900.

Should you forget to wear your NWS Decoder Ring, simply ask DUATS for a plain English translation (Phew!).

---

[125] from FAA-H-8083-25 ch. 11

TWEB (pronounced "Tweeb"). That's not an insult, as in, *"You stupid Tweb! Winds aloft are based on True not Magnetic North!"* Instead, TWEB stands for Transcribed Weather Broadcasts. Fairly rare, except in Alaska, and one day may be eliminated altogether, but you may need to know this for the test. TWEBs contain meteorological and aeronautical data (winds aloft, surface conditions, PIREPs and more) recorded and broadcast continuously on specified navaids. TWEBs usually apply to specific routes.

More Charts

Weather charts resemble battle maps with sweeping lines along the fronts and barbed armies attacking stationary positions. Instead of well-regulated militias, though, weather charts depict air masses swooping across vast sections of the globe. We'll use Surface Analysis Charts, Weather Depiction Charts and Radar Summary Charts. They're relatively easy to use and paint an image of the weather.

Surface Analysis Charts, as the name indicates, depict an analysis of current weather—not a forecast—on the…(*wait for it*)…surface. It's so easy even I can figure one out…mostly. (See Figure 10-19)

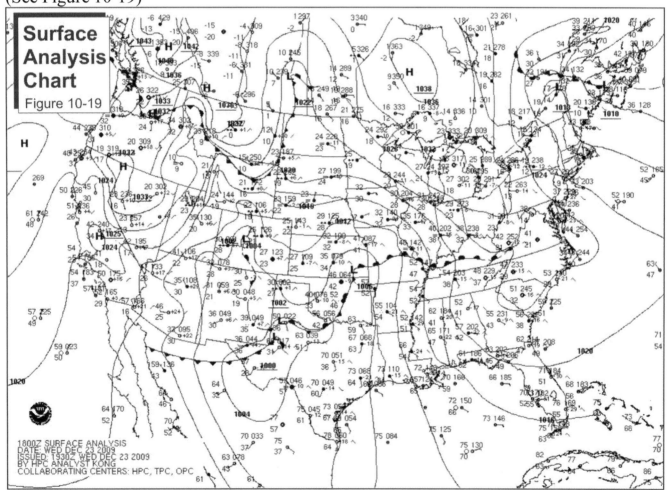

The Surface Analysis Chart is computer-generated and transmitted every 3 hours. It covers the lower 48 states and some adjacent territory. It depicts areas of High and Low pressure, fronts, temperatures and dew points, plus wind directions and speeds, local weather and visual obstructions. A handy thing this chart.

Reporting points across the country are depicted on the chart by a **Station Model**. (Figure 10-13. Each station model shows the following information (don't get hung up on the details):

Type of Observation: A round symbol means that an official obscrvcr was on duty. A square says that he lost his job to automation and an automated station took the observation.

Sky Cover: The symbol will show clear (empty) for Clear skies, ¼ filled for Scattered, ½ filled for Broken, all black for Overcast, an X indicates obscured/partially obscured.

Clouds: High and middle cloud type symbols are placed above the station model while low cloud symbols are placed below.

Sea Level Pressure: Expressed in three digits to the nearest tenth of a millibar.

Pressure Change/Tendency: Expressed in tenths of millibars over the past 3 hours.

Precipitation: Depth of what fell

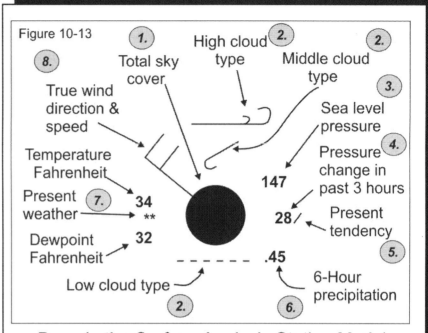

Decode the Surface Analysis Station Model:
1. Overcast, **2.** Predominant clouds, **3.** 1014.7 millibars (add a "10" to the 3-digit number), **4.** increased by 2.8 mbs., **5.** increased, **6.** precipitation in hundredths of an inch, **7.** continuous light snow, **8.** from the NW at 20 kts.

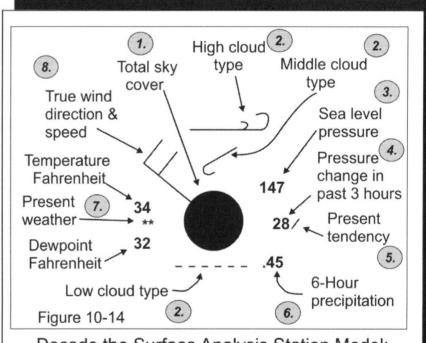

Decode the Surface Analysis Station Model:
1. Overcast, **2.** Predominant clouds, **3.** 1014.7 millibars (add a "10" to the 3-digit number), **4.** increased by 2.8 mbs., **5.** increased, **6.** precipitation in hundredths of an inch, **7.** continuous light snow, **8.** from the NW at 20 kts.

from the sky over the past 6 hours.

Dewpoint: In degrees Fahrenheit.

Present Weather: See Figure 10-14 for some of the 100 symbols used to depict actual weather. (Hint: These few are the ones you might need for the FAA test.)

Temperature: Again, given in Fahrenheit.

Wind: A feathered arrow depicts the True direction (referenced to True North) of the wind.

Weather Depiction Chart is similar to the Surface Analysis Chart and shares some of the same codes. The Weather Depiction Chart depicts what the hundreds of METARs and other surface observations are reporting. (See Figure 10-20 p. 225).

The chart is prepared

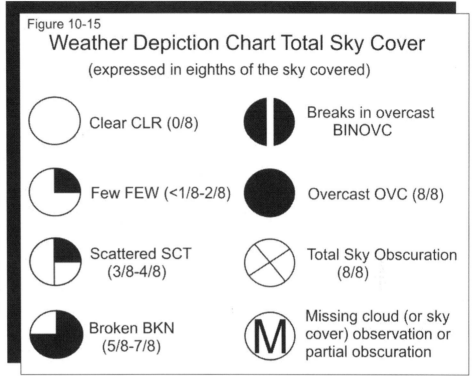

Figure 10-15

Weather Depiction Chart Total Sky Cover

(expressed in eighths of the sky covered)

Clear CLR (0/8)

Few FEW (<1/8-2/8)

Scattered SCT (3/8-4/8)

Broken BKN (5/8-7/8)

Breaks in overcast BINOVC

Overcast OVC (8/8)

Total Sky Obscuration (8/8)

Missing cloud (or sky cover) observation or partial obscuration

every 3 hours beginning at 0100Z. It depicts the big weather picture across the country. The Weather Depiction Chart uses a circle symbol for reporting stations. As with the Surface Analysis Chart you can determine the sky coverage by how filled the circle is (Figure 10-15).

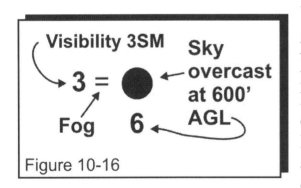

Visibility 3SM **Sky overcast at 600' AGL**

3 =

Fog 6

Figure 10-16

Weather Depiction Charts show fronts and graphically display large areas of IFR (ceilings less than 1000 feet or visibility less than 3 miles) with hatching encircled in a solid line. Even without the hatching each station model can be decoded to determine if the weather there is IFR, VFR or MVFR. Refer to Figure 10-16. The FAA written exam could ask you to decide if a station is reporting IFR, MVFR or VFR weather.

The number 3 indicates the visibility is 3 statute miles, so that doesn't make the area IFR. The symbol = means fog, but fog alone doesn't mean IFR, either. Below the solid black circle (overcast) is the number 6, which means ceiling 600 feet. That's IFR, ceiling less than 1000 feet or visibility less than 3 miles.

Marginal VFR (MVFR) is defined as ceilings 1000 to 3000 feet or visibility 3 to 5 miles. MVFR areas are depicted by encircling non-hatched areas in a solid line.

VFR areas are not outlined on the Weather Depiction Chart. Basically, if the area you want to fly though looks all hatched up with lines and filled in circles, then the weather is probably going to look just as grim. Conversely, if the weather map looks open and clear, then it's probably clear skies en route. Something to kccp in mind: If you'rc online digging through reams of weather charts that confuse and threaten more than help, then call Flight Service toll-free 1-800-WXBRIEF. A human will explain the weather

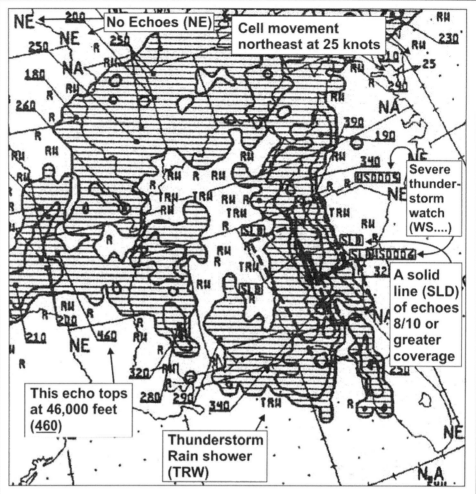

No Echoes (NE)

Cell movement northeast at 25 knots

Severe thunderstorm watch (WS....)

A solid line (SLD) of echoes 8/10 or greater coverage

This echo tops at 46,000 feet (460)

Thunderstorm Rain shower (TRW)

A portion of a Radar Summary Chart showing graphic depictions of radar echoes. Radar only shows precipitation and not cloud bases. Echo tops show how high the precip has been lifted. The higher the tops the stronger the storm (generally). **Figure 10-17**

in English, an option you won't have when taking the FAA's written exam, which is untouched by human hands. Never confuse exams with learning. Exams keep bureaucrats happy; real flight learning comes through good flight instruction, self-study and experience.

Radar Summary Charts should be used in conjunction with the other charts, and the textual **Radar Weather Reports** (not shown), to form the big weather picture in your mind before deciding go or no/go. Using the Radar Summary Chart in Figure 10-17 you can see at a glance that the eastern side of the country is wet. Underlined numbers with pointers indicate the measured maximum tops of precipitation in that area: 240 means tops 24,000 feet.

An arrow pointing out of a radar weather area with a number nearby indicates the direction in which the weather echo is moving and its speed. An example in Figure 10-17 is near Delaware. And arrow points northeast with an accompany number 25. That means the cell in that area is moving out to sea at 25 knots.

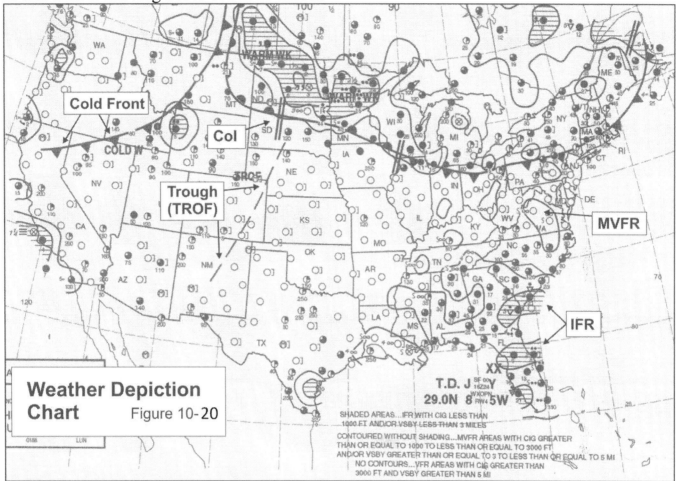

Weather Depiction Chart Figure 10-20

Significant Weather Prognostic Chart

You may never use one, but "Prog Charts" offer a quick, visual glance at forecast weather. You can actually see which geographic areas will likely be VFR, which MVFR and where the weather is forecast to be IFR. They're really pretty cool.

Significant Weather Prognostic Charts come in two flavors: One covers from the surface to 24,000 feet and the other from 25,000 feet to 60,000 feet. The low-level version is further subdivided into the 12-hour and 24-hour forecasts, and the other is the 36-hour and 48-hour surface-only forecast chart.
(See Figure 10-18 on the next page plus the four enlargements that follow.) The two upper panels depict significant weather such as: non-convective turbulence, freezing levels, and IFR or MVFR areas. Moderate or greater turbulence areas are enclosed inside dashed lines.

The numbers inside those dashed lines tell the upper limits of the turbulence in hundreds of feet MSL. IFR areas are circled in solid, and MVFR areas are enclosed in scalloped lines that sorta resemble clouds.

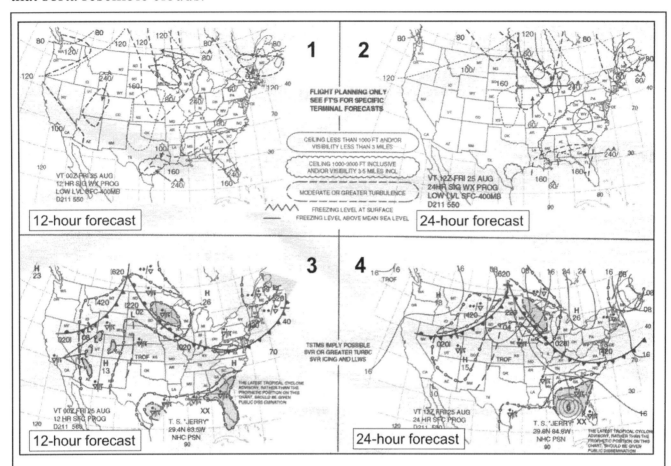

Significant Weather Prognostic Charts (aka Prog Charts) offer 12-hour and 24-hour forecasts or 36-hour and 48-hour forecasts. The FAA tests on the 12-24 charts like the one shown above. It's divided into four panels. Panels 1 and 2 forecast significant weather including areas of IFR and MVFR, moderate or greater turbulence and icing levels. The lower panels (3 and 4) forecasts surface weather and fronts. The Gulf states have a tropical storm moving ashore. A thunderstorm is forecast for western Pennsylvania in the 12-hour forecast. Panels 1 and 3 are 12-hour forecasts, while panels 2 and 4 are 24-hour forecasts. Figure 10-18

The lower panels show the weather forecast for the surface, including fronts, pressure systems and precipitation.

Figure 10-Prog-1 shows the 12-hour forecast depicting widespread areas of MVFR over southeast Texas plus much of the southeast in areas surrounded by scalloped lines. Moderate turbulence is

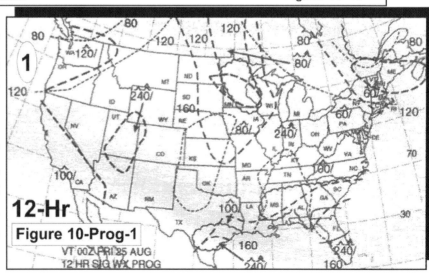

forecast for southern California from the surface to 10,000 feet as indicated by the 100 wearing a hat.

The 24-hour forecast (Figure 10-Prog-2) shows a dashed line running across Montana, Idaho and Oregon. At either end of the line is the number 120, meaning the freezing level is forecast for 12,000 feet MSL. IFR conditions are forecast southern West Virginia, western Virginia and western North Carolina, all encircled in a solid line.

In Figures 3 and 4 the prog chart draws an image of anticipated surface weather, such as a cold front headed into northwestern Wyoming, kicking off thunderstorms and rain showers ahead of it.

A trough (TROF dashed line in boxes 3 and 4) of low pressure is forecast to slowly move across Oklahoma, Kansas and Nebraska. A col separates a stationary front from a cold front over northern Kentucky. And Tropical Storm (T.S.) Jerry punches into the Florida Panhandle.

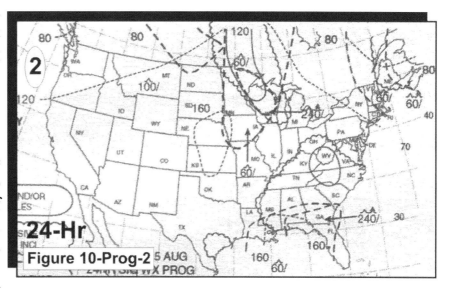

24-Hr

Figure 10-Prog-2

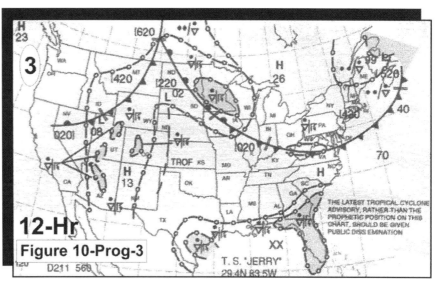

12-Hr

Figure 10-Prog-3

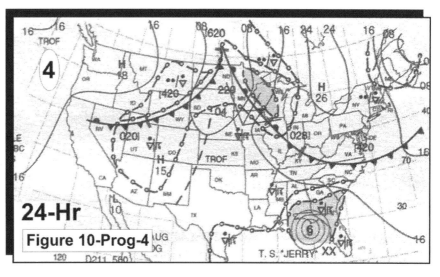

24-Hr

Figure 10-Prog-4

Test Question:

1. How are Significant Weather Prognostic Charts best used by pilots?

    a. For overall planning at all altitudes
    b. For determining areas to avoid (freezing levels and turbulence)
    c. For analyzing current frontal activity and cloud coverage
    d. As party hats

Answer:

1. **b**. For determining areas to avoid (freezing levels and turbulence). Significant Weather Prog Charts stare 12 and 24 hours into the future. Pilots will see forecasts for low level IFR and MVFR areas, plus moderate or greater turbulence areas and freezing levels. Answer **d**. is technically not correct, although I doubt you'd find one in 30 private or sport pilots who ever uses prog charts.

More Weather Test Questions:

1. To best determine general forecast weather conditions over several states, the pilot (Sport and Private) should refer to:

    a. Aviation Area Forecasts
    b. Weather Depiction Charts
    c. Satellite Maps
    d. Weather Channel

2. To determine freezing levels and areas of probable icing aloft, the pilot should refer to the:

    a. Inflight Aviation Weather Advisories
    b. Weather Depiction Chart
    c. Area Forecast

3. The section of the Area Forecast (FA) entitled "VFR CLDS/WX" contains a general description of:

    a. cloudiness and weather significant to flight operations broken down by states or other geographical areas
    b. forecast sky cover, cloud tops, visibility, and obstructions to vision along specific routes
    c. clouds and weather which cover an area greater than 3000 square miles and is significant to VFR flight operations

4. From which primary source should information be obtained regarding expected weather at the estimated time of arrival if your destination has no TAF?

   a. Low-Level Prognostic Chart
   b. Weather Depiction Chart
   c. Area Forecast

5. How will frost on the airplane's wings affect takeoff performance?

   a. Frost will disrupt the smooth flow of air over the wing, adversely affecting its lifting capability
   b. Frost will change the camber of the wing, increasing its lifting capability
   c. Frost will cause the airplane to become airborne with a higher angle of attack, decreasing the stall speed.

6. Clouds are divided into four families according to their

   a. outward shape
   b. height range
   c. composition

7. The suffix "nimbus" used in naming clouds means

   a. a cloud with extensive vertical development
   b. a rain cloud
   c. a middle cloud containing ice pellets

More Answers:

1. **a.** is correct. Aviation Weather Forecasts. Answer d. is a good source but not what the FAA's looking for on the written exam.
2. **a.** is again correct. Inflight Aviation Weather Advisories.
3. **c.** is correct (they can't all be **a.**) clouds and weather which cover an area greater than 3000 square miles and is significant to VFR flight operations
4. **c.** is correct (on any government test, when in doubt, answer **c.**) Area Forecast
5. **a.** Frost will disrupt the smooth flow of air over the wing, adversely affecting its lifting capability
6. **b.** height range
7. **b.** a rain cloud

This concludes the weather chapter. (*Phew, that was loaded with stuff...!*) You don't know everything about the weather, but at least now you can complain about it with some authority around the pilots lounge.

Learn From My Embarrassing Mistakes #999 and Counting

If you can't learn from others' mistakes you'll never become a good pilot. If you can't make mistakes from which to accelerate your education you'll never become a flight instructor. I've made a bunch of silly errors in 40+ years of flying, and one that makes me wince with chagrin happened on a summer day in Rawlins, Wyoming.

I'd purchased a Piper Cherokee 180 in California and was flying it home to Iowa. With me was Gary, a private pilot friend with no experience in mountain flying, and since I'd once flown near mountains I agreed to let him fly left seat while I instructed from the right. All went well, including his smooth landing at Rawlins, elevation 6816 feet.

We taxied to the fuel pump where an enthusiastic ramp rat asked, "How many gallons?" To which I replied, "Top 'er off!" That's 50 gallons at 6 pounds per gallon for a total of 300 pounds of fuel. No sweat for the 180-hp engine. "Have you checked density altitude?" the kid reeling out the hose asked. Insulted that he'd question a genuine flight instructor, I answered, "Yeah. Nice and cool today. Shouldn't be a problem." The outside air temperature was about 65 degrees F. Almost needed a jacket. He smiled and fueled the Cherokee to the brims. Later, inside the office after figuring my fuel bill, he casually said, "I'm curious what the density altitude is today," and he turned to a nearby weather display and then back to me with. "Hard to believe density altitude is almost 9000 feet."

Bong! Suddenly my flatlander CFI status shrank to rookie level. I'd forgotten that what felt like a cool day was actually quite warm for that elevation, and, subsequently, the density altitude (the altitude to which the airplane would react) was way higher than field elevation. I bowed to the "ramp rat's" superior intelligence and asked his advice about departing from the airport.

All went well—or you wouldn't be reading this book—and I learned a humble lesson about density altitude (always figure it) and personal CFI arrogance (don't be a know-it-all, especially when outside your home turf).

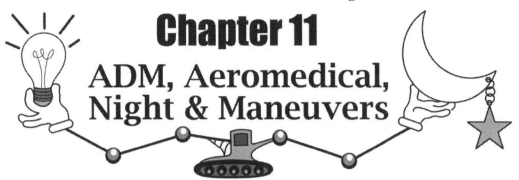

Chapter 11
ADM, Aeromedical, Night & Maneuvers

To many living in the farm belt ADM means the Archer Daniel Midland company, but pilots know that ADM means **Aeronautical Decision Making**. ADM is defined as: "A systematic approach to the mental process used by airplane pilots to consistently determine the best course of action in response to a given set of circumstances."[126] Frankly, I'm not sure why it's limited to "airplane pilots." Perhaps in stressful situations helicopter pilots revert to the old Army adage: "When in danger, when in doubt, run in circles, jump and shout."

This course is focused on the airplane pilot, but whatever type pilot you are, or will become, the FAA cautions that 75 percent of all aviation accidents can be blamed on "human factor" or "pilot error." That doesn't mean the three-quarters of all flights end in disaster, but, instead, that the small percentage of flights that become accidents are instigated by avoidable errors. Or in Teslavian logic: *Airplanes would be 75 percent safer without pilots on board.*[127]

Pilot In Command, Not Pilot In Error

The term Pilot Error gets tossed about rather cavalierly. Any accident not caused by mechanical failure or ATC error can be explained as pilot screw-ups. It's a common herd instinct after an accident, particularly a fatal accident, for pilots to distance themselves from the event by saying, "Wow, that guy really screwed up," as though: "*I'd* never do that," knowing full well that we could.

Pilot error means the pilot did something wrong or failed to do something right. Perhaps both. Oddly, the pilot often knows what went wrong and recognizes the danger while still making the wrong decisions. It could also mean that, perhaps, the pilot didn't recognize a small error, which began a chain of errors that ultimately overwhelmed the pilot, causing the accident. It's this "poor judgment chain" or "chain of errors" that we'll exam with an eye toward recognizing the weak links before they break.

---

[126] AC 60-22
[127] See how statistical analysis can influence a discussion?

Fatigue is one of the commonly recurring links in the error chain. We tend to ignore it or even treat fatigue as something any "real" pilot should be able to handle. Baloney! When you're tired, your brain gets clunky. Ask any high school student at 8:30 in the morning. Errors happen.

When I was an air traffic controller in a control tower operating 24/7, we were required to work in shifts, and for me the worst rotation was the eight-hour mid-shift, which ran from 11 PM to 7 AM. This after working an eight-hour shift from 6 AM the previous morning to 2 PM that afternoon. With nine hours between shifts, we were expected to sleep eight of those. Fat chance. I'd arrive zombie-like at 10:30 PM and drag my sorry self through the shift. When the morning rush of airline, cargo and corporate began at 5 o'clock, my mind was mush. Mistakes happened. Luckily, nothing serious, because at times when I knew I was exhausted I simply slowed the flow. I delayed aircraft rather than mistakenly clear someone into the clag when I wasn't fully functional. The FAA preaches against fatigue but to this day, ignores the issue with its own controllers. You, as pilot-in-command, have no excuse. Be rested or don't go.

What's the opposite of fatigue? Answer: Too much energy, which often manifests itself as **impatience**. In aviation it's called "Get-there-itis," the need to get to our destination no matter what, in order to meet self-imposed schedules or to please the boss or passengers. We might rush things in order to depart ahead of impending bad weather.
Rush, rush, rush = Crash, crash, crash.

The pilot in a hurry skimps on preflight planning and, maybe, skips the call to Flight Service, because the weather looks good so *why bother?* The pilot in a hurry doesn't check fuel tanks for contamination or check the oil level or might leave a fuel cap off, causing fuel to leak out in flight. The pilot in a hurry tries to taxi away with the tail still tied to a 500-pound block of concrete or tries to taxi over the wheel chocks by adding full power rather than "waste time" by shutting down and removing them. The pilot in a hurry tries to hand prop an engine to start it when the battery is dead, because the previous night—when in a hurry after landing—the pilot didn't use a shut-down checklist and left the Master Switch on, thus draining the battery for the morning flight.

- The hurried pilot doesn't check NOTAMs.
- The hurried pilot doesn't clean the windshield.
- The hurried pilot doesn't remove frost from the wings.
- The hurried pilot doesn't get the baggage door secured and takes off, spewing underwear all over the runway.
- Here's the kicker: The hurried pilot wastes more time (and money) than could be saved by slowing down. Although, the hurried pilot is always first on the accident scene.

At some point most pilots stretch the safety limits too far. Usually, the pilot escapes with a "Phew, I'll never do that again!" **Scud-running** is a key dumb idea. As ceilings lower, there's a temptation to get home by sneaking beneath a ceiling that only gets lower and lower. Sure, we all hear about the old crop duster pilot who regularly flies beneath the power lines on misty days to reach the fields, but that duster pilot probably has 10,000 hours of experience in the local area. More importantly, you might not hear about all the other duster pilots who didn't reach 10,000 hours when they wrapped a Pawnee wing around a telephone pole. Experience doesn't automatically make you safe; it should, however, make you aware of the traps and of your limits.

"Continuing VFR into instrument conditions," as we've discussed earlier, is a killer, no other word for it. VFR pilots cannot fly for long on the instruments alone. **Spatial Disorientation** inevitably ensues with fatal consequences. I'm not sure how to prevent these accidents other than to say when faced with the prospect of "punching through" a cloud deck as a VFR pilot—Don't do it.

Checklists should be called Memory Lists for repetitive tasks. My short-term (and long-term) memory is shot, so I need…ah, I need…(what was I talking about?) Oh, yeah, I need checklists to keep me from forgetting things, such as setting flaps before takeoff or advancing the mixture to rich.

ADM requires attitude adjustment. ADM recognizes **Five Dangerous Attitudes** and (this might be on the FAA test) offers five corresponding attitude Antidotes:

Hazardous Attitudes	**Antidote**
Anti-authority: "Don't tell me"	Follow the rules. The rules are usually right, so follow them. Than said, be ready to question authority: "Say again that heading."
Impulsivity: "Do it quickly"	Not so fast, think first.
Invulnerability: "It won't happen to me"	Wanna bet? It could happen to me. Bad things do happen to good pilots. It's not, however, a good pilot who thinks himself invulnerable. Risk taking isn't the same as risk analysis.

Hazardous Attitudes	Antidote
Macho: "I can do it"	<u>Taking chances is foolish.</u> While we applaud the "can do" attitude it takes to learn to fly, no one likes a show-off. Oh, yeah, machismo isn't limited to men, either. (Machisma?)
Resignation: "What's the use?"	<u>I am not helpless.</u> You're the pilot-in-command and not the pilot-in-the-seat-like-a-lump-of-laundry. Keep flying. You can make a difference.

Working hand-in-glove with ADM is **CRM**, which means **Crew Resource Management.** In my 1946 Aeronca Champ I'm a crew of one and think of CRM as Cockpit Resource Management. The term, **SRM, Single Pilot Resource Management**, is found in the ACS and captures the old CRM-for-one philosophy. Whatever the slogan, it means the pilot applies "team management concepts in the flight deck environment."

CRM was born in larger aircraft with impressive flight decks and crewmembers with epaulets on their uniform shoulders. Still, CRM can apply at some level to you and your passenger as the crew of a Cessna 150. With proper CRM the pilot "makes effective use of all available resources; human resources, hardware and information." This includes the pilot and everyone even remotely associated with the flight's operation, such as air traffic controllers, FSS briefers, your mechanic, and the ramp rat who drives the fuel truck—anyone. When you get your ATP (Airline Transport Pilot) certificate and go to work for CramPac Airlines, you'll learn CRM in the big iron. Initially, as a student and later as Private or Sport Pilot, CRM applies when flying your Cessna 172.

What is CRM, really? It can be many things. In our case, CRM means getting your stuff together before the flight. Have your charts and airport/facility directory (A/FD) handy in the cockpit where you can get to them, rather than in the baggage compartment or under the seat and out of reach when you need them. Perhaps, post a note on the panel or on your flight log with key frequencies noted.

CRM means utilize everything at hand. So, use the passengers. Explain to passengers what the charts are for and have them hold the charts you're not using. That serves two purposes: It gives you a secretary eager to please, and it gives an anxious rider something to do other than worry. Note: Don't trust passengers too much. Keep their cockpit role simple and well supervised.

The pilot's first duty in all phases of all flights is to *fly the airplane*. CRM includes a healthy glob of common sense. You can't be digging about for charts—or programming a

GPS—and ignore flying the airplane. Autopilots are fine but need to be monitored. An autopilot will blindly fly you into a TV tower or mountain without any warning, fear or guilt. ADM and CRM combine to help the PIC (lots of acronyms here) avoid CFIT (Controlled Flight Into Terrain). By applying a little cockpit housekeeping so that charts are accessible, so the pilot can more easily handle reroutes from ATC or for unforecast weather. ADM helps the pilot spot errors and threats and quickly deal with them.

ADM is more than an acronymed philosophy. It's a skill that includes a **Decision-Making Process**. That process addresses the fact that all flight involves risk. Face it, all of life involves risk. The goal is to manage the risk and enjoy your flying life. **Risk Management** is a part of ADM. It relies on (memorize these for the test): *Situational awareness, problem recognition and good judgment.*

To meet that goal the pilot needs to recognize the four fundamental **Risk Elements** that are found in the ADM process in any aviation situation. They are: *Pilot, aircraft, environment and mission.* Evaluating the factors in all four and relating them to each other helps the pilot (factor #1) make the **Go/No-Go** decision.

Pilot: That's you. Before any flight decide if you're fit, rested, healthy—mentally and physically.

Airplane: Is it safe for flight? Who decides, you or the mechanic? Answer: You.

Environment: We're not just talking about the weather, here, although that's a prime factor in making the Go/No-Go call. Also check the en route environment. Will ATC be busy? Any known traffic delays? Navaid outages? NOTAMs for runway restrictions? How's braking action after the recent snowfall? What does the destination airport look like? What's its environment? Don't wait and be surprised. Check the A/FD before you go.

Mission: How does this relationship between pilot, aircraft and environment apply to the operation, the flight itself? What are you trying to accomplish in this flight? Is it a trip? Aerobatics? Training? Or just sightseeing? Every flight has a purpose and every flight operation relates back to the other three elements. Is the aircraft appropriate for the mission? Is the pilot suited for the task? Is the weather, which might be okay for a local trip, good enough for a cross-country? Learn to relate each item to the others when analyzing the risk factors. And then mitigate those factors.

Test Questions:

1. Risk management, as a part of the aeronautical decision making (ADM) process, relies on which features to reduce the risks associated with each flight?

a.   Application of stress management and risk element procedures
b.   The mental process of analyzing all information in a particular situation and making a timely decision on what action to take
c.   Situational awareness, problem recognition, and good judgment

2. What is it often called when a pilot pushes his or her capabilities and the aircraft's limits by trying to maintain visual contact with terrain in low visibility and ceiling?

a. Scud running
b. Mind set
c. Peer pressure

3. The danger of spatial disorientation during flight in poor visibility conditions may be reduced by

a. shifting the eyes quickly between the exterior visual field and the instrument panel
b. having faith in the instruments rather than taking a chance on sensory organs
c. leaning body in the opposite direction of the motion of the aircraft

Answers:

1. **c.** Situational awareness, problem recognition, and good judgment

2. **a.** Scud running. Scud is slang for the bottom side of the overhanging clouds. Running under it, particularly in unfamiliar territory is dangerous and usually illegal.

3. **b.** having faith in the instruments rather than taking a chance on sensory organs. So: Unless you're instrument-rated and proficient, stay out of the clouds.

Aeromedical Factors

Sport Pilots may not need a medical certificate to fly, and Private Pilots may only need a one-time Class 3 medical, but all pilots need to be mentally and physically fit for flight. In other words, if you—the pilot—feel as though you're not up for the flight, don't go. Even the fit pilot, however, may encounter physiological issues in flight and must recognize and deal with them. Plus, of shorter-term importance, you need to answer a few questions about them on the FAA exam and during your check ride.

Hypoxia is a lack of oxygen getting to the brain. Flying would be so much easier if pilots didn't have brains. But we do (mostly), and those brains need oxygen to function. As we climb higher into the sky, we know that the air becomes thinner. There's less oxygen available for the brain, and this affects our thinking and decision-making abilities. We become fatigued. Lack of oxygen can cause a feeling of euphoria. (*Whoopee, I'm on top of the world...whoopee, the engine quit...!*) Lack of oxygen makes it tough for the brain to tell when euphoria is unwarranted. Ultimately, hypoxia leads to unconsciousness, and that leads to no good.

Hyperventilation is the opposite of Hypoxia. When a person becomes excited, stressed, tense, afraid or anxious it affects breathing. Too much Carbon Dioxide (CO_2) passes out of the system, retaining too much oxygen. The pilot becomes dizzy, may feel hot or cold and may become nauseated. Hyperventilation is relatively easy to treat: Slow the breathing rate. One way to retain CO_2 is to breath into a paper bag, it recycles the CO_2. (Now, make paper bags part of your flight kit for hyperventilating passengers or instructors.) Talking loudly will do the same thing. Of course, the sight of the pilot shouting into a paper bag may cause passengers to hyperventilate.

Carbon Monoxide (CO) can leak into the airplane's cabin from cracks in the exhaust system. Those stick-em-up Carbon Monoxide monitors you often see in small airplanes might not be reliable. Instead, be alert for CO danger signs: Dizziness, hazy (blurred) thinking, tightness across the forehead, headache and loss of muscle power. Carbon Monoxide poisoning susceptibility increases with altitude.

Spatial Disorientation results from losing reference to outside terrain, particularly the horizon. The pilot becomes disoriented in space, can't tell up from down. This happens— quickly—to the VFR-only pilot who attempts instrument flight inside the clouds or low visibility from dust, fog or snow. It can happen at night, even on a clear VFR night when the horizon is indistinct. Basic instrument scan and instrument flight attitude control prevents this. The pilot must not rely upon the natural-feeling sensations received from the inner ear or seat-of-the-pants. Instead, the pilot must rely upon the airplane's instruments to remain in control and oriented.

Night Flight

Some pilots consider night the best time to fly.[128] The skies are less crowded, turbulence from daytime heat lessens, and the air traffic controllers are so sleepy they're happy to have someone to help keep them awake. Night cross-country flight is easy, too, because you can see your destination shimmering in the distance. The civil airport's aerodrome beacon flashes white... green...white...green...., pulling the lonesome pilot in from the night sky. Even the runways are easier to spot at night, outlined in white and yellow lights with green threshold lights showing where the runway begins and red lights to show where it ends. Blue lights lead from runway to ramp where you discover the big disadvantage of night flight—everything's closed.   Check your A/FD for FBO hours of operation when planning your nighttime fuel stops.

---

[128] Sport pilots may not act as PIC at night

What is night? Seems like an easy question, but the FAA has its own definition of the time between the dark and the daylight, when the night begins to lower and there comes a pause in the day's occupations the FAA calls[129]: "the time between the end of evening civil twilight and the beginning of morning civil twilight." This official nighttime can be found in the *American Air Almanac*. Few pilots since the celestial navigation days have ever seen this almanac, but knowing the definition keeps test makers happy.

In order to carry passengers at night you must be night current: You must have made and logged 3 landings to a full stop within the past 90 days. These landings must be made between 1 hour after sunset to 1 hour before sunrise. You must have your position lights (nav lights) and anti-collision (rotating beacon) on between sunset and sunrise.

Weird Night Visions

As mentioned in chapter 5, the human eyes don't operate at night the way they do during the day. Usually, they're dormant beneath eyelids at night, but when you take off after dark, you need to understand a little about how your eyes adapt to low light.

> **Remember:** The airplane doesn't know it's dark outside. It flies the same way it does in daytime. Whatever approach speeds worked at noon will work at midnight.

I'm no ophthalmologist, but I'll play one for a moment by describing the rods and cones in the human eyeball. Both are receptors in the eye's retina and record the images transmitted through the optic nerve to the brain. The rods glean most of your nighttime images; they're more sensitive to light. Rods work best in the peripheral vision. Cones favor the center or fovea. So, at night, the pilot needs to know that the rods, favoring the periphery, will be dominant. This means that your best night vision is in the peripheral field. With your cones somewhat muted in the fovea you may have a blind spot when looking straight ahead. So, scan. Move your eyes. In general—day or night—the best scanning technique involves scanning small portions of the sky. At night, slowly work these small portions into the central vision area.

It may take 30 minutes for your eyes to adjust to nighttime light levels. Avoid bright lights before and during flight. Use red lights where possible in and around the airplane, even during preflight inspection.

The eye and brain play other tricks at night. **Autokinesis** happens when you stare at a single point of light against a dark background. After only a few seconds the light will appear to move. How to prevent this? Again, scan. Move your eyes, move your head.

---

[129] Nodding appreciation to Longfellow's "The Children's Hour"

False Horizon happens when the natural horizon is obscured. On a dark, moonless clear night, for instance, the twinkling stars can blend with the twinkling distant city lights and it's tough to figure out where the real horizon exists. Likewise, the same effect can happen along a shoreline. A dark ocean or lake looks an awful lot like dark sky and can disorient a pilot.

Landing Illusions are many at night. When flying at night over featureless terrain, pilots tend to fly lower than normal approaches. Rain, haze, or a dark runway environment might cause the same illusion. By contrast, bright lights, steep terrain and wide runways can cause a pilot to fly a higher than normal approach.

Streetlights often resemble runway lights. As a tower controller I've seen pilots (even in a Boeing 727) line up with a city road thinking it was the runway. Check the light colors and check runway alignment on final. Does your compass or heading indicator match the runway number? Why are cars on *your* runway?

Night flight is something you'll experience and appreciate with a small amount of instruction. The sky is beautiful at night. Fly the airplane as though it were daytime—same approach speeds—use the VASIs or PAPIs and you'll do fine. Remember: The airplane doesn't know it's dark outside and will fly just like it did in daytime.

Maneuvers

No book alone can teach you how to fly. That's why we have flight instructors hanging around the airport. They'll teach you the hands-on basics, and then you need to fly, fly and fly some more.

The FAA will ask a few questions on the written exam related to maneuvers, so let's review those.

The **Fundamentals of Flight** are (memorize):

1. Straight and Level
2. Turns
3. Climbs
4. Descents

While earning your pilot certificate you'll apply those fundaments to perform ground reference maneuvers including Rectangular Patterns, Turns Around a Point and S-Turns Across a Road. Both maneuvers require an awareness of the wind and how to correct for it.

The **Rectangular Pattern** resembles an airport traffic pattern. The pilot needs to crab into the crosswind on each leg. When making 90-degree course changes from one leg to the next, the airplane must turn either more or less than 90 degrees to compensate for the wind. (See Figure 11-1)

The turns to final and to the crosswind leg are less than 90 degrees, in order to roll out crabbed into the wind.

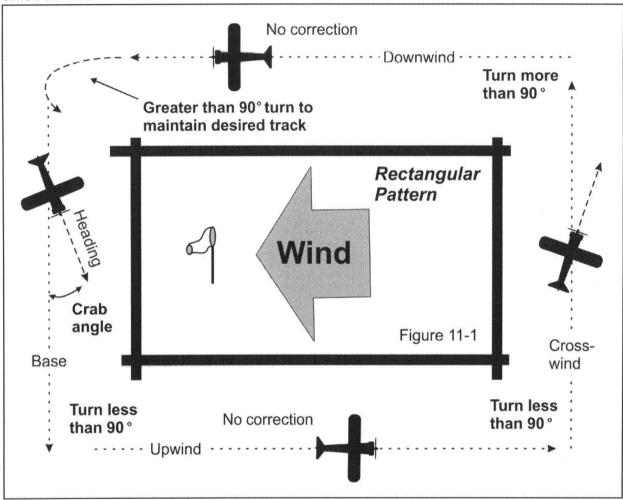

The turns to downwind and to base leg require more than a 90-degree change in heading to compensate for the crosswind.

When performing **S-Turns Across a Road**, (See Figure 11-2) the airplane never crabs along a straight line. Instead, the heading is always changing (same with Turns-Around-a-Point). So, the pilot must change the angle of bank to compensate for the wind. As groundspeed increases, bank angle must increase in order to maintain the same radius from the road. Bank angle is steepest when groundspeed is highest. If the pilot increases bank angle too quickly on the upwind half of the circle, then the radius of the circle will decrease.

Turns Around a Point utilize the same principles to control drift as the S-Turns Across a Road. Your instructor will demonstrate these maneuvers in the airplane. They're actually a lot of fun.

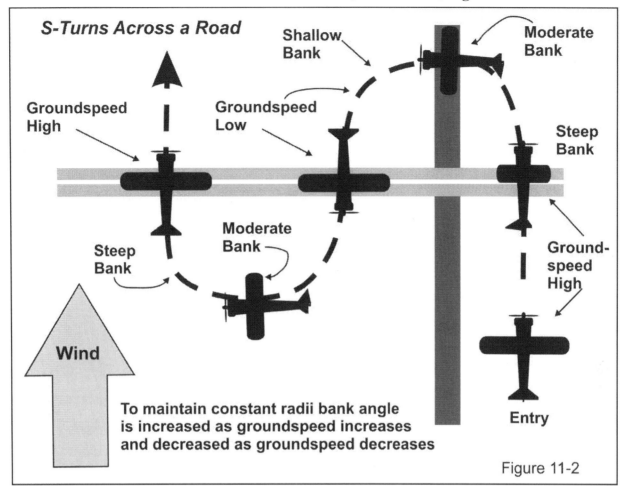

S-Turns Across a Road

Shallow Bank

Moderate Bank

Groundspeed High

Groundspeed Low

Steep Bank

Steep Bank

Moderate Bank

Ground-speed High

Wind

To maintain constant radii bank angle is increased as groundspeed increases and decreased as groundspeed decreases

Entry

Figure 11-2

Call Me A Taxi Redux

Tailwheel pilots are acutely aware of the effect of wind while taxiing the airplane. With the CG located behind the main gear there's a tendency for the airplane to weathervane into the wind. Therefore, the controls must be set to compensate for the wind and prevent tipping over or ground looping. Tricycle geared airplanes are less susceptible to these issues but not immune.

Here are some basic taxi techniques, with direct testable quotes from FAA manuals, regarding control input. (Remember, this is for ground operations only and has nothing to do with flight. See Figure 11-3)

Tailwheel or Tricycle Gear: "When taxiing with strong quartering tailwinds, the aileron should be down on the side from which the wind is blowing."

Tailwheel or Tricycle Gear: Generally, "when taxiing in strong quartering headwinds" the aileron should be "up on the side from which the wind is blowing."
A quartering tailwind "would be most critical when taxiing a nosewheel equipped high-wing airplane."

Generally, when taxiing a tricycle gear airplane into a headwind, the elevator should be neutral. When taxiing with a tailwind, the elevator should be down.

Generally, when taxiing a tailwheel gear airplane into a headwind, the elevator should be up. When taxiing with a tailwind the elevator should be down.

Finally…

In order to count a landing as successful—as opposed to just arriving—and "to minimize the side loads placed on the landing gear during touchdown, the pilot should keep the longitudinal axis of the aircraft parallel to the runway." (Chances are good that'll appear in a FAA test question.)

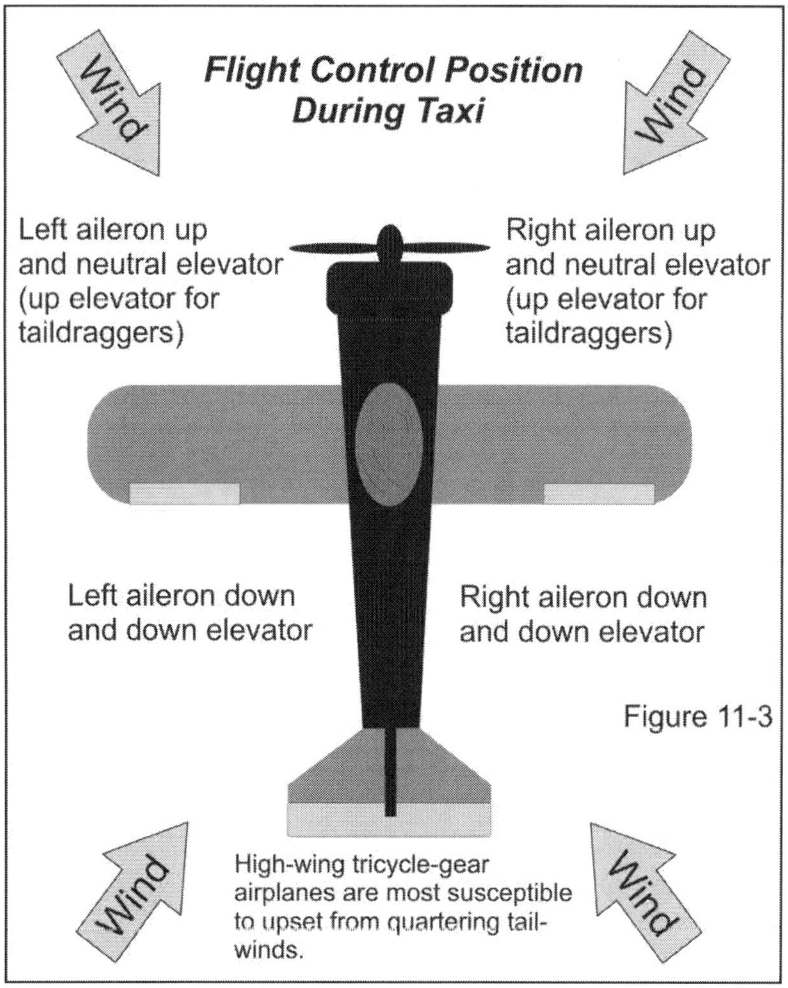

Flight Control Position During Taxi

Left aileron up and neutral elevator (up elevator for taildraggers)

Right aileron up and neutral elevator (up elevator for taildraggers)

Left aileron down and down elevator

Right aileron down and down elevator

Figure 11-3

High-wing tricycle-gear airplanes are most susceptible to upset from quartering tail-winds.

Test Question:

1. When landing VFR at night you should approach

a. at a higher airspeed
b. with a steeper descent
c. at the same as during the day

2. Nighttime is defined as:

a. Sunset to sunrise
b. 1 hour after sunset to 1 hour before sunrise
c. The time between the end of evening civil twilight and the beginning of morning civil twilight

Answer:

1. **c.** the same as during the day. The airplane doesn't know it's dark outside.

2. **c.** the time between the end of evening civil twilight and the beginning of morning civil twilight

Appendix 1 Glossary

Pilot Vocabulary and Abbreviations[130]

Terms you'll hear on the air or around the pilots lounge

A (Alpha)

AAA/APM: (See *Antique Airplane Association/Air Power Museum*)

Abeam: An aircraft is abeam a fix, point, or object when that fix, point, or object is approximately 90 degrees to the right or left of the aircraft track. Abeam indicates a general position rather than a precise point.

Above The Ordinary: An inspirational P-51 video on YouTube or at abovetheordinary.org

Absolute Altitude: The vertical distance of an airplane above the terrain, or above ground level (AGL).

Accessories: Components that are used with an engine, but are not a part of the engine itself. Units such as magnetos, carburetors, generators, and fuel pumps are commonly installed engine accessories.

Acknowledge: Radio terminology, means, "Let me know that you have received my message."

ACS: Airman Certification Standards, the FAA's testing process that's replaced the PTS

Active runway: Any runway currently in use as selected by ATC at an airport with a control tower in operation, sometimes referred to as the duty runway

ADF: Automatic Direction Finder (finds an NDB)

Adiabatic cooling: Cooling air through expansion. As air moves up, it expands from the reduced pressure. It cools as it expands.

Adiabatic heating: Heating air through compression. When air moves downward it's compressed, and temperature increases.

ADIZ (See *Air Defense Identification Zone*)

ADM: Aeronautical Decision Making

Administrator: The Federal Aviation Administrator or any person to whom he has delegated his authority in the matter concerned.

ADS-B: Automatic Dependent Surveillance-Broadcast

Adverse Yaw: A condition of flight in which the nose of an airplane tends to yaw toward the outside of the turn. This is caused by the higher induced drag on the outside wing, which is also producing more lift. Induced drag is a by-product of the lift associated with the outside wing.

---

[130] Most terms taken directly from FAA publications, including FAR 1.1 and 1.2, AIM, FAA-H-8083 series, P/C Glossary

Adverse Aileron Yaw (see *Adverse Yaw*)

Advisory Circulars (AC): Nonregulatory public information of interest

Aerodynamics: The science of the action of air on an object, and with the motion of air on other gases. Aerodynamics deals with the production of lift by the aircraft, the relative wind, and the atmosphere.

A/FD: (See **Airport/Facility Directory**)

Affirmative: Radio terminology, means, Yes.

AFM (See *Airplane Flight Manual*)

AFSS: Automated Flight Service Station

AGL: Above Ground Level

Aileron: Primary flight control surface mounted on the trailing edge of an airplane wing, near the tip. Ailerons control roll about the longitudinal axis.

Ailerona: Mythical airfield where avgas is free, the FAA pumps it, and the weather is always VFR. Oh, and TSA can't find it.

AIM: Aeronautical Information Manual (once called the Airmen's Information Manual)

Aircraft: A device that is used or intended to be used for flight in the air.

Aircraft Logbooks: Journals containing a record of total operating time, repairs, alterations or inspections performed, and all Airworthiness Directive (AD) notes complied with. A maintenance logbook should be kept for the airframe, each engine, and each propeller.

Aircraft Owners and Pilots Association (AOPA): Organization representing and protecting General Aviation. Go to: aopa.org

Air Defense Identification Zone (ADIZ): The area of airspace over land or water, extending upward from the surface, within which the ready identification, the location, and the control of aircraft are required in the interest of national security.

Airfoil: An airfoil is any surface, such as a wing, propeller, rudder, or even a trim tab, which provides aerodynamic force when it interacts with a moving stream of air.

Airframe: Fuselage, booms, nacelles, cowlings, fairings, airfoil surfaces (including rotors but excluding propellers and rotating airfoils of engines), and landing gear of an aircraft and their accessories and controls. Everything but the powerplant.

Air Guitar: Imaginary musical instrument found in Ailerona

Airmanship: A sound acquaintance with the principles of flight, the ability to operate an airplane with competence and precision both on the ground and in the air, and the exercise of sound judgment that results in optimal operational safety and efficiency

Air Mass: Not a religious ceremony held aboard Pontiff One but, instead, a weather term for an extensive body of air having fairly uniform properties of moisture and temperature

AIRMET: In-flight weather advisories issued only to amend the area forecast concerning weather phenomena which are of operational interest to all aircraft and potentially hazardous to aircraft having limited capability because of lack of equipment, instrumentation, or pilot qualifications. AIRMETs concern weather of less severity than that covered by SIGMETs or Convective SIGMETs. AIRMETs cover moderate icing, moderate turbulence, sustained winds of 30 knots or more at the surface, widespread areas of ceilings less than 1,000 feet and/or visibility less than 3 miles, and extensive mountain obscurement

Air Quotes: Lyrical musings by aviation authors. Never do that double-fingers on two hands gesture to signify quotes. It just looks stupid.

Airplane Flight Manual: A document developed by the airplane manufacturer and approved by the Federal Aviation Administration (FAA). It is specific to a particular make and model airplane by serial number and it contains operating procedures and limitations

Airport/Facility Directory (A/FD): A publication designed primarily as a pilot's operational manual containing all airports, seaplane bases, and heliports open to the public including communications data, navigational facilities, and certain special notices and procedures. This publication is issued in seven volumes according to geographical area.

Airspeed: The velocity of the airplane relative to the air mass through which it is flying

Airworthiness: A condition in which the aircraft conforms to its type certificated design including supplemental type certificates, and field approved alterations. The aircraft must also be in a condition for safe flight as determined by annual, 100 hour, preflight and any other required inspections.

Airworthiness Certificate: A certificate issued by the FAA to all aircraft that have been proven to meet the minimum standards set down by the Code of Federal Regulations.

Airworthiness Directives: A regulatory notice sent out by the FAA to the registered owner of an aircraft informing the owner of a condition that prevents the aircraft from continuing to meet its conditions for airworthiness. Airworthiness Directives (AD notes) must be complied with within the required time limit, and the fact of compliance, the date of compliance, and the method of compliance must be recorded in the aircraft's maintenance records.

Antique Airplane Association/Air Power Museum (AAA/APM): World's oldest organization dedicated to protecting, restoring and flying antique airplanes. Go to antiqueairfield.org

Anti-Servo Tab: A trim device generally found on the trailing edge of stabilators. Unlike a servo tab it moves in the same direction as the control surface, making the control input "heavier." This is ideal for airplanes with overly sensitive pitch control and prevents over controlling.

Altitude AGL: The actual height above ground level (AGL) at which the aircraft is flying.

Altitude MSL: The actual height above mean sea level (MSL) at which the aircraft is flying.

Angle of Attack (AOA): The acute angle between the chord line of the airfoil and the direction of the relative wind.

Angle of Incidence: The angle formed by the chord line of the wing and a line parallel to the longitudinal axis of the airplane.

Annual Inspection: A complete inspection of an aircraft and engine, required by the Code of Federal Regulations, to be accomplished every 12 calendar months on all certificated aircraft. Only an A&P technician holding an Inspection Authorization can conduct an annual inspection.

AOPA (See *Aircraft Owners and Pilots Association*)

Apron (See Ramp) "A defined area on an airport or heliport intended to accommodate aircraft for purposes of loading or unloading passengers or cargo, refueling, parking, or maintenance. With regard to seaplanes, a ramp is used for access to the apron from the water."

ARTCC: Air Route Traffic Control Center, aka, "Center"

ASOS: Automated Surface Observing System (weather). Provides continuous minute-by-minute observations and performs the basic observing functions necessary to generate an aviation routine weather report (METAR) and other aviation weather information.

Aspect Ratio: The aspect ratio is a factor that affects the lift and drag created by a wing. Aspect ratio is determined by dividing the wingspan (from wingtip to wingtip), by the average wing chord. Glider wings have a high aspect ratio

ASR: Airport Surveillance Radar (approach control ATC radar)

ATC: Air Traffic Control

ATCT: Air Traffic Control Tower, aka "Tower."

ATIS: Automatic Terminal Information Service or Automated Terminal Information System (the FAA switches the terms willy-nilly)

Attitude: The position of an aircraft as determined by the relationship of its axes and a reference, usually the earth's horizon.

Attitude Indicator: An instrument, which uses an artificial horizon and miniature airplane to depict the position of the airplane in relation to the true horizon. The attitude indicator senses roll as well as pitch, which is the up and down movement of the airplane's nose.

Authorized Flight Instructor: A catchall term for whatever instructor is authorized to give instruction (see CFI)

Autokinesis: This is caused by staring at a single point of light against a dark background for more than a few seconds. After a few moments, the light appears to move on its own.

Avgas: Aviation Gasoline

AWOS: Automated Weather Observing System

Axis of an Aircraft: Three imaginary lines that pass through an aircraft's center of gravity. The axes can be considered as imaginary axles around which the aircraft turns. The three axes pass through the center of gravity at 90-degree angles to each other. The axis from nose to tail is the longitudinal axis, the axis that passes from wingtip to wingtip is the lateral axis, and the axis that passes vertically through the center of gravity is the vertical axis.

Azimuth: A direction at a reference point expressed as the angle in the horizontal plane between a reference line and the line joining the reference point to another point, usually measured clockwise from the reference line.

B (Bravo)

Backside of the Power Curve: Flight regime in which flight at a higher airspeed requires a lower power setting and a lower airspeed requires a higher power setting in order to maintain altitude.

Back-taxi: "A term used by air traffic controllers to taxi an aircraft on the runway opposite to the traffic flow. The aircraft may be instructed to back-taxi to the beginning of the runway or at some point before reaching the runway end for the purpose of departure or to exit the runway." (ATC manual 7110.65)

Balked Landing: A go-around.

Bearing: The horizontal direction to or from any point, usually measured clockwise from true north, magnetic north, or some other reference point through 360 degrees.

BFR: Biennial Flight Review, every two years. Biannual means twice yearly.

Boost Pump: An electrically driven fuel pump, usually of the centrifugal type, located in one of the fuel tanks. It is used to provide fuel to the engine for starting and providing fuel pressure in the event of failure of the engine driven pump. It also pressurizes the fuel lines to prevent vapor lock.

Buffeting: The beating of an aerodynamic structure or surface by unsteady flow, gusts, etc.; the irregular shaking or oscillation of a vehicle component owing to turbulent air or separated flow.

Brake Horsepower: The power delivered at the propeller shaft of an aircraft engine.

Bus Bar: An electrical power distribution point to which several circuits may be connected. It is often a solid metal strip having a number of terminals installed on it.

Bus Tie: A switch that connects two or more bus bars. It is usually used when one generator fails and power is lost to its bus. By closing the switch, the operating generator powers both busses.

C (Charlie)

Camber: The wing's curvature. The camber of an airfoil is the characteristic curve of its upper and lower surfaces. The upper camber is more pronounced, while the lower camber is comparatively flat. This causes the velocity of the airflow immediately above the wing to be much higher than that below the wing.

CAP: Civil Air Patrol

Carburetor: 1. Pressure: A hydromechanical device employing a closed feed system from the fuel pump to the discharge nozzle. It meters fuel through fixed jets according to the mass airflow through the throttle body and discharges it under a positive pressure. Pressure carburetors are distinctly different from float-type carburetors, as they do not incorporate a vented float chamber or suction pickup from a discharge nozzle located in the venturi tube. 2. Float-type: Consists essentially of a main air passage through which the engine draws its supply of air, a mechanism to control the quantity of fuel discharged in relation to the flow of air, and a means of regulating the quantity of fuel/air mixture delivered to the engine cylinders.

CAT: Clear Air Turbulence

Category: (1) As used with respect to the certification, ratings, privileges, and limitations of airmen, means a broad classification of aircraft. Examples include: airplane; rotorcraft; glider; and lighter-than-air; and

(2) As used with respect to the certification of aircraft, means a grouping of aircraft based upon intended use or operating limitations. Examples include: transport, normal, utility, acrobatic, limited, restricted, and provisional.

CAS: Calibrated airspeed. The indicated airspeed (IAS) corrected for position and instrument error. Calibrated airspeed is equal to true airspeed in standard atmosphere at sea level.

Ceiling: The height above the earth's surface of the lowest layer of clouds or obscuring phenomena that is reported as "broken", "overcast", or "obscuration", and not classified as "thin" or "partial".

Center of Gravity (CG): The point at which an airplane would balance if it were possible to suspend it at that point. It is the mass center of the airplane, or the theoretical point at which the entire weight of the airplane is assumed to be concentrated. It may be expressed in inches from the reference datum, or in percent of mean aerodynamic chord (MAC). The location depends on the distribution of weight in the airplane.

Center of Gravity Limits: The specified forward and aft points within which the CG must be located during flight. These limits are indicated on pertinent airplane specifications.

Center of Gravity Range: The distance between the forward and aft CG limits indicated on pertinent airplane specifications.

CFI: Certificated Flight Instructor (an authorized instructor)

CFII: Certificated Flight Instructor-Instrument (an authorized instrument instructor)

CFIT: Controlled Flight Into Terrain (not good)

CFR: (see also *FAR*) Code of Federal Regulations

Checkpoint: A geographical point on the surface of the earth whose location can be determined by reference to a map or chart.

Check Ride: A practical flight test.

Children's Hour: (Longfellow) "Between the dark and the daylight, when the night begins to lower, comes a pause in the day's occupations that's known as The Children's Hour." (see *Night*)

Chord Line: Imaginary straight line from the airfoil's leading edge to its trailing edge.

Circuit Breaker: A circuit-protecting device that opens the circuit in case of excess current flow. A circuit breakers differ from a fuse in that it can be reset without having to be replaced.

Class: (1) As used with respect to the certification, ratings, privileges, and limitations of airmen, means a classification of aircraft within a category having similar operating characteristics. Examples include: single engine; multiengine; land; water; gyroplane; helicopter; airship; and free balloon; and

(2) As used with respect to the certification of aircraft, means a broad grouping of aircraft having similar characteristics of propulsion, flight, or landing. Examples include: airplane; rotorcraft; glider; balloon; landplane; and seaplane.

Clearance Delivery: ATC position from which VFR and IFR clearances are issued. Called "Clearance"

Controlled airspace: Airspace within which air traffic control service (not necessarily separation service) is provided to IFR and to VFR flights in accordance with the airspace classification. It's a generic term that covers Class A, Class B, Class C, Class D, and Class E airspace.

Cockpit: Place where the pilot and crew sit.

Cockpit (or Crew) Resource Management (CRM): Techniques designed to reduce pilot errors and manage errors that do occur utilizing cockpit human resources. The assumption is that errors are going to happen in a complex system with error-prone humans.

Common Traffic Advisory Frequency (CTAF): The common frequency used by airport traffic to announce position reports in the vicinity of the airport.

Complex Aircraft: An aircraft with retractable landing gear, flaps, and a controllable-pitch propeller, or is turbine powered.

Condensation: Water changes from gas (water vapor) to a liquid.

Cone of Ambiguity: Airspace over a VOR or TACAN station, conical in shape, in which the To/From ambiguity indicator is changing positions. Not to be confused with the Cone of Silence in *Get Smart*.

Controlled Airspace: Airspace in which ATC exerts some level of control over IFR and VFR traffic. Includes classes A, B, C, D, and E airspace.

Control Yoke: Also called the "yoke," this flight control comes in several shapes but is generally wheel-like or half-wheel and controls ailerons and elevator. In some Ercoupes, it's also linked to the rudders.

Convective SIGMET: A weather advisory concerning convective weather significant to the safety of all aircraft. Convective SIGMETs are issued for tornadoes, lines of thunderstorms, embedded thunderstorms of any intensity level, areas of thunderstorms greater than or equal to VIP level 4 with an area coverage of 4/10 (40%) or more, and hail 3/4 inch or greater.

Conventional Landing Gear: Landing gear employing a third rear-mounted wheel. These airplanes are also sometimes referred to as tailwheel airplanes.

Coordinated Flight: Application of all appropriate flight and power controls to prevent slipping or skidding in any flight condition.

Coriolis Force: Created by the earth's rotation; the force deflects air to the right in the Northern Hemisphere, causing it to follow a curved path instead of a straight line. The amount of deflection differs depending on the latitude and is greatest at the poles, diminishing to zero at the equator.

Course: The intended direction of flight in the horizontal plane measured in degrees from north.

Cowl: Engine cover

Cowl Flaps: Devices arranged around certain air-cooled engine cowlings, which may be opened or closed to regulate the flow of air around the engine.

Crab: A flight condition in which the nose of the airplane is pointed into the wind a sufficient amount to counteract a crosswind and maintain a desired track over the ground.

Critical Angle of Attack: The angle of attack at which a wing stalls regardless of airspeed, flight attitude, or weight.

CRM: Crew Resource Management or Cockpit Resource Management

Crosswind Component: The wind component, measured in knots, at 90° to the longitudinal axis of the runway.

D (Delta)

Datum (Reference Datum): An imaginary vertical plane or line from which all measurements of moment arm are taken. The datum is established by the manufacturer. Once the datum has been selected, all moment arms and the location of CG range are measured from this point.

DE: Designated Examiner, pilot designated by the FAA to give checkrides.

Dead Reckoning: Dead reckoning, as applied to flying, is the navigation of an airplane solely by means of computations based on airspeed, course, heading, wind direction, and speed, groundspeed, and elapsed time.

Density Altitude: Pressure Altitude corrected for non-standard temperature. When conditions are standard, pressure altitude and density altitude are the same. If the temperature is above standard, the density altitude is higher than pressure altitude. If the temperature is below standard, the density altitude is lower than pressure altitude. This is an important altitude because it is directly related to the airplane's performance.

Deposition: The direct transformation of a gas to a solid. The liquid state is skipped. You'll occasionally see the word sublimation used for that process. Go figure.

Detonation: The sudden release of heat energy from fuel in an aircraft engine caused by the fuel-air mixture reaching its critical pressure and temperature. Detonation occurs as a violent explosion rather than a smooth burning process.

Dewpoint: The temperature at which air can hold no more water.

Differential Ailerons: Control surface rigged such that the aileron moving up moves a greater distance than the aileron moving down. The up aileron produces extra parasite drag to compensate for the additional induced drag caused by the down aileron. This balancing of the drag forces helps minimize adverse yaw.

Directional Stability: Stability about the vertical axis of an aircraft, whereby an aircraft tends to return, on its own, to flight aligned with the relative wind when disturbed from that equilibrium state. The vertical tail is the primary contributor to directional stability, causing an airplane in flight to align with the relative wind.

Displaced Threshold: A threshold that is located at a point on the runway other than the designated beginning of the runway.

DME: (old school) Distance Measuring Equipment, mostly replaced by GPS, measures how far you are from a VORTAC. Gives mileage in slant range.

Downwash: Air deflected perpendicular to the motion of the airfoil.

DPE: Designate Pilot Examiner

Drag: An aerodynamic force on a body acting parallel and opposite to the relative wind. The resistance of the atmosphere to the relative motion of an aircraft. Drag opposes thrust and limits the speed of the airplane.

Dry Line*:* A boundary separating moist and dry air masses. Really nice to notice term when flying across the Great Plains. Usually, it's found running north to south across the central and southern high Plains states during the spring and early summer. The Dry Line separates moist Gulf of Mexico (to the east) air from dry desert air from the southwestern states (to the west). The dry line normally moves eastward during the afternoon and retreats westward at night. Don't bet on it, though. The Dry Line can stretch into Iowa and into the Mississippi Valley, or further east. Expect a sharp drop in humidity, clearing skies, and a wind shift from south or southeasterly to west or southwesterly. Severe weather often develops along a dry line or in the moist air east of it.

DTK: GPS/RNAV term. Direct Track (sometimes called Desired Path)

Dual Instruction: Flight instruction received from an authorized instructor, more commonly called a CFI (Certificated Flight Instructor)

DUATS: Direct User Access Service; a free weather briefing and flight planning service at duats.com. (Not to be confused with Duat, the ancient Egyptian realm of the dead.)

Dutch Roll: A combination of rolling and yawing oscillations that normally occurs when the dihedral effects of an aircraft are more powerful than the directional stability. Usually dynamically stable but objectionable in an airplane because of the oscillatory nature. Not to be confused with Dutch Letters, a sticky sweet alphabet-shaped pastry found in Pella, Iowa (KPEA)

Duty runway: (See, Active runway)

Dynamic Hydroplaning: A condition that exists when landing on a surface with standing water deeper than the tread depth of the tires. When the brakes are applied, there is a possibility that the brake will lock up and the tire will ride on the surface of the water, much like a water ski. When the tires are hydroplaning, directional control and braking action are virtually impossible. An effective anti-skid system can minimize the effects of hydroplaning.

Dynamic Stability: The property of an aircraft that causes it, when disturbed from straight-and-level flight, to develop forces or moments that restore the original condition of straight and level.

E (Echo, Echo, Echo...)

EFAS: (Decommissioned in 2016) En Route Flight Advisory Service; also known as "Flight Watch." An AFSS weather service that used to be on 122.0 Mhz

EFIS: Electronic Flight Instrumentation System

Elevator: The horizontal, movable primary control surface in the tail section, or empennage, of an airplane. The elevator is hinged to the trailing edge of the fixed horizontal stabilizer.

Emergency Locator Transmitter (ELT)*:* A small, self-contained radio transmitter that will automatically, upon the impact of a crash, transmit an emergency signal on 121.5, 243.0, or 406.0 MHz.

Empennage: The tail. Rudder, stabilizers and elevators or stabilator or even ruddervators in the case of Beechcraft V-tailed Bonanzas

FAR: (see also *CFR*) Federal Aviation Regulations

Equilibrium: A condition that exists within a body when the sum of the moments of all of the forces acting on the body is equal to zero. In aerodynamics, equilibrium is when all opposing forces acting on an aircraft are balanced (steady, unaccelerated flight conditions).

Evaporation: Liquid changes to gaseous state.

Exhaust Gas Temperature (EGT): The temperature of the exhaust gases as they leave the cylinders of a reciprocating engine or the turbine section of a turbine engine.

F (Foxtrot)

FAA: Federal Aviation Administration (unofficial: Funny Acronym Agency)

FADEC: Full Authority Digital Engine Control

False Horizon: An optical illusion where the pilot confuses a row of lights along a road or other straight line as the horizon.

FBO: Fixed Base Operator, a retailer on the airport where fuel, maintenance and flight instruction is sold

FDC: Flight Data Center

Fixation: A psychological condition where the pilot fixes attention on a single source of information and ignores all other sources.

Flaps: Secondary controls. Hinged portion of the trailing edge between the ailerons and fuselage. In some aircraft, ailerons and flaps are interconnected to produce full-span "flaperons." In either case, flaps change the lift and drag on the wing.

Flare (See *Round Out*)

Flicker Vertigo: A disorientating condition caused from flickering light off the blades of the propeller.

Flight Check: A call-sign prefix used by FAA aircraft engaged in flight inspection/certification of navigational aids and flight procedures.

Flight Following: Radar service for VFR flights.

Flight Time: Pilot time that commences when an aircraft moves under its own power for thepurposeofflight and ends when the aircraft comes to rest after landing.

Flight Level: A level of constant atmospheric pressure related to a reference datum of 29.92 inches of mercury, stated in three digits that represent hundreds of feet. For example, flight level 250 represents a barometric altimeter indication of 25,000 feet. All altitudes 18,000 feet and above over the US are called Flight Levels (e.g. FL 180, FL 190).

Flight Plan: Specified information, relating to the intended flight of an aircraft that is filed orally or in writing with Flight Service or air traffic control.

Flight Service Station: FSS (see also *AFSS*) a non-ATC entity responsible for giving pilot weather briefings, processing flight plans, PIREPs and other information critical to flight

Flight Visibility: The average forward horizontal distance, from the cockpit of an aircraft in flight, at which prominent unlighted objects may be seen and identified by day and prominent lighted objects may be seen and identified by night.

Flight Watch: (See *EFAS*) Decommissioned in 2016

Floating: A condition when landing where the airplane does not settle to the runway due to excessive airspeed.

Force: The energy applied to an object that attempts to cause the object to change its direction, speed, or motion. In aerodynamics, it is expressed as F, T (thrust), L (lift), W (weight), or D (drag), usually in pounds.

Form Drag: The part of parasite drag on a body resulting from the integrated effect of the static pressure acting normal to its surface resolved in the drag direction.

Forward Slip: A slip in which the airplane's direction of motion continues the same as before the slip was begun. In a forward slip, the airplane's longitudinal axis is at an angle to its flight path.

Friction Drag: The part of parasitic drag on a body resulting from viscous shearing stresses over its wetted surface.

Frise-Type Aileron: (pronounced "Freeze") An aileron having the nose portion projecting ahead of the hinge line. When the trailing edge of the aileron moves up, the nose projects below the wing's lower surface and produces some parasite drag, decreasing the amount of adverse yaw.

FSDO: Flight Standards District Office

FSS (See *Flight Service Station*)

Fuel Injection: A fuel metering system used on some aircraft reciprocating engines in which a constant flow of fuel is fed to injection nozzles in the heads of all cylinders just outside of the intake valve. It differs from sequential fuel injection in which a timed charge of high-pressure fuel is sprayed directly into the combustion chamber of the cylinder.

Fuel Load: The expendable part of the load of the airplane. It includes only usable fuel, not fuel required to fill the lines or that which remains trapped in the tank sumps.

Fuel Tank Sump: A sampling port in the lowest part of the fuel tank that the pilot can utilize to check for contaminants in the fuel.

Fuselage: The section of the airplane that consists of the cabin and/or cockpit, containing seats for the occupants and the controls for the airplane.

G (Golf)

GA: General Aviation. That's us, no military, no airlines

GAMA: General Aviation Manufacturers Association.

Glidepath: The path of an aircraft relative to the ground while approaching a landing.

Glide Ratio: The ratio between distance traveled and altitude lost during non-powered flight.

G-loading (See *Load Factor*)

Go-Around: Terminating a landing approach.

Go/No-Go: A major part of ADM in which the PIC weighs the briefing facts and decides to go or not to go

GPS: Global Positioning System. A satellite-based radio positioning, navigation, and time-transfer system.

Gross Weight: The total weight of a fully loaded aircraft including the fuel, oil, crew, passengers, and cargo.

Ground Controller: ATC position in an air traffic control tower. This controller works the ground traffic. Called "Ground"

Ground Effect: A condition of improved performance encountered when an airplane is operating very close to the ground. When an airplane's wing is under the influence of ground effect, there is a reduction in upwash, downwash, and wingtip vortices. As a result of the reduced wingtip vortices, induced drag is reduced.

Ground Instructor: An instructor authorized to give ground instruction. All CFIs are authorized to be ground instructors, but not all ground instructors are CFIs.

Ground Loop: A sharp, uncontrolled change of direction of an airplane on the ground.

Ground Loop Inn: Official eatery at Antique Airfield, Blakesburg, Iowa (IA27) www.antiqueairfield.com

Ground School: School for pilots that's taught on the ground

Groundspeed (GS): The actual speed of the airplane over the ground. It is true airspeed adjusted for wind. Groundspeed decreases with a headwind, and increases with a tailwind.

Ground Track: The aircraft's path over the ground when in flight.

Gyroscopic Precession: An inherent quality of rotating bodies, which causes an applied force to be manifested 90° in the direction of rotation from the point where the force is applied.

H (Hotel)

Hand-Propping: The art of starting an airplane engine by rotating the propeller by hand without losing one's hands in the process

Hangar: Building in which airplanes are stored

Hanger: Wire device on which pilots hang their jackets inside the hangar

Heading: The direction in which the nose of the aircraft is pointing during flight

Heading Bug: A marker on the heading indicator that can be rotated to a specific heading for reference purposes

Heading Indicator: An instrument, which senses airplane movement and displays heading based on a 360° azimuth, with the final zero omitted. The heading indicator, also called a directional gyro, is fundamentally a mechanical instrument designed to facilitate the use of the magnetic compass. The heading indicator is not affected by the forces that make the magnetic compass difficult to interpret. (Old terminology: Directional Gyro or DG)

Headwind Component: The component of atmospheric winds that acts opposite to the aircraft's flight path.

Heavy Aircraft: Aircraft capable of takeoff weights of more than 255,000 pounds whether or not they are operating at this weight during a particular phase of flight.

High Performance Aircraft: An aircraft with an engine of more than 200 horsepower.

HIRL: High Intensity Runway Light system

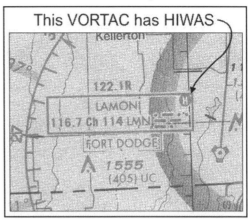

HIWAS: Hazardous In-Flight Weather Advisory. Broadcasts hazardous weather information in a continuous recorded message over select naviads, such as some VORs. Look for the H symbol in the upper right-hand corner of navaid frequency boxes on aeronautical charts.

Hollow, Jake: 1929 barnstorming protagonist in *Bootleg Skies*

Horizon: The line-of-sight boundary between the earth and the sky.

Horsepower: The term, originated by inventor James Watt, means the amount of work a horse could do in one second. One horsepower equals 550 foot-pounds per second, or 33,000 foot-pounds per minute.

Hot Spot or Airport Surface Hot Spot: A location on some airport movement areas with a history or risk of collision or runway incursion. These are marked on A/FD airport diagrams and numbered HS 1, HS 2, etc.

Hydroplaning (See *Dynamic Hydroplaning*)

Hypoxia: A lack of sufficient oxygen reaching the body tissues.

Hyperventilation: Too much oxygen. A condition caused when an abnormal increase in the volume of air is breathed in and out of the lungs. Hyperventilation "blows off" excessive carbon dioxide from the body

I (India)

IACRA: Integrated Airman Certification and/or Rating Application. Possibly one of the most confusing websites ever created.

IAPG (See *Iowa Aviation Promotion Group;* go to: www.flyiowa.org)

IAS (See *Indicated Airspeed*)

ICAO: International Civil Aviation Organization

IE: Author's operating initials when he was an air traffic controller (1979-1997).

IFR: Instrument Flight Rules that govern the procedure for conducting flight in weather conditions below VFR weather minimums. The term "IFR" also is used to define weather conditions and the type of flight plan under which an aircraft is operating.

ILS: Instrument Landing System

IMC: Instrument Meteorological Conditions (Below VFR minimums)

Inclinometer: An instrument consisting of a curved glass tube, housing a glass ball, and damped with a fluid similar to kerosene. It may be used to indicate inclination, as a level, or, as used in the turn indicators, to show the relationship between gravity and centrifugal force in a turn.

Indicated Airspeed (IAS): The direct instrument reading obtained from the airspeed indicator, uncorrected for variations in atmospheric density, installation error, or instrument error. Manufacturers use this airspeed as the basis for determining airplane performance. Takeoff, landing, and stall speeds listed in the AFM or POH are indicated airspeeds and do not normally vary with altitude or temperature.

Indicated Altitude: The altitude read directly from the altimeter (uncorrected) when it is set to the current altimeter setting.

Induced Drag: That part of total drag, which is created by the production of lift. Induced drag increases with a decrease in airspeed.

Inertia: The opposition, which a body offers to a change of motion.

Internal Combustion Engine: An engine that produces power as a result of expanding hot gases from the combustion of fuel and air within the engine itself. A steam engine where coal is burned to heat up water inside the engine is an example of an external combustion engine.

Inversion: An increase in temperature with altitude

Iowa Aviation Promotion Group (IAPG): Non-profit group promoting all aspects of aviation in Iowa. Go to: flyiowa.org

ISA (International Standard Atmosphere): Standard atmospheric conditions consisting of a temperature of 59°F (15°C), and a barometric pressure of 29.92 in. Hg. (1013.2 mb) at sea level. ISA values can be calculated for various altitudes using a standard lapse rate of approximately 2°C per 1,000 feet.

J (Juliet)

Jink: (slang, military) Sudden turn to avoid hazards

Joystick: Aircraft control. In airplanes, particularly older ones, the joystick is a vertical stick that controls ailerons and elevator

K (Kilo)

KIAS: Knots Indicated Airspeed

Kimchi: (slang) Stuff you don't wanna be in

Kinesthesia: The sensing of movements by feel

Knot: 1 nautical mile per hour or 1.151 statute miles-per-hour. ATC speeds are in knots

L (Lima)

Large Aircraft: Aircraft of more than 12,500 pounds maximum certificated takeoff weight

Lateral Axis: An imaginary line passing through the center of gravity of an airplane and extending across the airplane from wingtip to wingtip

Lateral Stability (Rolling): The stability about the longitudinal axis of an aircraft. Rolling stability or the ability of an airplane to return to level flight due to a disturbance that causes one of the wings to drop

Licensed Empty Weight: The empty weight that consists of the airframe, engine(s), unusable fuel, and undrainable oil plus standard and optional equipment as specified in the equipment list. Some manufacturers used this term prior to GAMA standardization

Lift: One of the four main forces acting on an aircraft. On a fixed-wing aircraft, an upward force created by the effect of airflow as it passes over and under the wing

Lift Coefficient (Coefficient of Lift C/L): A coefficient representing the lift of a given airfoil. Lift coefficient is obtained by dividing the lift by the free-stream dynamic pressure and the representative area under consideration

Lift/Drag Ratio: The efficiency of an airfoil section. It is the ratio of the coefficient of lift to the coefficient of drag for any given angle of attack

Line up and wait: Control tower ATC clearance authorizing an aircraft to taxi onto the runway, line up on the centerline and wait (with your back blind to oncoming traffic) for a takeoff clearance. *Line up and wait* replaces *Taxi into position and hold*

Load Factor: The ratio of the load supported by the airplane's wings to the actual weight of the aircraft and its contents. Also referred to as G-loading

Local Controller: ATC in-house term. Air traffic controller working the tower position known as Local

Log: (verb) To record flight and/or ground training time in a pilot logbook

Logbook: A book that looks a bit like a ledger, in which the pilot logs flight time. Separate logbooks are also used for aircraft engine airframe and propellers to record time in service and maintenance.

Longitudinal Axis: An imaginary line through an aircraft from nose to tail, passing through its center of gravity. The longitudinal axis is also called the roll axis of the aircraft. Movement of the ailerons rotates an airplane about its longitudinal axis

Longitudinal Stability: Stability about the lateral axis. A desirable characteristic of an airplane whereby it tends to return to its trimmed angle of attack after displacement.

LSA: (see appendix p. 281) Light-Sport Aircraft. Aircraft, other than a helicopter or powered-lift that, since its original certification, has continued to meet the following:

(1) A maximum takeoff weight of not more than--

(i) 1320 pounds (600 kilograms) for aircraft not intended for operation on water; or

(ii) 1430 pounds (650 kilograms) for an aircraft intended for operation on water.

(2) A maximum airspeed in level flight with maximum continuous power (V_H) of not more than 120 knots CAS under standard atmospheric conditions at sea level.

(3) A maximum never-exceed speed (V_{NE}) of not more than 120 knots CAS for a glider.

(4) A maximum stalling speed or minimum steady flight speed without the use of lift-enhancing devices (V_{S1}) of not more than 45 knots CAS at the aircraft's maximum certificated takeoff weight and most critical center of gravity.

(5) A maximum seating capacity of no more than two persons, including the pilot.

(6) A single, reciprocating engine, if powered.

(7) A fixed or ground-adjustable propeller if a powered aircraft other than a powered glider…

(8) A non-pressurized cabin, if equipped with a cabin.

(9) Fixed landing gear, except for an aircraft intended for operation on water or a glider.

(10) Fixed or retractable landing gear, or a hull, for an aircraft intended for operation on water.

M (Mike)

MAC (See *Mean Aerodynamic Chord*)

Mach: Speed relative to the speed of sound. Mach 1 is the speed of sound

Magenta: a purple-like color favored by the FAA

Magnetic Compass: A device for determining direction measured from magnetic north

Main Gear: The wheels of an aircraft's landing gear that supports the major part of the aircraft's weight

Maintenance: Inspection, overhaul, repair, preservation, and the replacement of parts, but excludes preventive maintenance

Maneuverability: Ability of an aircraft to change directions along a flight path and withstand the stresses imposed upon it

Maneuvering Speed (V_A): The maximum speed where full, abrupt control movement can be used without overstressing the airframe

Manifold Pressure (MP): The absolute pressure of the fuel/air mixture within the intake manifold, usually indicated in inches of mercury

Maximum Weight: The maximum authorized weight of the aircraft and all of its equipment as specified in the Type Certificate Data Sheets (TCDS) for the aircraft

Mean Aerodynamic Chord (MAC): Used in large aircraft CG computations, MAC represents the mean, or average, physical chord of a tapered wing. Or, the chord drawn through the geographic center of the plan area of the wing. (FAA-H-8083-1)

MEF: Maximum Elevation Figure. Indicates the height of the highest known obstacle within a quadrangle marked by Lat/Long (Latitude/Longitude) lines on a sectional chart.

MEL: Multi-Engine Land

METAR: Pronounced "Mee-tar," it's the Aviation Routine Weather Report for an airport

Minimum Controllable Airspeed: An airspeed at which any further increase in angle of attack, increase in load factor, or reduction in power, would result in an immediate stall

Minimum Drag Speed (L/D MAX): The point on the total drag curve where the lift-to-drag ratio is the greatest. At this speed, total drag is minimized

Mixture: The ratio of fuel to air entering the engine's cylinders.

Mode: The letter or number assigned to a specific pulse spacing of radio signals transmitted or received by ground interrogator or airborne transponder components of the Air Traffic Control Radar Beacon System (ATCRBS). Mode A (military Mode 3) and Mode C (altitude reporting) are used in air traffic control

MoGas: Automotive gasoline

Moment: The product of the weight of an item multiplied by its arm. Moments are expressed in pound-inches (lb-in). Total moment is the weight of the airplane multiplied by the distance between the datum and the CG

Moment Arm: The distance from a datum to the applied force.

Moment Index: A moment divided by a constant such as 100, 1,000, or 10,000. The purpose of using a moment index is to simplify weight and balance computations of airplanes where heavy items and long arms result in large, unmanageable numbers.

MSL: Mean Sea Level

MULTICOM: A non-government aviation frequency for activities of a temporary, seasonal, emergency nature or search and rescue, as well as, airports with no tower, FSS, or UNICOM. Usually 122.9 Mhz

Mushing: 1) A flight condition caused by slow speed where the control surfaces are marginally effective. 2) How Alaskan pilots get to the airfield in winter

MVFR: Marginal VFR. Ceiling 1000 to 3000 feet and/or visibility 3 to 5 miles inclusive

N (November)

Nacelle: A streamlined enclosure on an aircraft in which an engine is mounted. On multiengine propeller-driven airplanes, the nacelle is normally mounted on the leading edge of the wing

Nautical Mile (NM): 6076 feet. One latitude minute of arc; there are 60 minutes in a degree. ATC mileage is measured in nautical miles.

NAVAID: Any facility used in, available for use in, or designated for use in aid of air navigation, including landing areas, lights, any apparatus or equipment for disseminating weather information, for signaling, for radio direction finding, or for radio or other electronic communication, and any other structure or mechanism having a similar purpose for guiding or controlling flight in the air or the landing or takeoff of aircraft. VORs are NAVAIDS, for example.

NDB: Non-Directional Beacon. An L/MF or UHF radio beacon transmitting non-directional signals whereby the pilot of an aircraft equipped with direction finding equipment can determine bearing to or from the radio beacon and "home" on or track to or from the station.

NDH: No Damage History. A casually used phrase commonly found in used airplane ads. When you see it be suspicious, be very, *very* suspicious.

Negative: As it applies in radio terminology, means, No

Negative Static Stability: The initial tendency of an aircraft to continue away from the original state of equilibrium after being disturbed

Neutral Static Stability: The initial tendency of an aircraft to remain in a new condition after its equilibrium has been disturbed

NEXRAD: Next Generation Weather Radar

Night: The time between the end of evening civil twilight and the beginning of morning civil twilight, as published in the American Air Almanac, converted to local time

NORAD: North American Aerospace Defense Command

NORDO: No Radio

Normal Category: An airplane that has a seating configuration, excluding pilot seats, of nine or less, a maximum certificated takeoff weight of 12,500 pounds or less, and intended for non-acrobatic operation

NOTAM: Notice to Airmen

NTSB: National Transportation Safety Board

NWS: National Weather Service

O (Oscar)

OBS: Omni-Bearing Selector. An instrument capable of being set to any desired bearing of an omnirange station (VOR) and which controls a course deviation indicator.

Octane: The rating system of aviation gasoline with regard to its antidetonating qualities.

Operate: A word that's bandied about in FARs. With respect to aircraft, means use, cause to use or authorize to use aircraft, for the purpose (except as provided in 91.13 of this chapter) of air navigation including the piloting of aircraft, with or without the right of legal control (as owner, lessee, or otherwise)

P (Papa)

PAPI: Precision Approach Path Indicator

Parasite Drag: That part of total drag created by the design or shape of airplane parts. Parasite drag increases with an increase in airspeed

Payload: The weight of occupants, cargo, and baggage

Person: An individual, firm, partnership, corporation, company, association, joint-stock association, or governmental entity. It includes a trustee, receiver, assignee, or similar representative of any of them. Not to be confused with "people," which are much friendlier than "persons."

P-Factor: 1) A tendency for an aircraft to yaw to the left due to the descending propeller blade on the right producing more thrust than the ascending blade on the left. This occurs when the aircraft's longitudinal axis is in a climbing attitude in relation to the relative wind. The P-factor would be to the right if the aircraft had a counterclockwise rotating propeller. 2) Random Drug testing term.

PIC: Pilot In Command

Pilot: Person with wings who's convinced that gravity is a myth

Pilotage: Navigation by visual reference to landmarks

Pilot's Operating Handbook (POH): A document developed by the airplane manufacturer and contains the FAA approved Airplane Flight Manual (AFM) information

PIPR: *Pilot Induced Performance Restrictions*

PIREP: Pilot Report

Piston Engine: A reciprocating engine

Pitch: The rotation of an airplane about its lateral axis, or on a propeller, the blade angle as measured from plane of rotation.

Planform: A wing's shape when viewed from overhead

Porpoising: Oscillating around the lateral axis of the aircraft during landing

Position Lights: Lights on an aircraft consisting of a red light on the left wing, a green light on the right wing, and a white light on the tail. CFRs (FARs) require that these lights be displayed in flight from sunset to sunrise

Positive Static Stability: The initial tendency to return to a state of equilibrium when disturbed from that state

Power: Implies work rate or units of work per unit of time, and as such, it is a function of the speed at which the force is developed. The term "power required" is generally associated with reciprocating engines

Powerplant: A complete engine and propeller combination with accessories

Precession: The tilting or turning of a gyro in response to deflective forces causing slow drifting and erroneous indications in gyroscopic instruments

Preignition: Ignition occurring in the cylinder before the time of normal ignition. Preignition is often caused by a local hot spot in the combustion chamber igniting the fuel/air mixture

Pressure Altitude: The altitude indicated when the altimeter setting window (barometric scale) is adjusted to 29.92. This is the altitude above the standard datum plane, which is a theoretical plane where air pressure (corrected to 15°C) equals 29.92 in. Hg. Pressure altitude is used to compute density altitude, true altitude, true airspeed, and other performance data

Preventive Maintenance: means simple or minor preservation operations and the replacement of small standard parts not involving complex assembly operations

Preventative Maintenance: (irregular, see **Preventive Maintenance**)

PRN: As needed

Profile Drag: The total of the skin friction drag and form drag for a two-dimensional airfoil section

Prohibited Area: Airspace within which no person may operate an aircraft without the permission of the using agency.

Propeller: A device for propelling an aircraft that, when rotated, produces by its action on the air, a thrust approximately perpendicular to its plane of rotation. It includes the control components normally supplied by its manufacturer

Propeller Blade Angle: The angle between the propeller chord and the propeller plane of rotation. (Not to be confused with Propeller Pitch)

Propeller Pitch: The theoretical distance in inches that a propeller will move forward per rotation

Propeller Slipstream: The volume of air accelerated behind a propeller producing thrust

PTS: Practical Test Standards. Old school testing standards, replaced by ACS

Q (Quebec, pronounced "Keh-beck")

Q-Route: Q is the designator assigned to published RNAV routes used by the United States.

R (Romeo)

Radar: A device which, by measuring the time interval between transmission and reception of radio pulses and correlating the angular orientation of the radiated antenna beam or beams in azimuth and/or elevation, provides information on range, azimuth, and/or elevation of objects in the path of the transmitted pulses

a. *Primary Radar* - A radar system in which a minute portion of a radio pulse transmitted from a site is reflected by an object and then received back at that site for processing and display at an air traffic control facility.

b. *Secondary Radar/Radar Beacon (ATCRBS)* - A radar system in which the object to be detected is fitted with cooperative equipment in the form of a radio receiver/transmitter (transponder). Radar pulses transmitted from the searching transmitter/receiver (interrogator) site are received in the cooperative equipment and used to trigger a distinctive transmission from the transponder. This reply transmission, rather than a reflected signal, is then received back at the transmitter/receiver site for processing and display at an air traffic control facility

Radar Approach Control Facility: A terminal ATC facility that uses radar and non-radar capabilities to provide approach control services to aircraft arriving, departing, or transiting airspace controlled by the facility. Called "Approach" or "Departure" on the air

Radar Contact: ATC phraseology, means that an aircraft is identified on the radar display and radar flight following will be provided until radar identification is terminated

Radar Service Terminated: Self-explanatory, ATC radar service is discontinued

Radar Vector: An ATC assigned radar heading

Radiosonde: A weather instrument that's usually carried aloft by a balloon to observe and report upper atmosphere meteorological conditions.

RAIM: Receiver Autonomous Integrity Monitoring; "the capability of a GPS receiver to perform integrity monitoring on itself by ensuring available satellite signals meet the integrity requirements for a given phase of flight. Without RAIM, the pilot has no assurance of the GPS position integrity. RAIM provides immediate feedback to the pilot." (*AIM*)

Ramp (See Apron)

Rate of Turn: The rate in degrees/second of a turn

Rating: A statement that, as a part of a certificate, sets forth special conditions, privileges, or limitations

Reciprocating Engine: An engine that converts the heat energy from burning fuel into the reciprocating movement of the pistons. This movement is converted into a rotary motion by the connecting rods and crankshaft

Redux: (ri-duhks), adj., brought back or resurgent

Registration Certificate: A State and Federal certificate that documents aircraft ownership

Relative Humidity: The amount of water vapor contained in the air compared to the amount the air could hold

Relative Wind: The direction of the airflow with respect to the wing. It's parallel to and opposite the airplane's flight path

Reporting Point: A geographical location in relation to which the position of an aircraft is reported

Restricted Area: Airspace designated under Part 73 within which the flight of aircraft, while not wholly prohibited, is subject to restriction

Roger: radio terminology, means, "I have received all of your last transmission." It should not be used to answer a question requiring a yes or a no answer

Roll: The motion of the aircraft about the longitudinal axis. It is controlled by the ailerons

Round Out (Flare): A pitch-up during landing approach to reduce rate of descent and forward speed prior to touchdown.

RNAV: Area navigation (includes GPS)

Rudder: The movable primary control surface mounted on the trailing edge of the vertical fin of an airplane. Movement of the rudder rotates the airplane about its vertical axis

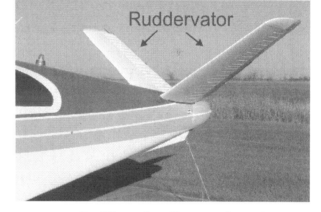

Ruddervator: A pair of control surfaces on the tail of an aircraft arranged in the form of a V (think Beech Bonanzas). These surfaces, when moved together by the control wheel, serve as elevators, and when moved differentially by the rudder pedals, serve as a rudder

Runway: That portion of an airport on which aircraft take off or land. May be paved, grass or dirt

Runway Centerline Lights: Runway centerline lights are installed on some precision approach runways to facilitate landing under adverse visibility conditions. They are located along the runway centerline and are spaced at 50-foot intervals. When viewed from the landing threshold, the runway centerline lights are white until the last 3,000 feet of the runway. The white lights begin to alternate with red for the next 2,000 feet, and for the last 1,000 feet of the runway, all centerline lights are red

Runway Centerline Markings: The runway centerline identifies the center of the runway and provides alignment guidance during takeoff and landings. The centerline consists of a line of uniformly spaced stripes and gaps

Runway Edge Lights: Runway edge lights are used to outline the edges of runways during periods of darkness or restricted visibility conditions. These light systems are classified according to the intensity or brightness they are capable of producing: they are the High

Intensity Runway Lights (HIRL), Medium Intensity Runway Lights (MIRL), and the Low Intensity Runway Lights (LIRL). The HIRL and MIRL systems have variable intensity controls, whereas the LIRLs normally have one intensity setting

Runway End Identifier Lights (REIL): One component of the runway lighting system. These lights are installed at many airfields to provide rapid and positive identification of the approach end of a particular runway

Runway Incursion: Any occurrence at an airport involving an aircraft, vehicle, person, or object on the ground that creates a collision hazard or results in loss of separation with an aircraft taking off, intending to take off, landing, or intending to land. A bad thing

Runway Threshold Markings: Runway threshold markings come in two configurations. They either consist of eight longitudinal stripes of uniform dimensions disposed symmetrically about the runway centerline, or the number of stripes is related to the runway width. A threshold marking helps identify the beginning of the runway that is available for landing. In some instances, the landing threshold may be displaced

RVR: Runway Visual Range

S (Sierra)

SAA: "Stabilize, Analyze, Anticipate" (author's in-flight mantra)

Satnav: Satellite navigation, think GPS

Scan: A procedure used by the pilot to visually identify all resources of information in flight

Sea Level: A reference height used to determine standard atmospheric conditions and altitude measurements

Segmented Circle: A visual ground-based structure to provide traffic pattern information

Service Ceiling: The maximum density altitude where the best rate-of-climb airspeed will produce a 100 feet-per-minute climb at maximum weight while in a clean configuration with maximum continuous power

Servo Tab: An auxiliary control mounted on a primary control surface, which automatically moves in the direction opposite the primary control to provide an aerodynamic assist in the movement of the control. Also know as a trim tab

Shall: Used in an imperative sense

Sideslip: A slip in which the airplane's longitudinal axis remains parallel to the original flight path, but the airplane no longer flies straight ahead. Instead, the horizontal component of wing lift forces the airplane to move sideways toward the low wing

SIGMET: A weather advisory issued concerning weather significant to the safety of all aircraft. SIGMET advisories cover severe and extreme turbulence, severe icing, and widespread dust or sandstorms that reduce visibility to less than 3 miles

Skid: A condition where the tail of the airplane follows a path outside the path of the nose during a turn

Slip: An intentional maneuver to decrease airspeed or increase rate of descent, and to compensate for a crosswind on landing. A slip can also be unintentional when the pilot fails to maintain the aircraft in coordinated flight

Slipstream (See ***Propeller Slipstream***)

Small Aircraft: Aircraft of 12,500 pounds or less maximum certificated takeoff weight

Solo: Flying alone

Solo, Han: Cool pilot in *Star Wars*, whom every pilot (at least the males) secretly wants to be

Special Equipment Suffixes: (partial list) /X no transponder, /T transponder with no Mode C (altitude encoder), /U transponder with altitude encoding, /G Global Navigation Satellite System (GNSS), including GPS or Wide Area Augmentation System (WAAS), with en route and terminal capability (save this one for when you go for your instrument rating in your Cirrus SR22)

Special VFR (SVFR) Conditions: Meteorological conditions that are less than those required for basic VFR flight in controlled airspace and in which some aircraft are permitted flight under visual flight rules (not student pilots or sport pilots and not authorized at night unless the pilot is instrument-rated and the aircraft is instrument-equipped)

Speed: The distance traveled in a given time

Spin: An aggravated stall that results in what is termed an "autorotation" wherein the airplane follows a downward corkscrew path. As the airplane rotates around the vertical axis, the rising wing is less stalled than the descending wing creating a rolling, yawing, and pitching motion

Spinner: Not one who spins, but, instead a cone-shaped cap over the propeller's hub

Spiraling Slipstream: The slipstream of a propeller-driven airplane rotates around the airplane. This slipstream strikes the left side of the vertical fin, causing the airplane to yaw slightly. Vertical stabilizer offset is sometimes used by aircraft designers to counteract this tendency.

SRM: Single Pilot Resource Management (See: CRM)

Stabilator: Similar to an elevator but comes in one piece and pivots around a central hinge point. It has a thin anti-servo tab attached to the trailing edge

Stability: The inherent quality of an airplane to correct for conditions that may disturb its equilibrium, and to return or to continue on the original flight path. It is primarily an airplane design characteristic

Stabilized Approach: A landing approach in which the pilot establishes and maintains a constant angle glidepath towards a predetermined point on the landing runway. It is based on the pilot's judgment of certain visual cues, and depends on the maintenance of a constant final descent airspeed and configuration

Stabilizer: Usually two of these on the tail. One is vertical and is called the Vertical Stabilizer; the other is horizontal and called (way ahead of me here…) the Horizontal Stabilizer. The Rudder attaches to the Vertical Stabilizer, and the elevator attaches to the Horizontal Stabilizer. And the shinbone attaches to the knee bone…

Stall: When the smooth airflow over the airplane's wing is disrupted, lift degenerates rapidly, when the wing exceeds its critical angle of attack. This can occur at any airspeed, in any attitude, with any power setting

Standard Atmosphere: At sea level, the standard atmosphere consists of a barometric pressure of 29.92 inches of mercury (in. Hg.) or 1013.2 millibars, and a temperature of 15°C (59°F). Pressure and temperature normally decrease as altitude increases. The standard lapse rate in the lower atmosphere for each 1,000 feet of altitude is approximately 1 in. Hg. and 2°C (3.5°F). For example, the standard pressure and temperature at 3,000 feet mean sea level (MSL) is 26.92 in. Hg. (29.92 - 3) and 9°C (15°C - 6°C)

Standard Rate of Turn: A turn at the rate of 3° per second, which enables the airplane to complete a 360° turn in 2 minutes

Station: For weight and balance computations, it's a location in the airplane that is identified by a number designating its distance in inches from the datum. The datum is, therefore, identified as station zero. An item located at station +50 would have an arm of 50 inches

Statute Mile (SM): 5280 feet. Visibility is measured in statute miles.

STOL: Short TakeOff and Landing

Sublimation: When a solid changes to a gas while bypassing the liquid stage

Supercharger: An engine- or exhaust-driven air compressor used to provide additional pressure to the induction air so the engine can produce additional power

Supercooled Water Droplets: Water droplets cooled below freezing but remain liquid

Supplemental Type Certificate (STC): A certificate authorizing an alteration to an airframe, engine, or component that has been granted an Approved Type Certificate

Swept Wings: A wing planform in which the tips of the wing are farther back than the wing root

T (Tango)

TACAN: Tactical Air Navigation

TAF: Aerodrome Forecast. A concise statement of the expected meteorological conditions at an airport during a specified period (usually 24 hours). TAFs use the same codes as METAR weather reports. They are scheduled four times daily for 24-hour periods beginning at 0000Z, 0600Z, 1200Z, and 1800Z

Tailwheel Aircraft (See ***Conventional Landing Gear***)

Takeoff Roll (Ground Roll): The total distance required for an aircraft to become airborne

Tarmac: (irregular) Tar Macadam, a type of paving process

TAS (See *True Airspeed*)

Taxi: Movement of an aircraft on the ground. 2.) The yellow car that takes you from the airport to a nearby hotel.

Taxi into position and hold (See: *Line up and wait*)

Taxiway: Portion of the airport used for taxiing aircraft

Taxiway Lights: Omnidirectional lights that outline the edges of the taxiway and are blue in color

Tetrahedron: A large, triangular-shaped, kite-like object installed near the runway. Tetrahedrons are mounted on a pivot and are free to swing with the wind to show the pilot the direction of the wind as an aid in takeoffs and landings

Throttle: The valve in a carburetor or fuel control unit that determines the amount of fuel-air mixture that is fed to the engine

Thrust: The force, which imparts a change in the velocity of a mass. This force is measured in pounds but has no element of time or rate. The term, thrust required, is generally associated with jet engines. A forward force, which propels the airplane through the air

Thrust Line: An imaginary line passing through the center of the propeller hub, perpendicular to the plane of the propeller rotation.

Total Drag: The sum of the parasite and induced drag. Also, what it feels like when bad weather grounds you for a week

Touch-and-Go: An operation by an aircraft that lands and departs on a runway without stopping or exiting the runway

Touchdown Zone Lights: Two rows of transverse light bars disposed symmetrically about the runway centerline in the runway touchdown zone

TRACON: Terminal Radar Approach Control

Track: The actual path made over the ground in flight

Trailing Edge: The portion of the airfoil where the airflow over the upper surface rejoins the lower surface airflow

Traffic in the area, please advise: A counterproductive phrase you should never, ever use on CTAF. See *AIM* 4-1-9(g)

Traffic Pattern: The traffic flow that is prescribed for aircraft landing at, taxiing on, or taking off from, an airport. The components of a typical traffic pattern are upwind leg, crosswind leg, downwind leg, base leg, and final approach.

a. Upwind Leg- A flight path parallel to the landing runway in the direction of landing.

b. Crosswind Leg- A flight path at right angles to the landing runway off its upwind end.

c. Downwind Leg- A flight path parallel to the landing runway in the direction opposite to landing. The downwind leg normally extends between the crosswind leg and the base leg.

d. Base Leg- A flight path at right angles to the landing runway off its approach end. The base leg normally extends from the downwind leg to the intersection of the extended runway centerline.

e. Final Approach. A flight path in the direction of landing along the extended runway centerline. The final approach normally extends from the base leg to the runway. An aircraft making a straight-in approach VFR is also considered to be on final approach.

Transponder: The airborne portion of the secondary surveillance radar system. The transponder emits a reply when queried by a radar facility.

Tricycle Gear: Landing gear employing a third wheel located on the nose of the aircraft

Trim Tab: A small auxiliary hinged portion of a movable control surface that can be adjusted during flight to a position resulting in a balance of control forces. (See also Servo Tab)

Tropopause: The boundary layer between the troposphere and the stratosphere, which acts as a lid to confine most of the water vapor, and the associated weather, to the troposphere

Troposphere: The layer of the atmosphere extending from the surface to a height of 20,000 to 60,000 feet depending on latitude

TRSA: Terminal Radar Service Area

True Airspeed (TAS): Calibrated airspeed corrected for altitude and nonstandard temperature. Because air density decreases with an increase in altitude, an airplane has to be flown faster at higher altitudes to cause the same pressure difference between pitot impact pressure and static pressure. Therefore, for a given calibrated airspeed, true airspeed increases as altitude increases; or for a given true airspeed, calibrated airspeed decreases as altitude increases

True Altitude: The vertical distance of the airplane above sea level - the actual altitude. It is often expressed as feet above mean sea level (MSL). Airport, terrain, and obstacle elevations on aeronautical charts are true altitudes

TSA: Transportation Security Administration. Large threat to GA freedom

T-Tail: An aircraft with the horizontal stabilizer mounted on the top of the vertical stabilizer, forming a T

Turbocharger: An exhaust-driven air compressor used to provide additional pressure to the induction air so the engine can produce additional power

Turboprop Engine: A turbine engine that drives a propeller through a reduction gearing arrangement. Most of the energy in the exhaust gases is converted into torque, rather than its acceleration being used to propel the aircraft

Type Certificate (TC): A certificate of approval issued by the FAA for the design of an airplane, engine, or propeller

Turbulence: An occurrence in which a flow of fluid is unsteady.

Turn and Slip Indicator: A flight instrument consisting of a rate gyro to indicate the rate of yaw and a curved glass inclinometer to indicate the relationship between gravity and centrifugal force. The turn-and-slip indicator indicates the relationship between angle of bank and rate of yaw. Also called a turn-and-bank indicator

Turn Coordinator: An instrument that displays the rate (not bank angle) at which an airplane turns and rolls. A standard rate turn is 3 degrees-per-second. At that rate it takes 2 minutes to complete a 360-degree turn (360/3 = 120 seconds or 2 minutes). It also has an inclinometer to reflect the quality of the turn.

Turning Error: One of the errors inherent in a magnetic compass caused by the dip compensating weight. It shows

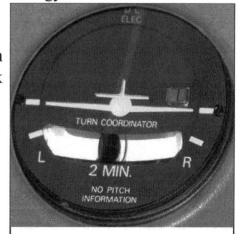

Above: *Turn Coordinator*

up only on turns to or from northerly headings in the Northern Hemisphere and southerly headings in the Southern Hemisphere. Turning error causes the compass to lead turns to the north or south and lag turns away from the north or south

Type: As used with respect to the certification, ratings, privileges, and limitations of airmen, means a specific make and basic model of aircraft, including modifications thereto that do not change its handling or flight characteristics. Examples include: DC-7, 1049, and F-27; and as used with respect to the certification of aircraft, means those aircraft which are similar in design. Examples include: DC-7 and DC-7C; 1049G and 1049H; and F-27 and F-27F

U (Uniform)

UCT: Coordinated Universal Time, aka Greenwich Mean Time or Zulu Time

Uncontrolled Airspace/Airports: Airspace (Class G) and airports over which ATC exerts no control. The vast majority of US airports are located inside Class G airspace and have no control towers

UNICOM: A non-government air/ground radio communication station, which may provide airport information at public use airports where there is no tower or FSS

Unusable Fuel: Fuel that cannot be consumed by the engine. This fuel is considered part of the empty weight of the aircraft

Useful Load: The weight of the pilot, copilot, passengers, baggage, usable fuel, and drainable oil. It is the basic empty weight subtracted from the maximum allowable gross weight. This term applies to general aviation aircraft only. Not the same as Payload

Utility Category: An airplane that has a seating configuration, excluding pilot seats, of nine or less, a maximum certificated takeoff weight of 12,500 pounds or less, and intended for limited acrobatic operation

V (Victor)

Vapor Lock: A condition in which air enters the fuel system and it may be difficult, or impossible, to restart the engine. Vapor lock may occur as a result of running a fuel tank completely dry, allowing air to enter the fuel system. On fuel-injected engines, the fuel may become so hot it vaporizes in the fuel line, not allowing fuel to reach the cylinders

Vector: A force vector is a graphic representation of a force and shows both the magnitude and direction of the force

Velocity: The speed or rate of movement in a certain direction.

Vertical Axis: An imaginary line passing vertically through the center of gravity of an aircraft. The vertical axis is called the z-axis or the yaw axis

Vertical Card Compass: A magnetic compass that consists of an azimuth on a vertical card, resembling a heading indicator with a fixed miniature airplane to accurately present the heading of the aircraft. The design uses eddy current damping to minimize lead and lag during turns

Vertical Speed Indicator (VSI): An instrument that uses static pressure to display a rate of climb or descent in feet per minute. The VSI can also sometimes be called a vertical velocity indicator (VVI)

Vertical Stability: Stability about an aircraft's vertical axis. Also called yawing or directional stability

VFR: Visual Flight Rules

VFRNR: (See also VNR) VFR Flight Not Recommended, AFSS lingo

VFR Terminal Charts: Depict Class B airspace which provides for the control or segregation of all the aircraft within the Class B airspace. The chart depicts topographic information and aeronautical information, which includes visual and radio aids to navigation, airports, controlled airspace, restricted areas, obstructions, and related data.

Vis: (slang) Visibility

Visual Approach Slope Indicator (VASI): The most common visual glidepath system in use. The VASI provides obstruction clearance within 10° of the extended runway centerline, and to 4 nautical miles (NM) from the runway threshold.

VHF: Very High Frequency

VMC: Visual Meteorological Conditions or VFR weather

VNR: (See also VFNR) VFR Flight Not Recommended

VOR: VHF Omni (directional) Range station

VORTAC: VOR plus TACAN

VOT: A ground facility, which emits a test signal to check VOR receiver accuracy. Some VOTs are available to the user while airborne, and others are limited to ground use only

V-Speeds (See below)*:* Designated speeds for a specific flight condition.

o V_A: maneuvering speed
o V_F: Design flap speed
o V_{FE}: Maximum flap extended speed
o V_{FO}: The maximum speed that the flaps can be extended or retracted
o V_H: Maximum speed in level flight (LSA)
o V_{NE}: Never exceed speed
o V_{NO}: Maximum structural cruising speed
o V_X: Best angle-of-climb speed. The speed at which the aircraft will produce the most gain in altitude in a given distance.
o V_Y: Best rate-of-climb speed. The speed at which the aircraft will produce the most gain in altitude in the least amount of time.
o V_S: Stalling speed or the minimum steady flight speed at which the airplane is controllable
o V_{S1}: Stalling speed or the minimum steady flight speed obtained in a specific configuration.
o V_{SO}: Stalling speed or the minimum steady flight speed in the landing configuration.
o V_{TOSS}: Means takeoff safety speed for Category A rotorcraft and not the speed at which passengers toss their cookies after excessive uncoordinated maneuvering in rough air.

W (Whiskey or Whisky for single-malt afficianadoes)

Wake Turbulence: Wingtip vortices that are created when an airplane generates lift. When an airplane generates lift, air spills over the wingtips from the high-pressure areas below the wings to the low-pressure areas above them. This flow causes rapidly rotating whirlpools of air called wingtip vortices or wake turbulence.

Warning Area: defined airspace extending from 3 nautical miles outward from the coast of the United States that contains activity that may be hazardous to nonparticipating aircraft. The purpose of such warning areas is to warn nonparticipating pilots of the potential danger. A warning area may be located over domestic or international waters or both.

Waypoint: A predetermined geographical position used for route/instrument approach definition, progress reports, published VFR routes, visual reporting points or points for transitioning and/or circumnavigating controlled and/or special use airspace, that is defined relative to a VORTAC station or in terms of latitude/longitude coordinates.

Weathervane: The tendency of the aircraft to turn into the relative wind.

Weight: A measure of the heaviness of an object. The force by which a body is attracted toward the center of the Earth (or another celestial body) by gravity. Weight is equal to the mass of the body times the local value of gravitational acceleration. One of the four main forces acting on an aircraft. Equivalent to the actual weight of the aircraft. It acts downward through the aircraft's center of gravity toward the center of the Earth. Weight opposes lift.

Weight and Balance: The aircraft is said to be in weight and balance when the gross weight of the aircraft is under the max gross weight, and the center of gravity is within limits and will remain in limits for the duration of the flight.

Wheelbarrowing: A condition caused when forward yoke or stick pressure during takeoff or landing causes the aircraft to ride on the nosewheel alone. Ugly maneuver.

Wilco: Radio phraseology. I have received your message, understand it, and will comply with it

Wind Correction Angle: Correction applied to the course to establish a heading so that track will coincide with course.

Wind Direction Indicators: Indicators that include a windsock, wind tee, or tetrahedron. Visual reference will determine wind direction and runway in use.

Wind Shear: A sudden, drastic shift in wind speed, direction, or both that may occur in the horizontal or vertical plane.

Windsock: A truncated cloth cone open at both ends and mounted on a freewheeling pivot that indicates the direction from which the wind is blowing.

Wind Tee: A T-shaped wind direction indicator

Wings: Airfoils attached to each side of the fuselage and are the main lifting surfaces that support the airplane in flight.

Wing Area: The total surface of the wing (square feet), which includes control surfaces and may include wing area covered by the fuselage (main body of the airplane), and engine nacelles.

Wing Span: The maximum distance from wingtip to wingtip.

Wingtip Vortices: The rapidly rotating air that spills over an airplane's wings during flight. The intensity of the turbulence depends on the airplane's weight, speed, and configuration. It is also referred to as wake turbulence. Vortices from heavy aircraft may be extremely hazardous to small aircraft.

Wing Twist: A design feature incorporated into some wings to improve aileron control effectiveness at high angles of attack during an approach to a stall.

With You: Bad phraseology, utilized by talkative pilots who don't realize that air traffic controllers hate hearing pilots say, "Ailerona approach, Cirrus 12345, with you at 5500 feet." If you're not actually in the radar approach control room, leave out "with you." Extra words clog the already crowded communication frequencies. Don't say, "feet," either. It's understood. Even "at" eats up a half-second that could otherwise be used for listening and thinking. And don't get me started on "Um…"

X (Xray)

(Intentionally left blank; if you can think of an aviation term beginning with X, please let us know.)

Y (Yankee)

Yaw: Rotation about the vertical axis of an aircraft.
Yoke (see **Control Yoke**)

Z (Zulu)

Zulu Time: Coordinated Universal Time (UCT) or Greenwich Mean Time (GMT) is written with the letter Z at the end, e.g.: 2145Z. Spoken: "Two One Four Five Zulu."

VOR ORIENTATION
© Paul Berge

There are four basic navigation forms available to the VFR Private Pilot: Pilotage, Dead Reckoning, Radio Navigation, and Radar Navigation...oh, plus satellite navigation (SatNav); so, make that *five* basics means of navigation.

Pilotage: The ancient art of looking out the window as you fly to identify checkpoints on the ground along your path.

Dead Reckoning: A somewhat morbid name, but it simply means drawing a course line, and then through the use of a few simple mathematical formulae the pilot applies wind correction and magnetic anomalies to that course to reckon a compass heading to fly. Also, the pilot can accurately estimate times en route and fuel burns.

Radar Navigation: Rare for the VFR sport pilot, but when working with ATC you may receive radar vectors for sequencing to a runway or for separation purposes. ATC radar guides the flight to the destination.

SatNav: Think **GPS** (Global Positioning System). This is the most commonly used form of navigation. Hikers, hunters, Uber drivers, paroled convicts, the military, boaters and especially pilots all rely upon this amazingly accurate, reliable and cheap navigation system. It's so good that the FAA recognizes its worth and encourages its use provided you still master the mid-20th Century art of….

Radio Navigation: Remember your Morse Code? (*My what?*) All those dots and dashes (-.- … ---) that made 19th Century commerce hum are still a part of 21st Century air navigation and used in both the NonDirectional Beacon (NDB) and the Very High Frequency (VHF) Omnidirectional Range, better known as the **VOR**. The names have a 1940s ring to them. Don't worry, you don't need to speak Morse to use either system. Just be aware that the Morse Code is still used to identify the stations.

The **NDB** has been around since the Jimmy Doolittle days and is a fairly simple and reliable device. Chances are, though, you'll never use one, because they're being phased out. Still, it's nice to know a little navigation history. Here's a quick description of the NDB and ADF:

The NDB is a transmitter. The receiver portion in the aircraft is called the Automatic Direction Finder (**ADF**), also dubbed by students, the Automatic Disorientation Facilitator. Personally, I like the ADF for two reasons: You can pick up baseball games on AM stations, and it's a stone-simple device. It is the only instrument that automatically tells you where you are *not*. When tuned to a radio station, its single pointer needle points to the station, thus telling you: "Hey, you're *not* over there!" To get over there, simple turn the airplane until the needle is on the nose. Follow it.

Enough ADF. You will need to become comfortable with the **VOR**. Again, the FAA has confusing test questions with diagrams and VOR indicator pictures and expects you to match up the correct indicator to the correct diagram. Poppycock! Useless! Memorize the answers and move on. On day, soon, we hope those useless test questions will be expunged. Here's what you need to know to operate the VOR in the real world:

First, despite GPS (and rosy promises of an ADS-B[131] future) the VOR is reliable and will be around for years to come.

There are three basic VOR types:
1. **VOR**—Very High Frequency (VHF) Omnidirectional Range.
2. **VOR/DME**—VOR with Distance Measuring Equipment (DME)
3. **VORTAC**—VOR plus TACAN (Tactical Air Navigation). TACAN is a military navigation device similar to VOR but works on UHF (Ultrahigh Frequency). You can't receive this, except through DME and, then, it's tuned automatically.

You'll use VOR, VOR/DME and VORTACs as though they were the same navaid. Don't sweat the differences. We'll call everything, "V-O-R" and not "Vor," like some medieval Norse god

The VOR is a ground-based navaid. It looks like a big bowling pin atop a round barn. Omni means "all," and the VOR transmits 360 distinct radials (001° clockwise to 360°) in all directions. Each radial is a straight-line course referenced to magnetic north. You don't have to figure in magnetic variation when using the VOR. Example: Radial 001 is 1 degree east of magnetic north, 002 is 2 degrees east…radial 090 is 90 degrees east of north, and so forth.

Think of the VOR as a bicycle wheel lying flat and viewed from above. Its hub is the radio station out of which 360 identifiable spokes radiate.

Remember: All VOR **radials** radiate *FROM* the VOR, but you can track a radial to or from the VOR.

A compass rose is often (not always) printed on the VFR sectional charts surrounding a VOR. This aids with orientation.

---

[131] Automatic Dependent Surveillance-Broadcast (NexGen Nav)

VORs have limitations. They transmit line-of-sight signals that are easily blocked by mountains or the curvature of the Earth,[132] so VORs are placed all over the landscape to provide continuous coverage in cross-country navigation.

VORs are also classified according to their range (service volume):

Class **T** (Terminal) VORs are useful from 12,000 feet and below and have 25-NM range.
Class **L** (Low) VORs are useful below 18,000 feet and have ranges to 40 NM.
Class **H** (High) can be subdivided into three types, but the VFR pilot operating below 18,000 feet will use Class H VORs that either have a range of 40NM or 100 NM.

The Comm/NAVAID Remarks section of the A/FD will detail what restrictions a particular VOR has. Frankly, this isn't a big issue for the VFR pilot. Nice to know, though.

The higher you fly the better the VOR reception. Plus, the further you fly from the VOR station the wider the radial becomes. It fans out, so your course navigation deteriorates with distance, which is about the time for you to tune in the next VOR along the route and use its signal.

How To Use The VOR (without making yourself crazy)

The VOR transmitter is on the ground. The VOR receiver is in the aircraft and has three component parts:

1. Omni Bearing Selector (OBS). Slang: "Course Selector"
2. Course Deviation Indicator (CDI) or "Left/Right" needle
3. TO-FROM ambiguity indicator

The **OBS** knob rotates the VOR receiver's compass azimuth face. With it, the pilot selects a radial or determines on which radial the VOR receiver in the aircraft is currently located.

Hint: Think of the receiver as sitting alone in space. It does not know that it's attached to your airplane. The VOR receiver does not know what the airplane's heading is. It senses which radial it is on and whether it's drifting from the selected radial.

As the pilot rotates the OBS, the CDI will move depending upon the receiver's position relative to the radial currently selected.

---

[132] Columbus had a helluva time picking up the Miami VOR until almost to Cuba, at which point he said, "Far enough, lads!"

Figure VOR-1

As the CDI centers, the TO-FROM ambiguity indicator will display either TO or FROM. If it reads **FROM**, simply read the number at the top of the azimuth dial. That is the radial on which the receiver (and the airplane) is currently located. If the top number is, say, "33", then you're on the 330-degree radial (add a 0 to 33) FROM the VOR. You're on that 330-degree "spoke" from the VOR's hub. Where's that? It's roughly northwest of the VOR. What's your heading? Don't know, don't care, doesn't matter. For that instant, you are located somewhere along the 330 radial. If your airplane's heading were 330° you'd be tracking outbound on the 330-degree radial. If your heading were 150°, then you'd be tracking inbound on the 330-degree radial. As long as you remain on the 330-degree radial, regardless of heading, the CDI needle remains centered.

With the OBS set to 330, if the CDI centered with the TO-FROM reading **TO**, then—in order to locate your position—you'd need to read the reciprocal of 330°, because you are not on the 330-degree radial from the VOR station. Instead, your are southeast of the station on the 150-degree radial FROM the station. If you turned the OBS until the CDI centered with a FROM indication, you'd see "15" (short for 150) at the top of the VOR receiver azimuth.

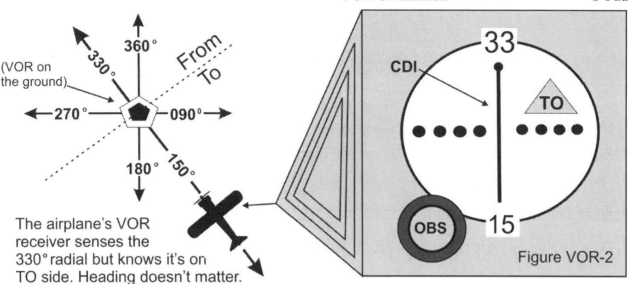

(VOR on the ground)

360°

330°

270° ← → 090°

180°

150°

From To

The airplane's VOR receiver senses the 330° radial but knows it's on TO side. Heading doesn't matter.

33

CDI

TO

OBS 15

Figure VOR-2

So, here's how you orient yourself from a VOR (without any math):

Step 1: Tune and identify the station (pretend to listen for the Morse Code dots and dashes or a voice stating the VOR's name).

Step 2: Rotate the OBS until the CDI needle centers with a FROM indication in the TO-FROM window.

Step 3: Read the number at the top of the VOR receiver's azimuth. Add a 0 to that number. That is the magnetic direction you are located from the VOR. If the number at the top read 6, add a 0 = 60° (or 060°), and if the TO-FROM window reads FROM, then you are northeast or 60° from the VOR station. You're oriented. You know where you are at that instant. Your heading is irrelevant when simply locating your position along a radial. But heading becomes important when you want to go *to* or away *from* the station along a radial.

In order to fly *to* the VOR station, turn the airplane until your compass heading (or DG) is equal to (in this case) the reciprocal of 060°. That's 240°. You are on (or close to) the 060-degree radial from the station, but now you are headed 240° to the station. The VOR receiver does not know your heading. It will still show the CDI centered (or nearly so) on 6 (060°). The TO-FROM will still read FROM, because you are still on the 60-degree radial from the VOR even though you're flying toward (headed to) the VOR on a 240-degree heading. The problem here is the DG or compass reads 240°, while the VOR receiver is set to 060° FROM. The VOR receiver "thinks" you'd logically be headed northeast bound, and if you drifted off course, the CDI needle would point toward the selected course. Unfortunately it's now "reverse sensing" and will point the wrong way. So, do not track inbound on the 060 radial with a FROM indication while heading 240. Instead, rotate the OBS to the reciprocal of 060 and track TO 240. When your compass (or DG) and OBS are both on the same number (in this case 240) you'll have correct CDI sensing. If the needle points right, fly right. If the needle points to the left, fly left. Keep things simple.

As you approach the VOR, the CDI will swing because the sensitivity becomes more accurate—the spokes jam together at the hub. As you cross the VOR, the TO-FROM ambiguity indicator will flip from TO (you're still heading 240) to NO FLAG as you cross, to FROM on the other side assuming you have not altered your course. This area where the TO/FROM indicator switches is known as the **Cone of Ambiguity**. For a few seconds the VOR receiver will appear not to work. Hold heading and wait until on the other side, the VOR receiver senses the 240-degree radial FROM the VOR. Sum up: Going to the station you'll have 240 TO. After crossing you'll see 240 FROM. Because you went from the TO side to the FROM side of the VOR without changing headings.

Had you kept the 060-degree radial FROM selected and tracked 240° to the station from the northeast, the TO-FROM flag would flip from FROM to TO as you crossed the VOR. The receiver would be telling you that in order to fly to the station you must now fly 060° TO.

Confused? Remember this: In order to track to a station, center the CDI needle with a TO flag and then turn the airplane to make your compass (or DG) match the number at the top of the VOR azimuth dial.

To track away from a station along a selected radial with a FROM flag, make your heading match the selected radial. When both match, thre CDI needle will tell you if you're left or right of that selected radial.

Drift Correction

In a perfect sky, the wind might never blow, clouds might never form, and ATC will always allow you to proceed direct to the runway using GPS navigation. Sorry, folks, but even though the sky is perfect in all its glory, how we navigate through it is subject to imperfect winds.

VOR radials are used to define federal airways. At low altitudes (below 18,000 feet MSL) these are called **Victor Airways**. They appear on your VFR sectional chart as blue lines identified with the letter V (and a number) such as V 235 or V 26. Think of them as federal Interstate Highways in the Sky…without the eighteen-wheelers and blandness of identical rest stops. Plus, no tolls (for now[133]). V 235 is simply a name. The number, 235, does not indicate its VOR radial. V 235 could have a magnetic course of 190° from one VOR to the next, and then change course to, say, 203° for the next segment.

---

[133] Contact AOPA at www.AOPA.org to keep then toll free.

The pilot can track a concrete highway or a radio beam highway. To track a paved highway you simply follow the road by looking out the window. A federal airway is like a road—it never moves—but you follow it by centering the VOR's CDI needle.

Except in exceptionally strong crosswinds cars normally don't blow off highways, because their wheels have contact with the pavement. Airplanes easily and routinely blow off course. That's called drift. Pilots need to crab the aircraft into the wind to correct for the crosswind in order to track a road. Likewise with a federal airway or any VOR radial.

Imagine tracking R090 (090-degree radial) from a VOR. On a calm day you'd head 090° along the radial with the CDI centered. But add a southerly wind and the airplane will drift north, just as it would if you'd been tracking a concrete highway. No problem. Turn into the wind to correct for drift. How much? *Dunno.* You'll have to experiment.

Once a radial is selcted the VOR receiver senses the aircraft drifting off course. The OBS is set to the 090 radial. A south wind pushes the airplane north. The CDI needle indicates the selected course is to the right.

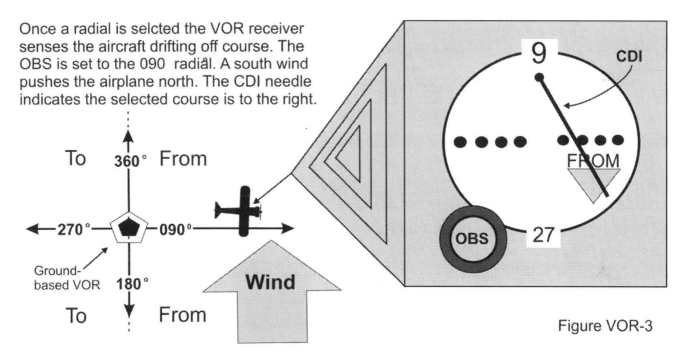

Figure VOR-3

Try a ten-degree cut into the wind, so in this case you'd head (compass or DG) 100° in order to track the 090-degree radial. If that crab angle is correct the airplane will track nicely along the radial, and the VOR receiver's CDI will stay centered.

But if the wind gets stronger, you'll drift again, and the CDI needle will once again point into the wind to inform you that the selected radial is, in this scenario, to the right. So, turn further right, perhaps, another five degrees. Now, you're heading 105°. For the remainder of the trip along that leg, make minor adjustments to heading in order to hold your track along the radial. It's a trial-and error method.

That's basic VOR orientation and tracking. Review the steps and imagine your position. Remember that the VOR receiver does not know your airplane's heading. It merely senses where the selected radial is. To track to a station, select TO in the TO-FROM window and match your compass heading to the number at the top of the VOR azimuth. To track away from the station, select FROM and match your heading to the selected radial.

How do you track a radial to Carnegie Hall? *Practice, practice, practice...*[134]

The VOR combined with DME or GPS will give you an exact position along a radial rather than simply which radial you're on.

By using two radials from separate VOR stations, the pilot can positively identify position by where those two radials cross. If your VOR receiver is tuned to the Omaha VOR, and the CDI needle centers with a FROM flag on the 270 degree radial, you're somewhere west of Omaha VOR. If you tune in the Scribner VOR and center the CDI with a FROM flag on radial 180, then you are south of Scribner VOR. Where those two radials cross is your exact position. Draw a line west of Omaha and south of Scribner, and there you are. Where you want to go in Nebraska, however, is your business.

Test: Because VOR receivers deteriorate with age (what doesn't?) you should periodically check your VOR receiver's accuracy. IFR pilots *shall* check VOR receiver accuracy every 30 days. The best way to test your VOR is to use an FAA VOR Test Facility (VOT).

The **VOT** is free for anyone to use. Check your A/FD for an airport with a VOT on the field. With the aircraft on the ramp, you simply dial in the VOT frequency and center the VOR receiver's **OBS** (Omni Bearing Selector) needle on 360°. The VOR receiver's TO-FROM ambiguity indicator window should read FROM. Rotate the OBS 180 degrees until it's set on 180°. The TO-FROM should read TO. The OBS should be accurate within +/-4° with this test.

***

---

[134] See chapter 4 to understand that lame joke.

Sport Pilot Appendix

The Private Pilot Beginner's Manual (for Sport Pilots, Too) admittedly focuses on the airplane Private Pilot, which is a shame since the sport pilot certificate offers a great way to get into flying in roughly half the required training time. It's also the certificate of last resort for already licensed pilots who haven't been denied a medical certificate and don't want to risk doing so. The candidate for a Sport Pilot certificate will be expected to know most of what's appeared in the previous chapters and appendices. The basics of aerodynamics, flight control, weather, cross-country planning and airspace apply to any airplane pilot certificate. What follows are direct quotes from various FAA sources, mainly FAA-H-8083-27A and samplings from FARs 61.305 through 61.327, that should answer some question regarding the sport pilot certificate:

The FAA Speaks:

FAQs (from FAA-H-8083-27A)

Q. What aircraft can I fly as a sport pilot?
A. You are limited to flying an aircraft that meets the definition of a light sport aircraft (LSA). An LSA is any certificated aircraft that meets the following performance parameters:
1320 pounds Maximum Gross Weight (1430 pounds for seaplanes)[135]
45 knots (51 mph) Max Landing Configuration Stall
120 knots (138 mph) Max. Straight & Level
Single or Two seat Aircraft
Fixed Pitch or Ground Adjustable Propeller
Fixed Landing Gear (except for amphibious aircraft)

Q. What are the restrictions on a sport pilot?
A. Sport pilots cannot make flights:
- at night;
- in controlled airspace unless you receive training and a logbook endorsement;
- outside the U.S. without advance permission from that country(ies);
- for the purpose of sightseeing with passengers for charity fundraisers;
- above 10,000' MSL;
- when the flight or surface visibility is less than 3 statute miles;
- unless you can see the surface of the Earth for flight reference;

---

[135] This includes, but is not limited to, Aeronca 7AC Champs, some series 11 Chiefs, Piper J-3 Cub, Taylorcraft BL65 and BC12D, plus some Luscombes, Interstates and some Ercoupes. Sadly, the Cessna 120, 140 and 150 series are not eligible.

• in LSA with a maximum speed in level flight with maximum continuous power (V$_H$) of greater than 87 knots (100 mph), unless you receive training and a logbook endorsement;

      • if the operating limitations issued with the aircraft do not permit that activity;

      • contrary to any limitation listed on the pilot's certificate, U.S. driver's license, FAA medical certificate, or logbook endorsement(s); and

      • while carrying a passenger or property for compensation or hire (no commercial operations).

FARs:

61.305
Eligibility

Above: Light Sport Aircraft (LSA). The two-seat CTLS has room for two full-sized adults (below)

To be eligible for a sport pilot certificate you must:
(1) Be at least 17 years old (or 16 years old if you are applying to operate a glider or balloon).
(2) Be able to read, speak, write, and understand English. If you cannot read, speak, write, and understand English because of medical reasons, the FAA may place limits on your certificate as are necessary for the safe operation of light-sport aircraft.

61.309
Aeronautical knowledge to apply for a sport pilot certificate

Except as specified in 61.329[136], to apply for a sport pilot certificate you must receive and log ground training from an authorized instructor or complete a home-study course on the following aeronautical knowledge areas:
(a) Applicable regulations of this chapter that relate to sport pilot privileges, limits, and flight operations.
(b) Accident reporting requirements of the National Transportation Safety Board.
(c) Use of the applicable portions of the aeronautical information manual and FAA advisory circulars.

---

[136] 61.329 refers to "special provisions for obtaining a sport pilot certificate for persons who are registered ultralight pilots with an FAA-recognized ultralight organization."

(d) Use of aeronautical charts for VFR navigation using pilotage, dead reckoning, and navigation systems, as appropriate.

(e) Recognition of critical weather situations from the ground and in flight, wind shear avoidance, and the procurement and use of aeronautical weather reports and forecasts.

(f) Safe and efficient operation of aircraft, including collision avoidance, and recognition and avoidance of wake turbulence.

(g) Effects of density altitude on takeoff and climb performance.

(h) Weight and balance computations.

(i) Principles of aerodynamics, powerplants, and aircraft systems.

(j) Stall awareness, spin entry, spins, and spin recovery techniques, as applicable.

(k) Aeronautical decision making and risk management.

(l) Preflight actions that include--

(1) How to get information on runway lengths at airports of intended use, data on takeoff and landing distances, weather reports and forecasts, and fuel requirements; and

(2) How to plan for alternatives if the planned flight cannot be completed or if you encounter delays.

61.311
Flight proficiency requirements for a sport pilot certificate

Except as specified in 61.329[137], to apply for a sport pilot certificate you must receive and log ground and flight training from an authorized instructor on the following areas of operation, as appropriate, for airplane single-engine land or sea, glider, gyroplane, airship, balloon, powered parachute land or sea, and weight-shift-control aircraft land or sea privileges:

(a) Preflight preparation.

(b) Preflight procedures.

(c) Airport, seaplane base, and gliderport operations, as applicable.

(d) Takeoffs (or launches), landings, and go-arounds.

(e) Performance maneuvers, and for gliders, performance speeds.

(f) Ground reference maneuvers (not applicable to gliders and balloons).

(g) Soaring techniques (applicable only to gliders).

(h) Navigation.

(i) Slow flight (not applicable to lighter-than-air aircraft and powered parachutes).

(j) Stalls (not applicable to lighter-than-air aircraft, gyroplanes, and powered parachutes).

(k) Emergency operations.

(l) Post-flight procedures.

61.313

---

[137] 61.329 pertains to "special provisions for obtaining a sport pilot certificate for persons who are registered ultralight pilots with an FAA-recognized ultralight organization."

Aeronautical experience to apply for a sport pilot certificate

Airplane category and single-engine land or sea class privileges,
(1) 20 hours of flight time, including at least 15 hours of flight training from an authorized instructor in a single-engine airplane and at least 5 hours of solo flight training in the areas of operation listed in 61.311,
(i) 2 hours of cross-country flight training, (ii) 10 takeoffs and landings to a full stop (with each landing involving a flight in the traffic pattern) at an airport, (iii) One solo cross-country flight of at least 75 nautical miles total distance, with a full-stop landing at a minimum of two points and one segment of the flight consisting of a straight-line distance of at least 25 nautical miles between the takeoff and landing locations, and (iv) 3 hours of flight training on those areas of operation specified in 61.311

61.315
Privileges and limits of a sport pilot certificate

(a) If you hold a sport pilot certificate you may act as pilot in command of a light-sport aircraft, except as specified in paragraph (c) of this section.
(b) You may share the operating expenses of a flight with a passenger, provided the expenses involve only fuel, oil, airport expenses, or aircraft rental fees. You must pay at least half the operating expenses of the flight.
(c) You may not act as pilot in command of a light-sport aircraft:
(1) That is carrying a passenger or property for compensation or hire.
(2) For compensation or hire.
(3) In furtherance of a business.
(4) While carrying more than one passenger.
(5) At night.
(6) In Class A airspace.
(7) In Class B, C, and D airspace, at an airport located in Class B, C, or D airspace, and to, from, through, or at an airport having an operational control tower unless you have met the requirements specified in 61.325.
(8) Outside the United States, unless you have prior authorization from the country in which you seek to operate. Your sport pilot certificate carries the limit "Holder does not meet ICAO requirements."
(9) To demonstrate the aircraft in flight to a prospective buyer if you are an aircraft salesperson.
(10) In a passenger-carrying airlift sponsored by a charitable organization.
(11) At an altitude of more than 10,000 feet MSL.
(12) When the flight or surface visibility is less than 3 statute miles.
(13) Without visual reference to the surface.
(14) If the aircraft has a V_H that exceeds 87 knots CAS, unless you have met the requirements of 61.327.

(15) Contrary to any operating limitation placed on the airworthiness certificate of the aircraft being flown.

(16) Contrary to any limit or endorsement on your pilot certificate, airman medical certificate, or any other limit or endorsement from an authorized instructor.

(17) Contrary to any restriction or limitation on your U.S. driver's license or any restriction or limitation imposed by judicial or administrative order when using your driver's license to satisfy a requirement of this part.

(18) While towing any object.

(19) As a pilot flight crewmember on any aircraft for which more than one pilot is required by the type certificate of the aircraft or the regulations under which the flight is conducted.

FARs in the form of FAQ:

61.317

Q. Is my sport pilot certificate issued with aircraft category and class ratings?

A. Your sport pilot certificate does not list aircraft category and class ratings. When you successfully pass the practical test for a sport pilot certificate, regardless of the light-sport aircraft privileges you seek, the FAA will issue you a sport pilot certificate without any category and class ratings. The FAA will provide you with a logbook endorsement for the category, class, and make and model of aircraft in which you are authorized to act as pilot in command.

61.319

Q. Can I operate a make and model of aircraft other than the make and model aircraft for which I have received an endorsement?

A. If you hold a sport pilot certificate you may operate any make and model of light-sport aircraft in the same category and class and within the same set of aircraft as the make and model of aircraft for which you have received an endorsement.

61.321

Q. How do I obtain privileges to operate an additional category or class of light-sport aircraft?

A. If you hold a sport pilot certificate and seek to operate an additional category or class of light-sport aircraft, you must--

(a) Receive a logbook endorsement from the authorized instructor who trained you on the applicable aeronautical knowledge areas specified in 61.309 and areas of operation specified in 61.311. The endorsement certifies you have met the aeronautical knowledge and flight proficiency requirements for the additional light-sport aircraft privilege you seek;

(b) Successfully complete a proficiency check from an authorized instructor other than the instructor who trained you on the aeronautical knowledge areas and areas of operation specified in 61.309 and 61.311 for the additional light-sport aircraft privilege you seek;

(c) Complete an application for those privileges on a form and in a manner acceptable to the FAA and present this application to the authorized instructor who conducted the proficiency check specified in paragraph (b) of this section; and

(d) Receive a logbook endorsement from the instructor who conducted the proficiency check specified in paragraph (b) of this section certifying you are proficient in the applicable areas of operation and aeronautical knowledge areas, and that you are authorized for the additional category and class light-sport aircraft privilege.

61.323

Q. How do I obtain privileges to operate a make and model of light-sport aircraft in the same category and class within a different set of aircraft?

A. If you hold a sport pilot certificate and seek to operate a make and model of light-sport aircraft in the same category and class but within a different set of aircraft as the make and model of aircraft for which you have received an endorsement, you must--

(a) Receive and log ground and flight training from an authorized instructor in a make and model of light-sport aircraft that is within the same set of aircraft as the make and model of aircraft you intend to operate;

(b) Receive a logbook endorsement from the authorized instructor who provided you with the aircraft specific training specified in paragraph (a) of this section certifying you are proficient to operate the specific make and model of light-sport aircraft.

61.325

Q. How do I obtain privileges to operate a light-sport aircraft at an airport within, or in airspace within, Class B, C, and D airspace, or in other airspace with an airport having an operational control tower?

A. If you hold a sport pilot certificate and seek privileges to operate a light-sport aircraft in Class B, C, or D airspace, at an airport located in Class B, C, or D airspace, or to, from, through, or at an airport having an operational control tower, you must receive and log ground and flight training. The authorized instructor who provides this training must provide a logbook endorsement that certifies you are proficient in the following aeronautical knowledge areas and areas of operation:

(a) The use of radios, communications, navigation system/facilities, and radar services.

(b) Operations at airports with an operating control tower to include three takeoffs and landings to a full stop, with each landing involving a flight in the traffic pattern, at an airport with an operating control tower.

(c) Applicable flight rules of part 91 of this chapter for operations in Class B, C, and D airspace and air traffic control clearances.

61.327

Q. How do I obtain privileges to operate a light-sport aircraft that has a V_H greater than 87 knots CAS?

A. If you hold a sport pilot certificate and you seek to operate a light-sport aircraft that has a V_H greater than 87 knots CAS you must--

(a) Receive and log ground and flight training from an authorized instructor in an aircraft that has a V_H greater than 87 knots CAS; and

(b) Receive a logbook endorsement from the authorized instructor who provided the training specified in paragraph (a) of this section certifying that you are proficient in the operation of light-sport aircraft with a V_H greater than 87 knots CAS.

Printed in Poland
by Amazon Fulfillment
Poland Sp. z o.o., Wrocław

58201174R00163